# Advances in Information and Communication Research

Volume 3

**Series Editor**

Hitoshi Mitomo, Graduate School of Asia-Pacific Studies, Waseda University, Tokyo, Japan

This book series focuses on socioeconomic aspects of information and communication. Information and communication technology (ICT) is now indispensable as an infrastructure supporting the advancement of society. ICT has benefited modern civilization, and its influence has spread over numerous aspects of our life and economy. Along with technological progress, much has happened in this arena, with new developments continuing at a rapid pace.

Constructive use of ICT makes our society more efficient. On the other hand, however, inappropriate use of ICT causes serious social problems that have not been experienced until now. In such a rapidly changing area, our attention tends to be drawn to superficial phenomena rather than gaining deep insight into them. In order to understand the role of ICT in modern life, social science is essential for capturing the impact of the development of networks and the advancement of information and communication services and applications. Social sciences shed light on a variety of issues and provide a framework for promoting the utilization of ICT while avoiding the potential drawbacks.

The series Advances in Information and Communication Research helps to provide academics, government officials, and practitioners with the information and expertise necessary for understanding social phenomena and making policies appropriate for those new trends. Many ideas and suggestions are offered that are practical not only in the developed world but that can be applied in developing nations as well. In emerging countries ICT is highly anticipated as a means of improving the quality of life, promoting economic growth, and bridging the gaps among people and regions.

Readers will gain deep insight into the impacts of utilizing ICT in diverse societies. Interdisciplinary approaches help in understanding how those influences can be captured both qualitatively and quantitatively through studies stemming from various social sciences — economics, sociology, legal studies, media studies, marketing, regional studies, socioeconomic planning, and other relevant disciplines.



More information about this series at http://www.springer.com/series/16002

Hidenori Tomita
Editor

# The Second Offline

## Doubling of Time and Place

Springer

*Editor*
Hidenori Tomita
Faculty of Sociology
Kansai University
Suita, Osaka, Japan

ISSN 2524-3322 ISSN 2524-3330 (electronic)
Advances in Information and Communication Research
ISBN 978-981-16-2424-7 ISBN 978-981-16-2425-4 (eBook)
https://doi.org/10.1007/978-981-16-2425-4



This Springer imprint is published by the registered company Springer Nature Singapore Pte Ltd.
The registered company address is: 152 Beach Road, #21-01/04 Gateway East, Singapore 189721, Singapore

# Preface

With the increasing popularity of mobile devices such as smartphones, people always have information at their fingertips, enabled by access to the Internet. The transition from feature phones to smartphones began with the launch of the iPhone, making it easy to access the Internet through a smartphone. In addition, social media platforms such as Facebook, Twitter, WhatsApp, and LINE have become popular, with numerous people regularly accessing online information. In this book, this phenomenon is referred to as "second offline." If not being connected to the Internet is considered first offline, then being offline with the ability to access the Internet at any given time can be called second offline. AR technology has provided several ways to display online information. With the advent of the mobile AR technology that made Pokémon GO possible, the appearance of second offline is now unambiguous. When you launch Pokémon GO, your smartphone displays a map of your surroundings with Pokémon and other icons displayed. In other words, you play the game while navigating an actual space. Thus, the game space overlaps with a real space. Another app, "ModiFace," involves beauty simulation using AR technology. This allows for a realistic simulation where you can change your appearance in real time by applying makeup virtually. In addition, many AR apps are now available as online services superimposing on real spaces, thus becoming increasingly diversified. What are the characteristics of such a second offline society? What exactly is the difference between the first and second offline? These answers are perhaps most evident in various real-life situations. Therefore, I will focus on these changes in the basic aspects of our lives.

In a second offline society, people's sense of time and place is constantly evolving. Traditionally, we could not "be in two places at the same time." However, electronic media has made this possible. The media has made it possible to overlay two different places. Focusing on broadcast media, Paddy Scannell (1996) referred to this scenario as the doubling of place. In addition, Shaun Moores (2012) reassessed the concept of doubling of place, arguing that similar phenomena occur on the Internet and smartphones. However, duplication is not limited to place. Time can also be duplicated. In this book, I refer to this event as the doubling of time. The duplication of time and place has already become evident in various facets of modern society.

We received a Grant-in-Aid for Scientific Research (Fundamental Research (B)) to conduct "a sociological study on the post-mobile society" from FY2015 to FY2017, with the results of this research published in 2016 ("The Post-Mobile Society: From the Smart/Mobile to Second Offline," Routledge). In July 2017, we invited overseas and domestic researchers to attend a symposium (Are You Second Offline? The Diversity of Post-Mobile Society) at the Kansai Meeting of the Japan Society of Information and Communications Research. Overseas researchers invited to participate at the event included James E. Katz (Boston University), Michael Bjorn (Ericsson Inc. & Lund University), Jason Farman (University of Maryland), and Larissa Hjorth (RMIT). With new analytical concepts, these researchers produced noteworthy reports on the second offline. We subsequently received a research grant (Kansai University Fund for Supporting Outlay Research Centers) from Kansai University that spanned FY2019 to FY2020. In October 2020, a second international symposium (Doubling of Reality: Everyday Lives in Post-Mobile Society) of the Kansai Meeting of the Japan Society of Information and Communications Research was held. This book, published with the support of the Japan Society of Information and Communications Research, is the result of this research.

In this book, we established an analytical framework for the second offline and the doubling of time and place. To comprehensively analyze the second offline phenomenon, in each chapter, we discuss theory, history, society, culture, community, school, workplace, and similar areas by introducing concrete examples. The second chapter discusses Professor Katz's keynote speech at the International Symposium on Mobile Media held at Kansai University in July 2017. Using historical sources, Professor Katz reveals that today's new communications technology was anticipated in the 19th century. He then points out the risks inherent in today's media-society, and the concept of so-called second offline laziness. We apologize for not being able to publish most of the historical material introduced in the keynote speech in this chapter owing to space limitations. We would like to express our sincere gratitude to Professor Katz for permitting us to publish this manuscript.

The year 2020 saw the novel coronavirus become a worldwide epidemic with the WHO declaring it a "pandemic" on March 11 when the outbreak had spread to 114 countries, with 118,319 infected and 4,292 deaths. Governments issued curfews and lockdowns (city-wide lockdowns) in an attempt to stop the spread of infection, with little effect. This, in turn, resulted in a sharp increase in telecommuting, online coursework, online medical care, mail-order sales, online drinking parties, and the like. As a result, the second offline society, in which online is a superimposed offline, is growing rapidly. It is our hope that, by the time this book is published, the fight against the virus will have been won and the world will have returned to being a peaceful second offline society.

Suita, Japan Hidenori Tomita

# Acknowledgements

This book is published as the third volume in the book series of the Japan Society of Information and Communication Research (JSICR). As an academic organization focusing on the policies and socioeconomic aspects of ICT, JSICR is making an international contribution to the enhancement of ICT. This volume is based upon discussions at international symposia at the JSICR Kansai Meeting in 2017 and 2020. This is a product of research financially supported by the Kansai University Fund for Supporting Outlay Research Centers, 2019–2020, "sociology research on a mobile media society and the second offline phenomenon" (principal investigator: TOMITA, Hidenori).

Thank you to everyone involved to the publication of this book. In particular, I would like to thank Naoko Fukuda of JSICR and Yutaka Hirachi of Springer Japan for their editorial support.

Hidenori Tomita

# Contents

# Editor and Contributors

## About the Editor

**Hidenori Tomita** is a professor at Kansai University in Osaka, Japan. His present research interests are mobile AR application, mobile media culture and sociology of mobile media. His publications include The Post-Mobile Society : From the Smart/Mobile to Second Offline (Routledge, 2016), Intimate Stranger: The cultural sociology about anonymity and intimacy (in Japanese) (Kansai University Press, 2009), Digital media training (in Japanese) (with Katsuya Minamida and Izumi Tsuji, Yuhikaku, 2007) and 'Keitai and Intimate Stranger' in Personal, Portable, Pedestrian: Mobile Phones in Japanese Life (edited by Mizuko Ito, Daisuke Okabe, and Misa Matsuda, MIT Press, 2005). Translation book is Perpetual Contact: Mobile Communication, Private Talk, Public Performance, (edited by James E. Katz and Mark Aakhus, Cambridge Univ Press, 2002): Hidenori Tomita (Translation Supervised), Keiji, Tachikawa (Supervised), Taemanaki Koshin no Jidai (in Japanese), NTT Press, 2003.

## Contributors

**Kunikazu Amagasa** Faculty of Humanities and Social Sciences, Showa Women's University, Tokyo, Japan

**Michael Björn** Ericsson Consumer and IndustryLab, Stockholm, Sweden

**Jason Farman** Department of American Studies, University of Maryland, College park, USA

**Kenichi Fujimoto** Faculty of Human Environmental Sciences, Mukogawa Women's University, Hyogo, Japan

**Ichiyo Habuchi** Faculty of Humanities and Social Sciences Section, Hirosaki University, Aomori, Japan

**Larissa Hjorth** School of Media and Communication, Royal Melbourne Institute of Technology University, Melbourne, Australia

**Kota Ito** Faculty of Informatics, Kansai University, Osaka, Japan

**James E. Katz** College of Communication, Boston University, Boston, USA

**Kyoung-hwa Yonnie Kim** Department of International Communication, Kanda University of International Studies, Chiba, Japan

**Yuichi Kogure** Deputy Director, Digital Society Promotion Section, New Business Promotion Department, Regulatory Division, SoftBank Corp., Tokyo, Japan

**Misa Matsuda** Faculty of Letters, Chuo University, Tokyo, Japan

**Keita Matsushita** Faculty of Sociology, Kansai University, Osaka, Japan

**Tomoyuki Okada** Faculty of Informatics, Kansai University, Osaka, Japan

**Ingrid Richardson** School of Media and Communication, Royal Melbourne Institute of Technology University, Melbourne, Australia

**Hidenori Tomita** Faculty of Sociology, Kansai University, Osaka, Japan

**Eriko Uematsu** Department of International Communication, Musashino Gakuin University, Saitama, Japan

# Introduction: Are You Second Offline ?

# The Doubling of Time and Place

**Hidenori Tomita**

**Abstract** In the mobile Internet society, social time is separated from physical time. As a result, modern peoples' sense of time has changed. In this chapter, I call that situation "no sense of time." Peoples' sense of time and place has changed. Televisions and telephones allow us to overlap two distant places. VR and AR now allow us to overlap two different times. In short, the synchronization of time creates the Doubling of Place, and the reproduction of place creates the Doubling of Time. Furthermore, a phenomenon in which our concept of "here" is superimposed with another "here," and our concept of "now" is superimposed with another "now" has also appeared. In this chapter I call such a state "second offline". I describe the historical changes in the sense of time and place and explain the sense of time and place in the second offline society.

## 1 Introduction: the movie "The Lake House"

We cannot meet with people from different times even if we both exist in the same place. However, we can now achieve this with electronic media. This chapter refers to this phenomenon as the doubling of time. In the American movie, *The Lake House* (Warner Bros. Entertainment Inc. 2006), a curious mailbox makes an appearance.

The main character, Kate (played by Sandra Bullock), moved to Chicago from a lake house on Maple Lake to work at a hospital. She left a note for the next resident in the mailbox. In the same mailbox, a letter from Alex Wyler (Keanu Reeves) arrived. Strangely, the date on it was two years prior. They began to exchange letters using this mysterious mailbox. They fell in love and promised to meet. The day of their meeting was the next morning for Kate, but two years later for Alex. Both live in the USA. However, they are separated by a period of two years. Will they ever meet? Smartphones provide access to many people and provide us with a

H. Tomita (✉)
Faculty of Sociology, Kansai University, Osaka, Japan
e-mail: h-tomita@kansai-u.ac.jp

 
H. Tomita (ed.), *The Second Offline*, Advances in Information and Communication Research 3, https://doi.org/10.1007/978-981-16-2425-4_1

myriad of information. Can they allow us to access the sweet nothings of two lovers separated not only by distance but also by time, much like the mailbox in The Lake House? This chapter will discuss the sense of time in the age of smartphone technology.

## 2 The Second Offline

### *2.1 What is the Second Offline?*

The Internet and mobile media are obligatory when discussing today's media society. People use the Internet via mobile media devices such as smartphones. Smartphones are always on, and we can always receive online information. Referred to as the second offline (Tomita 2016) in this book, the term refers to the state of being offline while simultaneously being online. So far, we have understood being online as being connected to the Internet, and offline when disconnected. We were either online or offline. Now, it is possible to be both online and offline at the same time. The second offline refers to the state where virtual information is superimposed onto real space, where people are always browsing online information in their daily lives. It is offline where the online information is constantly received. Today, the second offline phenomenon has already impacted various aspects of our lives.

Many augmented reality (AR) apps are created for smartphones, and smart glasses are an AR device in and of themselves. AR is the concept proposed by Milgram and Kishino (1994). It is a technology that superimposes the virtual onto the real environment, a technology that makes real space into a virtual space. Smartphones or smart glasses allow online information to be superimposed onto the landscape in front of you. These devices make it possible for people to conduct their daily activities while always being online.

The development of the second offline started with the launch of the first iPhone which facilitated transition from feature phones to smartphones. This was followed by the emergence of new devices such as smart glasses, and the functions and usage of mobile media, which mainly focused on communication and information retrieval, expanded. In particular, new AR technology that made Pokémon GO possible has brought the second offline to the forefront.

### *2.2 Pokémon GO and the Second Offline: The Fusion of the Real and the Virtual*

Tojinbo (Sakai, Fukui Prefecture) is famous in Japan for its picturesque cliffs and for being a suicide hotspot. Signboards and poem monuments stand erect to dissuade suicides along with telephone cards and 10-yen coins placed in public phones to call suicide hotlines. Consequently, it has come to be known as a site for ghosts, accompanied by a multitude of ghost photos on the Internet. Still, the youth flock to Tojinbo in search of rare Pokémon. As a result, the cloud of association with suicide has lifted from Tojinbo, and the number of suicides is reported to have decreased. A popular television program also attributed the decreased rate of suicides to the game.

Pokémon GO is the smartphone version of the Game Boy handheld system game Pocket Monsters (known generally as Pokémon) made by Nintendo. Booting the program displays an exact map of an individual's surroundings on his/her smartphone. The Pokémon and in-game items appear on this map and the player plays the game by moving around in real space. In short, the real space is transformed into a game space. The AR function in the game allows Pokémon to appear in front of players when they hold up their smartphones. Pokémon can suddenly pop up when walking around and players catch them by throwing virtual balls at them. Caught Pokémon are saved in the Pokédex, a personal repository of players' captured Pokémon. The mobile AR of smartphones that this chapter focuses on is a function that allows users to receive useful information only when arriving at one place. Pokémon GO is a great research example for discussing mobile AR.

There is great potential for VR and AR. The reason lies in the concept of the word "virtual." This is translated as "supposed" or "pseudo-" in Japanese. However, according to the American Heritage Dictionary, the primary meaning of this term is "Existing or resulting in presence or effect not in actual fact, form, or name."[1] Virtual money does not mean counterfeit money, but electronic money or online currency. Although it does not appear as coins or bills, it still is "de facto" money. What would happen if AR were to project this kind of virtuality in real space? There are already apps that do so. Apps that show curtains of stars in the metropolitan night sky, apps that show encroaching rain clouds even if one is in a valley of skyscrapers, or apps that show historical buildings. All these examples do not display anything that is fictitious. It is necessary to reconsider the definition of a virtual person and a virtual self.

## 2.3 *Time and Place in the Second Offline*

This section covers issues of time and place in the second offline. It is a simple task to overlap a distant place to one's current place in the second offline situation. Here, the offline situation has a superimposed online situation. Televisions and phones already provide us with the feeling that we exist in faraway places. Scannell (1996)

[1]The American Heritage Dictionary of the English Language, https://ahdictionary.com/word/search.html?q=virtual. Accessed on 30 March 2019, The Virtual Reality Society of Japan, https://vrsj.org/about/virtualreality/. Accessed on 30 March 2019.

and Moores (2004, 2012, 2017) referred to this as the doubling of place. The doubling of place had already emerged at that time. Mobile phones have made this doubling of place possible anywhere and have gone even further with smartphones: making it possible to manifest things that do not exist in the current space and display scenes of distant locations by using AR technology.

Places are not the only things that overlap, AR can also cause an overlap in time. This book will refer to this phenomenon as the "doubling of time." The doubling of time also occurs in many instances of doubling of place. Live television broadcasts of incidents that occur in distant countries are known to have time differences. For instance, while it may be evening where you are watching, it may be daytime in the place being broadcast. Television facilitates the overlap of these two times. The same happens when making international phone calls. What occurs in the "Second Offline", in contrast, is the superimposition and visualization of information of the same place but from a different time. We walk around with another time in our pockets.

The words "overlap" and "superimpose" are integral to this chapter. de Souza e Silva et al. (2006) posited that the word "doubling" connotes a division or separation and thus it is not appropriate for discussing mobile technology. Accordingly, this chapter uses the word "superimpose" in lieu of "overlap" when explaining the "doubling" that arises in the second offline phenomenon so as not to conjure up images of division or separation. "Overlap" is used when two entities are layered equally on each other, while "superimpose" is used when one entity covers another unilaterally or is inserted and fused together.

## 3 Sociology of Time and Place

How have concepts of time and place been covered in sociology? In this chapter, Giddens' (1984, 1990) research will be used to clarify time and place in sociology. According to Giddens, a characteristic of modern society is the division of time and space. Location-based services have been highlighted in the topic of modern mobile media. Therefore, I will focus on place and not space. I will clarify how time and place have changed in the evolution of society from the premodern to industrial society, to Internet society, and finally to mobile Internet society.

### *3.1 Premodern Society: Calendar and Locale*

According to Giddens, time and place largely coincided in premodern society. The place was locale, and time was the calendar. "'Where' was almost universally either connected with 'where' or identified by regular natural occurrences" (Giddens 1990: 17). The rising and setting of the sun determined what people did and where they did it.

Time in premodern society was imprecise and unstable. Modern society adopted the fixed time method, in which the length of one hour does not change depending on the season. In premodern society, however, temporal hour systems were used. This was because the length of day and night changed with the seasons. In addition, people did not need exact times to go about their daily lives; it sufficed to have general time slots and time periods delineated by morning, noon, and night, as per the four seasons. Places in premodern society were locale. Basically, the space was to be understood from the eye level and be embedded in daily life. Giddens defined locale as: "A physical region involved as part of the setting of interaction, having definite boundaries that help to concentrate interaction in one way or another" (Giddens 1984: 375). To the people of this period, place was the physical domain in front of them and was the setting of interaction. According to Poster's *The Mode of Information* (1990), this is an *oral stage* and "the self is constituted as a position of enunciation through its embeddedness in a totality of face-to-face relations" (Poster 1990: 6). Time and place coincided, and work and life had a traditional meaning. There was a reason for everything an individual did from the moment they woke up to the moment they slept. Time, place, and actions were relegated to a world of traditional significance.

## 3.2 *Industrial Society: Clock and Map*

With the advent of modern society and industrialization, time and place in people's daily lives changed significantly. Society advanced toward a period of mass production, mass communication, and mass consumption. In this period, city workers began to conceptualize time based on clock time. They began to live in accordance with the clock time rather than sunrise or sunset. The measurement of time, which had changed with the seasons, also became fixed. No matter where they were, or what they were doing, their lives became dominated by clock time. Efficiency in work was also desired. The mechanical clock became more widespread, calendars were standardized worldwide, and time was standardized across regions. Giddens referred to this as "the emptying of time." Time had lost its traditional significance and became merely a way to measure "when."

During this period, place became one's position on a map. In premodern societies, people understood from place at the eye level but now people view their surroundings from a bird's eye view. Of course, eye level still gave people an understanding of their daily surroundings; however, it was now possible to view one's place via a precise map. That place became divorced over time. The diffusion of the universal map separated place from locale and caused the "emptying of place." Place had also lost its traditional significance and simply became one's position on a map. As a result, the separation of time and place occurred. Giddens called this process "disembedding" which signifies the "lifting out of social relations from local contexts of interaction" (Giddens 1984: 21).

The emptying of time and place caused the recombining of time and place. Giddens dubbed this "reembedding and zoning." One example of this is the timetable. Liberated from the traditional world, time and place were recombined through the logic of industry.

Meyrowitz (1985) explained this process by asserting that because of the development of mass media, a division in social place and physical place caused a loss of one's sense of place. This was an analysis of the state of mass media and communication media developed through the system of mass production, mass communication, and mass consumption spawned in modern society. According to Meyrowitz, physical places and social places were linked in both oral and print culture. The emergence of electronic technology such as the telephone, radio, television, and computers, has caused a split between social and physical places. Electronic media made it possible to be in a social space without being in the physical space. Therefore, the recombination and zoning of place and time were formed by the social place without a physical place and the clock time.

In a society of developed media, clock time is connected to a social place independently from a physical place. For example, time and work are detailed in business schedules. The physical place where that work occurs is not important. This is akin to a timetable of television programs. The place where a program is broadcast cannot be known just from a timetable. The content of the program tells us. It is not a timetable that shows the fusion of time and place in the era of no sense of place. It is a schedule book in which only tasks are written.

## *3.3 Internet Society*

**Timeless Time and No Sense of Time**

The advent of the Internet has made such a situation more apparent, and the sense of physical place continues to fade while clock time is also becoming more nebulous. Physical time refers to clock time, namely, "when." However, when playing online games over the Internet, a time separate from clock time passes. One's local time is irrelevant when chatting with people around the globe. In 1998, Swatch announced a watch that displayed Internet time.[2] This Internet time marked 24 h into 1000 periods. The uselessness of a standardized time for each country caused by the spread of the Internet was the reason for creating a globally shared unit of time.

Castells (1996, 2009) referred to time in Internet society as "timeless time." In Internet society, time is compressed by multitasking processes, and the order of past, present and future is also randomized (Castells 2009: 33–36). As a result,

[2]Swatch Internet, *Time*: Available from: https://2020.swatch.com/ja_jp/internet-time/. Accessed on 14 November 2020: Available from: http://www.swatchclock.com/. Accessed on 14 November 2020.

social time is separated from physical time in Internet society. The separation of social time and physical time gives rise to a "no sense of time." Then the zoning of time and place becomes vague and time separates from place again.

**Placeless Place and Space of Flow**

Castells (2009) called space in the Internet age a "space of flows." According to Castells, "the space of flows is the material organization of simultaneous social interaction at a distance by networking communication, with the technological support of telecommunications, interactive communication systems, and fast transportation technologies" (Castells et al. 2006: 171). "The space of flows" is not a placeless place. Castells stated that "places do not disappear, but their logic and meaning become absorbed in the network" (Castells 2009: 443). He asserted that place becomes a node of the network (Castells et al. 2006; Castells 2009) and added that "it does have a territorial configuration related to the nodes of the communication networks" (Castells et al. 2006: 171).

As Moores (2017) pointed out, Castells used financial systems as an example, and explained that nodes are "stock exchange markets and their ancillary advanced services centers around the world" (Moores 2017: 33). However, service centers are also places that exist physically. Moores (2017) pointed out that this is where the argument becomes mixed. Moores stated that Castells distinguishes between space of flow and space of place, "in his view, the subordinated live in locations that are not only disconnected from the space of flows but also increasingly segregated and disconnected from each other" (Moores 2017: 33). Moores criticized Castells' initial argument that "space of flow" is for a select elite, and all other people live in spaces that are placed distant from the flow of information. Castells et al. (2006) later amended this dualism when discussing the relationship between mobile media and space of flow. In addition, considering Internet places as nodes or links raises questions. Referring to them as spaces in which information also flows does not align with what is discussed in this text. In this chapter, I do not use the term "space," but use the term "place." Considering the arguments that have been made chronicling the changes in the concept of place throughout history, the concept of "places of flow" also creates some misgivings. The concept of place in modern society is defined as one's location on a map. The concept of a place cannot be considered applicable to Internet society. In short, a place in an Internet society is not based on a location on the map. In that sense, the term "placeless place" is appropriate.

## *3.4 Mobile Society (Real-Time Society)*

Around the same time that the use of the Internet became more widespread, the mobile phone was introduced to the masses as well. Townsend (2000) referred to cities in which mobile phones are popular as real-time cities. He posited that in these cities "as decision making and management of everyday life is increasingly decentralized, the complexity of these systems becomes greater and, therefore, less predictable" (Townsend 2000: 89). He also stated: "this decentralization creates myriad new interactions and potential interactions between individuals that dramatically speed up the metabolism of urban systems, increasing capacity and efficiency. The "real-time city," in which system conditions can be monitored and reacted to instantaneously, has arrived" (Townsend 2000: 89). He considered: "Information can be updated in real time, negating the need to plan anything. In a sense, accessibility becomes more important than mobility" (Townsend 2000: 96). These new decentralized networks make decisions in social, economic and political metropolitan systems mutable until the very last minute.

Townsend's decentralized networks enabled by mobile phones can be applied not only to businesses but also to people's daily lives. Human relationships in modern society have become decentralized networks, and actions in private lives have accelerated.

As Townsend pointed out that it is difficult to predict events that occur in a real-time city, it is impossible to predict decentralized and complex interindividual interactions in daily life. This has also become the cause of conflict in select cases. Given its flexible usability, the mobile phone has caused the times when we undertake activities in our daily lives to change. This is especially true for salesmen. Salesmen can receive work calls at all hours of the day leading to greater opportunities for businesses. They do not work within specific work hours as factory workers do. It is possible for them to flexibly adjust their work hours according to the job type or the client's business hours. I would like to refer to these kinds of hours as "flextime."

With the convenience of the mobile phone, work outside the workplace is possible. Further, people can talk to their friends as if they were at the workplace or in their home. Townsend pointed out that mobile phone users were the first to confirm their locations with "where are you now?" He also pointed out that many users falsify their locations. While conventional places have been lost in Internet society, place has become more important than ever in a mobile media society. Moreover, while this kind of place in the mobile society can be anywhere—an arbitrary place on a map—place is not always placeless.

## *3.5 Mobile Internet Society*

Initially, the Internet was accessed from offices, university research laboratories, and home PCs. At the same time, text messaging (or short message service) permeated the mobile phone market, and messaging among mobile phone users became possible. In Japan, e-mail via mobile phone also became possible. Then, the i-mode emerged in Japan, and it became possible to use the Internet from one's mobile phone. With the iPhone's foray into the market, the shift toward smartphones began, and Internet usage through mobile media began in earnest.

Mobile Internet fundamentally changed Internet use allowing us to use smartphones anytime, anywhere. If we have a smartphone, we can use the Internet to instantly access information around the world. Downloading applications on the smartphone became cheaper than on the PC. Smartphones enabled performing many tasks, such as research, e-mail/messaging, or playing video games, in places ranging from the workplace to one's home, which was not possible earlier. It eventually became integral to both our work and private lives.

With the advent of AR applications for smartphones, it became possible to superimpose graphics and images onto the users apparent surroundings by them holding the phone in front of themselves. The use of this technology is expanding rapidly. AR technology can be used to project directions to a destination in front of the user by using navigation applications. There are also applications that replicate old buildings at tourist sites. These are not possible using a home computer, but it is possible to see things for the first time by going to their actual location and holding up the mobile phone. The second offline refers to these phenomena, the mobile Internet world accessed through smartphones.

While there is not much sociological research in this field at present, some researchers are making contributions. Among these are mobile media researchers de Souza e Silva (2006), de Souza e Silva and Frith (2010), de Souza e Silva and Sutko (2011), de Souza e Silva and Frith (2012), Goggin (2012), Hjorth (2009, 2010), Hjorth and Mechael (2013), Hjorth and Richardson (2014) and Farman (2012). de Souza e Silva explains the same phenomenon through the terms "hybrid reality" and "net locality." In her research, a constant connection to the Internet was assumed. However, these researchers focus on the fusion of the real and the virtual and not the superimposition of information onto a space. This superimposed information cannot take just any form; however, the superimposed information needs to be virtual information that demonstrates the essential elements of a certain locale, place, or object. The second offline network is different from the conventional ubiquitous network. The ubiquitous network refers to a network environment that enables all kinds of information to be accessed anywhere at any time. The mobile phone has been highlighted as a form of media that is available anywhere at any time. In mobile Internet society, it has become important to be able to access necessary information here and now. The second offline presented in this book refers to the state where a certain type of information can be accessed immediately, here and now.

# 4 Doubling of Time and Place

## *4.1 Doubling of Place*

I would now like to discuss time and place in the world of the second offline. "It is only ever possible for any individual to be in one place at a time physically" (Moores 2004: 21). We cannot exist in two different places at the same time. Electronic media has drastically changed this. Media has made it possible to overlap two different places. Scannell (1996) called this the doubling of place in the context of broadcast media. We can watch a soccer match on the television while sipping tea in the comfort of our own living rooms. In this situation, my "here" overlaps with the "there" on television. Moores (2012) re-focused attention on the concept of Doubling of Place, considering that the same kind of phenomenon is emerging for the Internet and the telephone. It applies to a broad swathe of topics including travel, video games, marketing, geology, self-theory, and mass communication research.

Doubling of place in the age of the second offline differs vastly from the doubling of place in the mass media, the Internet, and mobile media ages. In discussing hybrid reality Adriana de Souza e Silva claims the difference is that mobile Internet is tied to the virtual world. In other words, a new doubling of place has been produced where the real world and the virtual world overlap. Not only do these two places overlap, but they can also fuse into one.

## *4.2 Doubling of Time*

Places are not the only things that overlap. Time can also overlap. Focusing on instant replay techniques, Marriott (1996) pointed out that the action replay onscreen is established by that which is live and non-live. When analyzing television programs, Scannell (1996) called the overlap of time the "doubling of time." In this chapter, I use the concept of doubling time according to his idea. There have been examples where the past and present overlap. For example, it is possible to read letters and postcards from people of ages past in writing. The same applies for images or audio. To be precise, that is only reading messages from the past. The past and present are still separate. In contrast, the doubling of time, as discussed in this chapter, refers to the fusion of past and present, the phenomenon whereby the past is superimposed onto the present.

Nowadays, with the prevalence of smartphones, our society is transitioning to a real and virtual overlapping society. In this kind of society, people are constantly utilizing online information in their daily lives (offline). The introduction of iPhones pushed the market toward smartphones over feature phones and this promulgated various applications such as the social media including social networking services (SNS) and mobile instant messengers (MIM). Subsequently, many people come to browse online information (virtual/online) in their daily lives (reality/online). In this book, we call this the second offline. We cannot meet with people from different times even if we both exist in the same place. However, electronic media has started to facilitate overlap two times. The doubling in time and place occurs in the second offline age.

Although there is little previous research on the doubling of time in mobile Internet society, this does not mean that there is none. Research on the doubling of place also discusses time, and several examples of the doubling of time can be observed. For example, the Japanese movie *Chakushin Ari* (2003), which has also received a Hollywood theatrical release (titled *One Missed Call* (2008)), has become a social phenomenon in Japan. The characters in this world received calls from their future selves. Recently, a movie where an application that allowed people to talk to the deceased called *Talk to the Dead* (2012), became a topic of conversation. These movies utilize mobile media to connect the past and the future and this is particularly prevalent in horror movies.

In contrast, there are also positive evaluations of the doubling of time. In the 2013 television advertisement (Misunderstood) for the iPhone, a smartphone that connects yesterday and today is depicted. After winning the 66th Emmy Award for outstanding commercial, the video was released online and gained popularity. In the spectacularly popular Korean movie *Il Mare* (directed by Lee Hyun-seung Lee, Production: Sidus Pictures, 2000), and Makoto Shinkai's animation *Your Name* (directed by Makoto Shinkai, Production: Your Name Production Committee 2016), a man and a woman from different times fall in love through once they are connected by media. *Il Mare* also had a Hollywood theatrical release, as did *The Lake House* (2006), which was previously mentioned. In these stories, the blossoming of relationships between men and women in situations where different times overlap is depicted as a kind of ideal.

In my research that highlights the overlap of time, I focus on the research of Farman (2012). His study covered services that use AR technology, such as the London Museum's Streetmuseum app, utilizing the projection method, which depicts events from the same location but at different periods, by overlapping them onto the London cityscape. In the application of *Virtual Asukakyo* (Asuka Lab, Japan), users can experience historical events synthesized in real time on the scenery of Asuka Village in Nara Prefecture by using AR technology.

## 4.3 Time Travel

VR can allow us to access the past. Unlike watching TV or movies, with VR goggles we are made to feel as if are in the scene. Currently, there are a number of VR apps for experiencing time travel. Time travel using AR has also appeared. In many cases, when using VR time travel, users move between locations and times. By contrast, when using AR time travel, users only move between times. For example, *TimeScope*[3] is rapidly spreading in France. It is a time travel machine, which is set up in tourist spots. Located throughout France, tourists see the state of the area in the old days, with a 360-degree view by using *TimeScope*. The growing popularity of time travel apps on smartphones in recent years has seen apps like the tourist app, *AR Time Traveler* (Seraphgames)[4] be approved by Niigata City in Japan. It allows you to view events that are not currently visible in Niigata City, or to overlay old photos of the scenery around you. More advanced than other AR apps, *Rembrandt Reality*[5] allows you to go back and forth between two times and places. When you start this app, a gate will appear on the screen of your smartphone, and when you "go through the gate" you will be able to enter inside the painting *De anatomische les van Dr Nicolaes Tulp* (The Anatomy Lecture of Dr. Nicolaes Tulp) by Rembrandt Harmenszoon van Rijn. Players can view the room at 360°. Players can see the real world when they look back at the gate from inside the room. Players can go back and forth between the two eras and places while looking at the screen of their smartphone. The Japanese telecommunications company KDDI (au) is also developing a similar app called *XR Door*.[6]

The doubling of time presented in this chapter is slightly different from these time travel experiences. I would like to consider that point next (Photograph 1).

## 4.4 Mechanical Replication and the Doubling of Time

Maruta (2008) made the following exceedingly important remarks about places on the Internet. Communication technologies cause spatial gaps to fade. Real-time network connections bring together actions performed in different places instantaneously. As a result, it creates the feeling that the actions are being done "here." Replication technology fades temporal gaps as it always replicates something with a temporal delay connecting actions done in different times as if they were being done "now." Maruta clarified that *synchronization* fades spatial gaps, and *coordination* fades temporal gaps (Maruta 2008: 188). According to Maruta, coordination signifies a similar location or identical position. This means that temporal gaps can become seemingly nonexistent by connecting to the information replicated in the same location as the sender. Maruta cited Niconico Douga, the largest video distribution service provided by Dwango in Japan as an example. On Niconico Douga, users can post comments and *Danmaku* ("barrage") that scroll across the screen, sometimes covering the video itself. Although the posting times for these comments

[3]https://timescope.com/. Accessed on 19 November 2020.

[4]http://seraphgames.com/Products/Order/time/index.html/. Accessed on 20 November 2020.

[5]https://www.mauritshuis.nl/en/explore/the-collection/rembrandt-reality/. Accessed on 20 November 2020.

[6]https://www.xrdoor.xreality.au.com/. Accessed on 20 November 2020.

**Photograph 1** XR door (au) (©2020KDDI)

differ, the comments are displayed in conjunction with the video, creating the illusion that all viewers are watching the video at the same time.

### Coordination

Until now, the concept of *coordination* in mobile media research has been used to explain changing the time and/or place of a meeting with one's mobile phone when it appeared one would be late for a meeting. The concept of *microcoordination* proposed by Ling and Yttri (2002) accurately captures how people use smartphones in the mobile phone age. What we thought of as coordinated time and place with our mobile phones; was only making two misaligned times coincide. Two people at different times cannot meet even if they are in the same place. It is *coordination* that adjusts the time lag. In the age of mobile phones, people who were likely to arrive earlier delayed their arrival. If you are two hours late, I can meet you without waiting if I arrive two hours later.

Ling and Lai (2016) called *coordination* in the age of smartphones, *microcoordination 2.0*. In their study, they covered *coordination* practices that utilized mobile instant messaging applications, such as WhatsApp, Line, and Facebook Messenger. Ling called "coordination with physical objects and different types of systems, such as that in the developing Internet of things" (Ling and Lai 2016: 853) *microcoordination 3.0*. This chapter covers *microcoordination* in the sense of a world being constantly connected to the Internet. It is the *microcoordination of 3.0*.

In the new *coordination* of the second offline age, it is important that two people are in the same place. The new *coordination* makes it seem as if that two people in different times are together. In the smartphone age, the doubling of time occurs even when two people do not meet. It was possible to enjoy a seemingly shared "now" in the mobile phone age by using asynchronous media, such as e-mail and text messages, to repeatedly exchange messages. However, this was using asynchronous media in different places. This chapter focuses on the feeling of sharing time between two people who are in the same place holding their smartphones. *Coordination* in the age of the second offline allows two people to feel like they share time even though they are in the same place at different times.

**Correspondence**

Maruta (2008) found that the pseudo-synchronicity created by the scrolling comments on *Niconico Douga* created a state of facing the same direction. It is easy to understand in terms of the corresponding angles in mathematics. Maruta called the state of facing the same direction *coordination*, yet the act of changing time and place of meeting in the mobile phone age has also been called *coordination*. I will use the term *correspondence* to distinguish it from *coordination* in the mobile phone age. Using the once-popular *Sekai Camera*, it was once possible to hang messages, such as a message for a boyfriend who was an hour late, in a space called *air tags*. The fact that she was in the same place and wrote a message to him gave him a feeling that they were connected over time. *Correspondence* is the two lovers' perception of sharing time because they are in the same place but at two different times. The AR application, *Sekai Camera*, made such a *correspondence* possible.

The two characters in the movie *The Lake House* live in the same house (although Kate had already moved to Chicago), but are two years apart. Sharing the Lake House, however, allows them to be so close to each other that they can ignore the two-year time gap. Although it is unclear whether the two would have been in love if they existed at the same time, their love deepens because of the overlap of their two different times. This is like to the online love experienced by two strangers. *Correspondence* in the age of smartphones has birthed a new type of love.

**The Doubling of Time and Place**

Using Maruta's theory of space, I would like to cross the axes of time and place to pinpoint the doubling of time and the doubling of place. The offline world is the world unsynchronized by communication technology and unreplicated by replication technology. Other quadrants are the world of the second offline, where time or place is superimposed. The world of the doubling of time and place is the world of the mobile Internet where time has been synchronized and place have been replicated (Fig. 1).

I would like to set communication technology (synchronization) and mechanical replication technology (correspondence) at each end of the axes of time and place. On *Niconico Douga*, which is popular among Japanese youth, and China has *Bilibili*, viewer comments fly across the screen of the video that is currently being watched. It is also possible for users to write comments on their favorite scenes in the video. As a result, it seems as if all viewers are watching the video at the current moment when the comments are displayed on screen, regardless of whether they have been written at different times. This is a form of the doubling of time used in this study.

However, it is also possible to experience this by using the Internet on a computer. In this case, the physical place is not shared. In contrast, this study focuses on Internet usage through mobile media. It is possible to post *air tags* in a physical place using the aforementioned *Sekai Camera*. When you are looking at a friend's

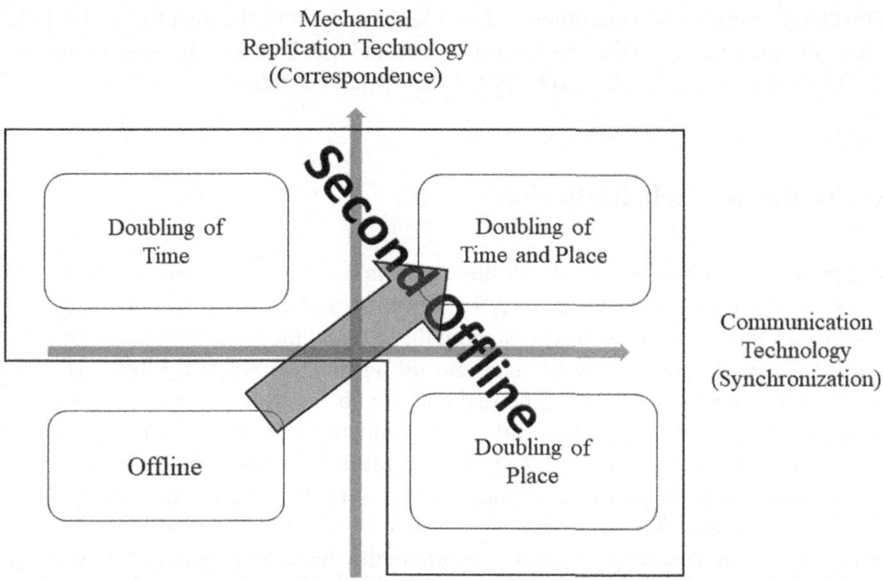


**Fig. 1** The doubling of time and place

*air tag*, you need to be at that same place. In other words, you and your friend share the place.

**Substitutional Reality**

Further, a new technology dubbed substitutional reality (SR) has garnered attention (Suzuki et al. 2012). We have been able to simulate the future and see the past with photos and videos. SR is a technology that depicts people who have existed in a certain place in the past as if they existed in the present moment. It uses VR and AR and enables one to experience a place's past as if it were the present. Replicating the images of the past in a place engenders a feeling of synchronicity between the past and present, and it becomes impossible to distinguish between them. SR also produces the phenomenon of doubling time.

What is important is that time synchronization creates the doubling of place, and place replication creates the doubling of time. In the doubling of place, the times of the two places are synchronized, but the two places are separate. In the same way, the doubling of time means that the places are superimposed, but the times are different. The synchronization of time produces the feeling of being at the same place, and the replication of the place produces the feeling of being at the same time.

Maruta posited that reading a letter in the place where the sender wrote it triggers the same kind of phenomenon. This chapter focuses on the usage of smartphones to access information by going to the place where the information exists. The Museum of London's Streetmuseum app, which Farman (2012) focused on, included a service that enabled users to see pictures in the museum's possession in front of the viewer by using their smartphone. The user could view the picture at the place where the picture was taken. As a result, a virtual "now" occurs. In other words, the doubling of time is equally easily possible with a smartphone.

## 5 Media for Self-Reflection

The previous discussion considered the superimposition of two different times and two separate places. The AR concept by Milgram and Kishino (1994) had a problem. It was an interesting idea that they put the real and the virtual on a line. But still, their idea was the dualism of the real and the virtual. de Souza e Silva and Sutko (2011) criticized this dualism of the real and the virtual, referring to "virtuality as a simulation." According to her, the same dualism appeared in the concept of Baudrillard's book *Simulacra and Simulation* (1994), a topic of focus in the 1980s. In essence, it was the dualistic relationship between the original and the copy. de Souza e Silva called this "technological virtuality". She asserted that such a dualistic theory of the real and the virtual was gradually becoming insufficient with the promulgation of mobile Internet. Following Deleuze's (1968) ideas, de Souza e Silva asserted that the real lurked in the virtual. She called this "the virtual as potential."

Thinking about it in this way, it is possible to establish the real and the virtual in both time and place. It becomes possible to establish a virtual place contained in the *here* and virtual time contained in the *now*. The second offline is the state in which virtual time and place are superimposed onto the time and place of everyday reality. The Virtual Reality Society of Japan defines virtuality as "existing or resulting in essence or effect though not in actual fact, form, or name."[7] This chapter abides by this definition.

### *5.1 Superimposing Here on Here*

Let us consider the case of superimposing one "here" onto another "here." A typical example of this would be navigation applications for cars and smartphones. Information displayed by a car navigation system or a navigation application of a smartphone is the position information of the current location. This information informs the user where they are now. Until recently, there have been limited instances where a person did not know their location. This would only occur when traveling or lost. However, there are now many people who search their current locations using Google Maps or similar applications. This is most frequent when traveling to a destination. We can display the destination location on the

[7] *The American heritage dictionary*, Second College Edition, Boston: Houghton Mifflin (1985: 1351).

smartphone by entering the store name, destination address, and searching for location information. The route to the destination is then displayed from the current location and the user can use the navigation function to reach their destination. It takes time to search for one's current location and destination on paper maps and the traveler would then have to figure out the route themself. Moreover, the paper map is rendered useless if one was to get lost in an unknown town. With Google Maps, this is highly unlikely.

What does this mean? We are aware of the current location by always using the smartphone's GPS functionality. The road signs in front, the shops on the right, and the restaurant on the left only serve to confirm that GPS information. The place where the individual exists is not first confirmed by using the information of the apparent location, but by superimposing the information gleaned from the smartphone. The virtual place is superimposed on the real place where one exists. A separate place is not being superimposed on the location; rather, it is another place hidden in the real location.

## 5.2 Superimposing Now on the Now

The same phenomenon occurs with time. An example is the replay images seen in TV sports programs. As mentioned previously, Marriott (1996) focused on instant replay techniques and posited that "live" and "non-live" create the action replay onscreen. This is an intriguing finding. Scannell (1996) also focused on Marriott's analysis. However, it was television broadcasts on which Marriott and Scannell focused, where the overlapping video was a replay of a live video. By contrast, this chapter focuses on images of us, our very selves. An example would be *real-time end roll movie* played at the end of a wedding ceremony that are popular in Japan. Recently, one such movie was played against the backdrop of the House of Peace after the banquet following the Inter-Korean Summit on April 27, 2018. The movie summarized the events of the day's meeting. Since these movies are screened immediately after the ceremony, they are created by repeating filming and editing short snippets. Even though these movies are images of the past, those who view them feel like they are watching the current image. A strange feeling occurs when individuals see themselves from an hour ago displayed on the screen, where the two "nows" overlap. The end roll is a video that plays at the end of a movie in which the names of the actors scroll across the screen. In the case of the *real-time end roll movie*, the movie does not exist on the screen. The movie is an event in which the individual performs. On the screen is an edited digest of the "now" occurring at the event. It becomes impossible to tell which now is the real now. Many people who watch these images are moved. But why? This is because of the superimposition of the current now. They are moved because the now has been superimposed and saved as an enjoyable moment. The distant past or the far-flung future is not currently being superimposed. They are moved because the enjoyable now, edited by media, has been superimposed onto the real now.

Smartphones automatically make short movies out of pictures that users take. The moments shared with friends can be enjoyed with these short movies if one has a smartphone. The revelry resulting from the superimposition of the now is becoming more popular.

## *5.3 Real-Time Simulation of the Self*

Recently, an interesting technology that is deeply intertwined with this chapter's discussion has gained attention. This is a real-time simulation that utilizes AR. ModiFace is a cosmetic simulation that uses AR technology. ModiFace makes it is possible to create a life-like simulation of one's face as if it was painted with makeup. It is also possible to edit one's face in real time as the user sees fit. It is not the act of applying makeup to one's face in a picture; rather, it applies makeup to one's face in a mirror in real time. Self-portrait applications such as SNOW and B612 are not merely self-portrait applications but they enable one to modify one's own face as well. Not only can one apply makeup, but it is also easy to sculpt one's face. The app includes feature to give oneself a double eyelid, eliminate wrinkles, and blemishes, in addition to changing the contours and shape of one's face, eyes, nose, and mouth. It is possible to change one's face into one that is desired by someone else. The app also enables video calls using these edits and modifications. One's unmodified real face will not be exposed to other users on this platform. In the list of features, it is also possible to draw on one's face, add bunny ears, or even change one's face into that of an animal. Further, the app allows real-time modification of every face that appears on the smartphone's LCD screen. Editing is now a characteristic of real-time simulation.

As Maruta (2008) found, replication always creates temporal delays. Therefore, real-time simulations, such as SNOW, have a slight time delay. However, because the delay is extremely small, face simulations are attached to real faces one after another. One's current face is the previously edited face from just moments ago. In other words, the now from just moments ago is mapped on top of the current now. This is the most novel form of the doubling of time and the newest form of now.

The defining characteristic of the second offline is the superimposition of another here and now on top of the here and now. What happens when synchronization and correspondence occur at the same time? Continuous replication in the form of real-time simulation blurs time sense, and continuous synchronization blurs place sense. The doubling of time and place liberates our sense of here and now from the here and now shown by clocks and maps, respectively. This is time and place in the second offline, where social time and place are fused with virtual time and place (Photograph 2).

**Photograph 2** AR camera app "SNOW" (©2020 SNOW Corp). https://apps.apple.com/jp/app/snow-%E3%82%B9%E3%83%8E%E3%83%BC/id1022267439

## 6 Conclusion: The Destination of a Love Transcending Time

Let us return to *The Lake House* in our introduction. Kate and Alex live in the same country and exchange letters to each other using the same mailbox. However, they are separated by two years. Alex looks for Kate's place and goes to see her. Kate does not know who Alex is. Because Kate receives Alex's letters two years later.

We live in our designated times and places which Giddens (1984) called regionalization or zoning. Giddens defined regionalization as "the temporal, spatial or time–space differentiation of regions either within or between locales" (Giddens 1984: 376). Giddens provided an example of a modern hospital, where regionalization and zoning are strictly managed, and posits that regionalization is not conducted using space but with times such as night shifts and afternoon shifts. He continued: "'Regionalization' should be understood not merely as localization in space but as referring to the zoning of time–space in relation to routinized social practices" (Giddens 1984: 119). He suggested that the rooms of a house are zoned by times. For example, the bedroom is used for sleeping at night. There are strict separations for the two different zones. However, there are places where the two zones are mixed. Giddens cites tea rooms and restrooms as back regions that exist in workplace settings (Giddens 1984: 127). These are a mixture of place zones; however, the same occurs with time zones.

In Japan, there are high schools that have night classes. In those high schools, daytime class students and night class students study in the same classroom. The times in which daily activities are undertaken differ between day time and night class students. They lead high school lives at the same high school; however, they never meet because they live in two different zones. One day, an night class student wrote a message on his desk. The next day, a daytime class student studying at the same desk read the message written on her desk. The two students then write messages on the desk in their shared classroom and become friends over time. They exist in the same place, but their times are misaligned. They encounter each other in two different time zones that exist in the same place. Here, correspondence rears its head again.

The curious reality depicted in *The Lake House* is due to the shared location of The Lake House between the two main characters. The house is Alex's current residence while the house was a residence for Kate in the past. In addition, there is the same mailbox in front of them. They use the same mailbox to exchange letters. Sharing a place engenders the feeling of the two-year gap as one that has been overcome. The replication of place creates a doubling of time. The mysterious mailbox in *The Lake House* is a replication technology that enables the doubling of time, and what is being replicated is not time, but possibly The Lake House. Mobile media, such as smartphones, coincide with the mailbox in the film. The smartphone is a form of communication media, but also a form of media that replicates places. My smartphone replicates my office. I wonder what kind of person it will bring to me. Let us hope that it is Sandra Bullock.

## References


Baudrillard J (1994) Simulacra and simulation. University of Michigan Press, Ann Arbor

Castells M (1996) The rise of the network society, the information age: economy, society and culture, vol I. Oxford, Malden, MA; Blackwell, UK

Castells M (2009) Communication power. Oxford University Press, Oxford

Castells M, Fernández-Ardèvol M, Linchuan Qiu J, Sey A (2006) Mobile communication and society. The MIT Press

de Souza e Silva A (2006) From cyber to hybrid: mobile technologies as interfaces of hybrid spaces. SAC 9(3):261–278

de Souza e Silva A, Frith J (2010) Locative mobile social networks: mapping communication and location in urban spaces. Mobilities 5(4):485–505

de Souza e Silva A, Sutko DM (2011) Theorizing locative technologies through philosophies of the virtual. Commun Theory 21(1):23–42

de Souza e Silva A, Frith J (2012) Mobile interfaces in public spaces: locational privacy, control and urban sociability. Routledge, New York

Deleuze G (1968) Différence et répétition. Presses Universitaires de France, Paris

Farman J (2012) Mobile interface theory: embodied space and locative media. Routledge Press, New York

Giddens A (1984) The constitution of society: outline of the theory of structuration. Polity Press

Giddens A (1990) The consequences of modernity. Polity Press

Goggin G (2012) Encoding place: the politics of mobile location technologies. In: Wilken R, Goggin G (ed) Mobile technology and place. Routledge

Hjorth L (2009) Mobile media in the Asia-Pacific. Routledge

Hjorth L (2010) Games and gaming. Berg

Hjorth L, Mechael A (2013) Online@AsiaPacific. Routledge

Hinton S, Hjorth L (2013) Understanding social media. Sage

Hjorth L, Richardson I (2014) Gaming in social, locative and mobile media. Palgrave
Ling R, Yttri B (2002) Hyper-coordination via mobile phones in Norway. In: Katz JE, Aakhus M (eds) Perpetual contact: mobile communication, private talk, public performance. University Press, Cambridge
Ling R, Lai C (2016) Microcoordination 2.0: social coordination in the age of smartphones and messaging apps. J Commun 66(5):834–856
Marriott S (1996) Time and time again: 'live' television commentary and the construction of replay talk, vol 18. Media Cultural and Society, London, Thousand Oaks and SAGE, New Delhi, pp 69–86
Maruta H (2008) Basho'ron: uebu No Riarizumu, Chiiki No Romanchishizumu. NTT Publishing Co., Ltd.
Milgram P, Kishino F (1994) A taxonomy of mixed reality visual displays, IEICE transactions on information systems, vol E77-d (12, December). http://etclab.mie.utoronto.ca/people/paul_dir/IEICE94/ieice.html. Accessed 23 Feb 2019
Meyrowitz J (1985) No sense of place: the impact of electronic media on social behavior. Oxford University Press
Moores S (2004) The doubling of place: electronic media, time-space arrangements and social relationships. In: Couldry N, Mc. Carthy A (ed) MediaSpace: place, scale and culture in a media age. Routledge, London
Moores S (2012) Media, place and mobility. Palgrave MacMillan, New York
Moores S (2017) Digital orientations: non-media-centric media studies and non-representational theories of practice. Peter Lang Pub. Inc.
Poster M (1990) The mode of information: poststructuralism and social context. Polity Press
Scannell P (1996) Radio, television and modern life: a phenomenological approach. Blackwell, Oxford
Suzuki K, Wakisaka S, Fujii N (2012) Substitutional reality system: a novel experimental platform for experiencing alternative reality. Sci Rep 2(459). https://doi.org/10.1038/srep00459
Tomita H (ed) (2016) The post-mobile society: from the smart/mobile to second offline. Routledge
Townsend AM (2000) Life in the real-time city: mobile telephones and urban metabolism. J Urban Technol 7(2):85–104

**Hidenori Tomita** is a professor at Kansai University in Osaka, Japan. His present research interests are mobile AR application, mobile media culture and sociology of mobile media. His publications include The Post-Mobile Society : From the Smart/Mobile to Second Offline (Routledge, 2016), Intimate Stranger: The cultural sociology about anonymity and intimacy (in Japanese) (Kansai University Press, 2009), Digital media training (in Japanese)(with Katsuya Minamida and Izumi Tsuji, Yuhikaku, 2007) and 'Keitai and Intimate Stranger' in Personal, Portable, Pedestrian: Mobile Phones in Japanese Life (edited by Mizuko Ito, Daisuke Okabe, and Misa Matsuda, MIT Press, 2005). Translation book is Perpetual Contact: Mobile Communication, Private Talk, Public Performance, (edited by James E. Katz and Mark Aakhus, Cambridge Univ Press, 2002): Hidenori Tomita (Translation Supervised), Keiji, Tachikawa (Supervised), Taemanaki Koshin no Jidai (in Japanese), NTT Press, 2003.

# Mobile Communication Technology and the Lifeworld: Examining the Implications of the Second Offline Concept from a Phenomenological Perspective

**James E. Katz**

**Abstract** The second offline perspective, as introduced by Hidenori Tomita and explored in his edited volume, *The post-mobile society: From the smart/mobile to second offline* (2015), offers a valuable way of perceiving how the world works from a communication viewpoint as well as what problems may arise. In this chapter, I examine historical precedents, drawing on both my own research and that presented in the Hidenori volume. These precedents offer insight into the way technology consistently affects lives as well as the enduring human inclinations that seek realization through our modes of communication, no matter the ambient technology. Using material from the Tomita volume, I delve into the second offline concept, connecting it to retrospective views of analog precursors from the nineteenth and early twentieth centuries. Selected issues from the Tomita volume chapters as they concern the second offline in today's society are explored along with a mini-theory that helps explain some micro-behavior, especially in an environment of dyadic relationships and mobile communication. I close the chapter by offering my gloss on the second offline construct, connecting it to significant issues concerning social realities stemming from the rise of the second offline throughout our lives.

This chapter was developed from the keynote speech of the International Symposium (Are You Second Offline?—The Diversity of Post-Mobile Society—). This symposium was held as a joint event of the Kansai University Faculty of Sociology's 50th Anniversary, the 2017 Japan Society of Information and Communications Research (JSICR) Kansai Meeting, and the 2017 Telecommunications Month Participatory Event.

J. E. Katz (✉)
College of Communication, Boston University, Boston, USA
e-mail: katz2020@bu.edu

 
H. Tomita (ed.), *The Second Offline*, Advances in Information and Communication Research 3, https://doi.org/10.1007/978-981-16-2425-4_2

# 1 Introduction

In this chapter, I examine the second offline perspective, which was introduced by Hidenori Tomita and explored in his fine edited volume, *The post-mobile society: From the smart/mobile to second offline* (2015). This collection of papers offers valuable material on how what he terms the "second offline" arose in the first place and how it has been unfolding during the early twenty-first century. As a scholar long interested in all matters digital, the Tomita thesis concerning the second offline offers me an inviting subject for further analysis; this is especially so given its implications for technological practices of everyday life and the quality of the lived experience. Hence this chapter offers a phenomenological exploration of the second offline thesis. By drawing on selected chapters from the Tomita volume, I will pursue several vectors to explore the second offline online concept. I will first look at the concept, then connect it to a retrospective view of the second offline as depicted by our analog precursors from the nineteenth century. Next, I will look at the selected issues from the Tomita volume contributors concerning the second offline, which will constitute the bulk of the chapter. Finally, I will close by offering my gloss on the second offline construct, connecting it to significant issues concerning social realities stemming from the rise in technological capabilities.

# 2 Contextualizing Second Offline Society

Drawing on the words of volume editor Tomita, the "second offline" concept refers to a real-world environment whose elements are augmented by virtual information and one in which "individuals are constantly referring to the online world." This statement succinctly defines far more than the concept but rather directly characterizes the profound changes that are taking place in most parts of the world. But despite all the dramatic recent changes in technology, and our at-times full absorption into technology's thrall, we must never lose sight of the important fact that it is through communication that we become human.

Not only do we come to exist through communication, we cannot long survive without it. The seemingly insatiable lust for communication with others, increasingly instantiated through our ever-more capable mobile devices, is a theme incorporated within the Tomita volume. It also underpins the book that Mark Aakhus and I edited in 2002, which was also translated into Japanese (2003). We intentionally chose the term "perpetual contact" to serve as a metaphor to stress communication's compelling force drawing us social animals together, as the second offline is a metaphor for the reality that enriches and complicates these interactions. The emphasis on interaction implicit in both the terms perpetual contact and second offline is appropriate when analyzing the organizing concepts underlying the second offline thesis.

To contextualize what we have today, we can look to the past to see what constants there might be in human behavior vis-à-vis communication technology. Although a detailed examination is far beyond the scope of this chapter, it may profit us to consider how "yesterday's tomorrow" expected our world of the new millennium to look like. As I aim to demonstrate, the pre-digital era's vision of the contemporary world can show us a perspective that will help us understand the issues people are now facing as the second offline continues to proliferate. It reveals both continuities and novelties in their expectations and our realities.

## 3 Historical Predictions of What is Today's Second Offline Society

Poring over historical materials, one can encounter astounding examples of prescient visions of what we might playfully call Analog Internet 1.0. Futurists of the nineteenth century drew on the available technology and predominating worldview to predict how we would be living in the twenty-first century. Let's pick a few examples to see how they did.

As may be seen from the first example, global video conferencing was envisioned shortly after the telephone was invented, in fact a mere two years after it was publicly demonstrated. The image (Fig. 1), taken from the English satirical magazine *Punch*, was published in 1879. It depicts a scene in which, from the comfort of their Victorian mansion, a father and mother chat with their daughter who is halfway around the world in Ceylon (now Sri Lanka). And what do they talk about? Perhaps the great political or economic issues of the day? New scientific discoveries? The latest news? No, they gossip about a potential romantic match for their daughter. This was computer dating before they even had computers! And parental concerns about a suitable partner for children also endure.

The French illustrator Albert Robida (1848–1926) clearly foresaw the processes and activities that people would be using for virtual interaction in Analog Internet 1.0. These ranged from education to socializing and squabbling (Fig. 2). Even the forerunner of videoconferencing, a technology now commonplace, was seen with remarkable accuracy (Robida, 1883; 1893). About the only thing he missed was the role of automation, specifically failing to foresee how a computer could substitute for the human operator depicted in his illustration. The importance of social interaction and "face-time" is prominent (Fig. 3). Although one must not read too much into the illustration, one may observe from the fashions illustrated the continuing importance of "lookism" and attractive appearance as an influence in human interaction at a distance no less than face-to-face.

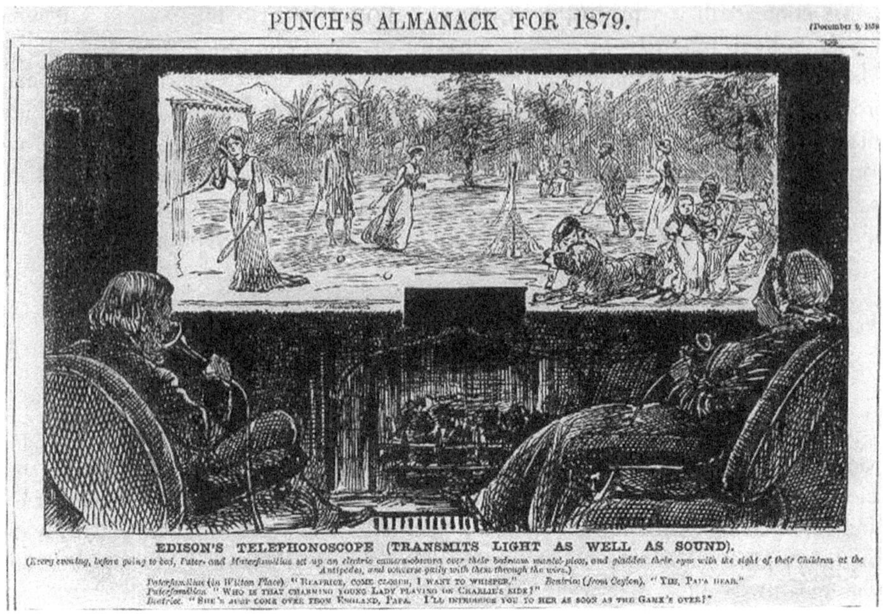


**Fig. 1** "Telephonescope" from the English satirical magazine *Punch* (1879)[1]

Technologically enabled remote surveillance was foreseen by some other illustrators. Observe such activity in colored illustration (Fig. 4), which depicts an angry wife spying on her inebriated husband. Of particular note is that the focus is much more on the prospects of interpersonal social conflict rather than on Panopticon-style surveillance operations that others feared and foresaw, and which another Frenchman, Michel Foucault (1926–1974), has made infamous in contemporary academic discourses. In this context, it is perhaps worth pointing out that my research on privacy often finds that people are more concerned about what their neighbors may know about them than remote or faceless bureaucracies of big business and government, although the threats these latter entities pose must not be underestimated.

Returning to Robida's vision, he was also able to capture with striking insight people's use of customized entertainment and news services. Note his depiction (Fig. 5) of urban commuters. In this drawing, one may see the various offerings via on-board stations. These programs include financial news, philosophy, romance novelettes and, for the little baby, a discourse on political economy. Robida foresaw our future multimedia delivery system, with the exception of having missed the wireless/personal possession dimension of the technology, as may be seen if one rides in today's public transportation systems. The point is that by extrapolating

[1]http://internet.kelasekstensi.co.id/IT/2615-2507/Videophone_22402_internet-kelasekstensi.html. Accessed 25 Dec 2020.

**Fig. 2** Virtual activities envisioned by Albert Robida, 1880s[2]

from our analog experiences with socializing and entertainment capabilities, the direction that people would take their communication technologies becomes clear.

This image of public transport echoes the mobile dimension of the second offline perspective. Those early forecasters saw the inherent need for perpetual contact even while on the move and the equally inherent drive toward a bourgeois level of personal comfort enabled via media. And of course, they also saw the continued central role, let alone existence, of gossip, conflict, social comparison and interpersonal communication that underlies all societies (Katz, 1999). They caught the interpersonal and customization notions but, as stated, not the role of a computer. They also missed the mobile phone and all that has followed in a wireless world. Neither did they see the next step after the first introduction of digital network technologies. That is, what would happen as the world of the second offline began to flourish. (I should mention that the question of how a new regime of automated vehicles will affect personal communication and social interaction is severely under-explored, which leaves vast terrain to be investigated by enterprising researchers.)

How big of a change in our lives did these foretellers miss? Let's briefly turn our attention to the recent transformation in the domain of mobile communication. The global success of the mobile phone is well known; there are more mobile phone subscriptions than there are people in the world. But in consideration of moving the process of mobile communication usage beyond the voice and texting facilities, much credit must be paid to the smartphone app. Unquestionably, the iPhone put

[2]https://archive.org/details/gri_33125008772267/page/n99. Accessed 25 Dec 2020. https://archive.org/details/levingtimesiclel00robi/page/n10. Accessed 25 Dec 2020.

**Fig. 3** Video chats foreseen by Albert Robida, ca. 1910[3]

the mobile phone revolution in high gear beyond voice. As part of that revolution, throughout the world Apple's iPhone became an aspirational icon that some even found literally worth killing to obtain. And why? A major part of the answer is the easy usability and ready access to connected apps. This facility has opened worlds of experience, information and support. As such this domain of activity has enjoyed unprecedented growth in popularity, as well as economic impact.

So we have seen that some critical human aspects were effectively captured when more than a century ago people imagined what our world might look like today. That is, they accurately extrapolated the consistencies of human nature. They even understood how we might be dealing with the "second offline." They were less sure-footed with the technology. Augmented reality, mobile phone apps, and Facebook were not seen when futurists extrapolated from what I have called Analogue Internet 1.0 to the world of the transistor and wireless network. Despite this, however, we could argue that they did catch much of the phenomenological sense of what we now call web 2.0.

With mobile communication, the built (and even the natural) environment has become much richer environments from which to gather and access information on the move. Likewise, there was reciprocity: those in stationary places could also track the location of people on the move, and obtain information about the local environment around those travelers as they were passing through.

---

[3]https://vsemart.com/french-artist-predictor-albert-robida/. Accessed 27 Dec 2020.

**Fig. 4** Spousal monitoring envisioned in 1902: "future possibilities of wireless telegraphy," (Eskergian, *St. Louis Star*, 2-20-1902)[4]

Returning our attention from the setting of futuristic projections and consumer demand to another phase of the Tomita volume, namely the portion addressing the "post-mobile society," which I find to be one of its most compelling aspects. This section delves into a historically rich perspective on several domains surrounding communication technology practices, the human psyche, and physical mobility. I shall discuss a few ideas in this section, especially in terms of the phenomenology of the second online.

[4]https://commons.wikimedia.org/wiki/File:Future_Possibilities_of_Wireless_Telegraphy_(Eksergian).jpg. Accessed 27 Dec 2020.

**Fig. 5** Podcasts envisioned: transit users listening to the reading of works (Uzanne and Robida 1895)[5]

# 4 Exploring the Tomita Volume Chapters

Addressing the matter at a high level, the Tomita volume allows the reader to see how the many parts of his perspective have come together to construct the contemporary digitally informed world.

## *4.1 Telepresence, Teledistance; the Camera and the Selfie*

For example, in part one of the books, there is a chapter on the genealogy of telepresence. Chapter author Kyoung-hwa Yonnie Kim reintroduces the reader to the profoundly disturbing Austrian writer Franz Kafka (1883–1924). Kim tells us of the tantalizing pleasures of contact via remote communication (in this case the mail) even while ostensibly denying interacting parties the pleasures of physical connection. Indeed, the parties may have intentionally sought to maintain this physical distance, isolating and conveying emotion solely by the written word of their letters. In Kim's retelling, Kafka relied on correspondence to conduct his social relationship with his romantic partner; though this may have been fulfilling for him, it did not seem so for his fiancée who broke off the relationship, presumably because of

---

[5]https://archive.org/details/UzanneContesBibliophiles1895bnf/page/n159/mode/2up. Accessed 27 Dec 2020.

the lack of direct physical interaction. Generally speaking, the use of letters required text to effectuate their communication purpose. Kim alludes to the convergence of mass production, the printing industry and photographs, along with a postal system, in creating an industrial-era form of "augmented reality," namely the postcard. (This frustration with the limitations of written language may help explain the popularity of emoji and other ornamentations to correspondence of the era; stamps and their positioning could be an effective way to visually supplement correspondence.)

Kim describes the nationalistic uses of the postcards, but the postcard remains a quintessential status gift that is designed to create an impression both explicit and latent, in the eye of the beholder.

It is worth mentioning another nineteenth-century form of augmented reality, also predominantly deployed by the bourgeoisie—the stereoscope. Just as the postcard allowed one to envision faraway places, so too did the stereoscope. Just as one can visit today a mobile phone store to try out a virtual reality system, including a chair from which one can go skiing or swimming with manta rays, so too did our predecessors troop to centers where the distant reality, augmented through technology, could make the Egyptian pyramids or Parisian street scenes come alive before one's eyes. Various public parlors were established where people could view stereoscopic presentations of exotic places and people, and in wealthier homes, the stereoscope itself was installed. Indeed, even complete libraries of views from around the world were available via mail, and public libraries (Fig. 6) also provided this educational resource for anyone who wished to see them.

Tomoyuki Okada sheds valuable light on the perennial argument concerning technological determinism and the role of affordances. By telling the story of the rise of visual communication via Japan's photo-sharing culture (e.g., photo-stickers), he demonstrates how it helped stimulate the birth of the camera phone. Okada also points to the role of Yamamoto Shinsuke of Sharp Corp. who was able to leapfrog the competing company KDDI. KDDI had earlier introduced a camera that could be attached to the cell phone and Kyocera produced a PHS device with a built-in camera; both of these innovations were greeted by the marketplace with indifference. Part of this indifference was due to the fact that the 1999 PHS camera phone by Kyocera had the camera pointing in the same direction as the operator. Presumably with much better and cheaper cameras available, both film and digital, this was not an impressive feature for users. It was Sharp's innovation —putting it on the camera's backside—that made a huge difference in consumer interest, dramatically translating into mushrooming purchases. Yet as Okada shows, and has been confirmed by subsequent experiences around the globe, there does seem to be a practically universal desire to have a camera on both the front side and back side of the phone. In the West, many experts have been puzzled by the excitement over the selfie. Nonetheless, by drawing on the insight from the experience of Japan, most notably with the wildly popular photo sharing of young people, the unbridled enthusiasm could be perhaps understood. In other words, no one knew people wanted to take selfies in abundance until the capability to do so came into existence. Theories of "hard technological determinism" do not seem to

**Fig. 6** Children viewing stereoscopic images in the Cincinnati Public Library, ca. 1895[6]

be appropriate here. Nothing about having a camera on the phone physically compels people to take pictures. Despite this, with the rise of the visual capability technologically speaking, and the availability of photo curation services such as Instagram, the camera has become a vital component, if not the most important aspect, of the smartphone.

Another topic of enduring concern is that of romantic relationships and the use of mobile communication. This topic is dealt with in the chapter by Ichiyo Habuchi in terms of university students' relationships. The desire for "non-present" attachments and interaction has often been overlooked, inverting as it does traditional understandings of the seemingly ultimate objective in romantic partnerships, namely colocation. Yet this inversion is shown in Kafka's communication processes, as sketched out by Kim. She reveals the strange brilliance of Kafka, and the insight he sheds on the human condition through his writing, and exemplified in his biography; these work well as case studies that complement statistical survey data.

This concern about relationships, especially the self vis-à-vis the other, brings us back to the topic of selfies, which is discussed by Ito. The curation of mobile phone photos, which grew out of the processes analyzed in Okada's chapter mentioned

[6]https://www.messynessychic.com/2014/06/17/seriously-though-how-did-the-most-beautiful-library-in-america-get-demolished/. Accessed 4 January 2021.

above, is another unexpected development that did not seem to be predicted by those who have tried to peer into the future. Yet as I have shown elsewhere, it is but a continuation of earlier practices, amplified and enhanced by advancing technological capabilities.

How does the selfie-taking process affect relationships for both those in the selfie and those around the selfie-takers themselves? In this regard, I will mention a study that I did with Daniel Halpern, my former student and now a professor in Chile. Using panel data—that is, surveying the same couples at one time and then again a year later. What we found was that the more individuals who were in a couple of relationship gave attention to, and curated, their selfie photos, the more likely they were to experience relationship problems. The study was done in a careful way to identify which came first: the selfie activity or the problem in the relationship. We wanted to make sure that the direction of causality was clear. The data indicated that curation came first; it was a practice presumably adopted because the relationship developed problems rather than the relationship problems leading to selfie attention and curation. This finding held only for those who took selfies of themselves. By contrast, when couples took selfies together, we detected no deleterious effect; rather, this practice seemed to act as a cement to strengthen the relationship. The positive effect of couples taking selfies together is illustrated by the pose assumed by the people in Fig. 7.

**Fig. 7** A couple taking a selfie together. *Source* James E. Katz

## 4.2 Medical and Healthcare

Health is important to everyone so it is no surprise that mobile communication would be directed toward assisting people in this area. Yuichi Kogure's chapter addresses the second offline perspective in the medical field. Highlighted is the use of the second offline domain for diagnostic and surgical procedures. Complementing the discussion of the usefulness of these technologies is a description of the encumbrances imposed on second offline by older legalistic procedures. To comply with defined ethical standards and professional expectations, the medical practitioner is required to have face-to-face contact with the subject. While Kogure sees this reliance on paper as a distinctive problem, it is also the case that it is reflective of a higher-level issue, namely the retrograde sensibility among officialdom. As such, it hobbles the ability to deliver both quality medical care and adds strain on both physician and patient. Further, it requires administrative oversight with all the psychological, economic, and infrastructural costs associated with those processes.

This is a diagnosis (pun intended) I agree with. Still, one must not overlook the structural consequences of a move to electronic medical systems and the subsequent "big data" regimes that will perforce follow. Having looked at this with Ronald Rice when a similar revolution was taking place in the US, we observed how problems immediately arise with the move to electronic record-keeping (Rice & Katz, 2000). First, it represents a major stumbling block for physicians. Not only is there the educational and operational demands, but from a phenomenological viewpoint, it interferes with physicians' ability to have useful and valued face-to-face contact with patients. Many patients complain about the incessant demand of the physician's attention by the computer terminal and the fact that the physician must turn their back on the patient, something that is "read" by the patient, no matter how unintentionally, as disrespectful. Also unintentional is the impression generated that form completion takes precedence over patient treatment. Yet all is not hopeless: via mobile devices and data collection, harnessed with artificial intelligence, both patients and physicians can be better served. Data can be remotely and silently collected both prior to and during the examination. This is but one way that with further development the second offline can be of great service to the public's health in Japan and elsewhere. The second offline perspective, if properly understood, can allow a reconceptualization of the medical data adjunct to healthcare delivery as a social process.

## 4.3 Education

The potential insights to be yielded by the second offline perspective for education are also profound, as suggested in the chapter by Uematsu Eriko. She highlights several ways the second offline can help achieve the benefits of technologically enabled education once the concomitant technological obstacles are removed. Her insightful analyses focus on three major impediments to deploying technology and thus take advantage of a second offline approach. The first of these is the technology infrastructure. Do all students have access to the needed device and software? It's difficult to foresee how new technology can be made available equally to students, given the varying socio-economic situations of families. This problem is exacerbated when combined with the question of individual initiative and mastery of the relevant educational technology. For example, some students might have work-arounds, tutors, or money for technical tools that advantage them relative to their fellow students. The second dimension is teacher preparation. Teachers already have a difficult job, and it may be unreasonable to suddenly expect them to not only master the technology but then also understand how best to lead the class in teaching them how to use the technology.

Conversely, training in the use of such technologies, and having technical support in addressing the inevitable problems that are encountered, is both logistically and pedagogically challenging. It need hardly be mentioned that these initiatives can be expensive in terms of both infrastructure and training. Moreover, there is an understandable reluctance on the part of teachers to adopt new innovations given the unpromising history of failed gadgetry. Too often teachers have been forced to adopt the latest and greatest "new thing" only to see their students become baffled and disheartened as the innovation falls short of promises. Additionally, such innovations may undermine the authority of, and respect students have for, the classroom instructors, harming their ability to properly exercise their leadership, with all the negative learning and psychological fallout that accompanies it. Drawing on an understanding of the larger structure and phenomenology of what's going on, which the second offline invites, sounder solutions can be advanced, ones that are integrated with the realities of the educational system.

## *4.4 Interpersonal Communication and the Problem of the Present Other*

The second offline perspective also sheds light on how people manage their communication practices, especially those involving portable or mobile devices. This may be seen in a study of the so-called "triple junction model" of mobile media by Fujimoto. The triple junction model addresses something that parallels a concept called phone snubbing, or phubbing. Both terms are related to what happens when there are people co-present during a mobile phone call. I myself explored this topic, without developing a specialized term for it in my book *Connections*. The spillover effects were also addressed by Kenneth Gergen. It may be safely said that consequences for the people around the mobile phone user can be both incremental and far-reaching. Complementing Kenichi Fujimoto's idea, these works cumulatively find that getting calls can be isolating for those not included in the call. Although I have not collected data systematically on the question, I do have sufficient case studies and examples to support the argument that these processes affect people at every level, in settings from diplomatic missions to bowling clubs. This chapter is not an occasion to explore the process in depth, yet we can elucidate it at a broad level that exemplifies the second offline phenomenology.

More particularly, even as these models of phubbing are fundamental to understanding the use of communication technology, as far as I'm aware their analyses overlook the crucial issue of what the relationship is between the "phubber," that is the person doing the snubbing, and the "phubee," the person being snubbed. The focus for this critical distinction arises less in terms of what the relationship is between the phubber and phubee but rather between the phubee and the person that the phubber is engaging with.

My model of this interpersonal situation is straightforward and based on implicit knowledge of the participants. When I first published on the subject, in a 2004 piece entitled "A nation of ghosts," I referred to the problem as the choreography of mobile communication (Katz, 2004). Consider an abstract example, which is depicted in Fig. 8. Take two people who are friends with each other, and call them Alter and Ego. They are in a face-to-face conversation (Fig. 8①) Alter then gets a phone call and decides to accept it (Fig. 8②); Ego is in a suspended state awaiting implicit or explicit identification of the calling party. Then Ego will react to the scenario as follows, all else being equal (that is to say that Ego does not have an antipyretic relationship with the caller). If caller is known to both members of the dyad (and assuming that Ego is not antipathetic to the caller) the reaction of Ego will be friendly toward Alter and the outside caller (Fig. 8④). Ego will not experience negative emotions due to the call. On the other hand, if the phone call Alter receives is from a caller not known to Ego, then Ego will experience negative emotions (Fig. 8③), directed to Alter and the outside caller. Alter may not be directly aware of this reaction. The large negative sign in Fig. 8③ and positive sign in Fig. 8④ indicate the direction of Ego's emotional state upon Alter's accepting the outside call.

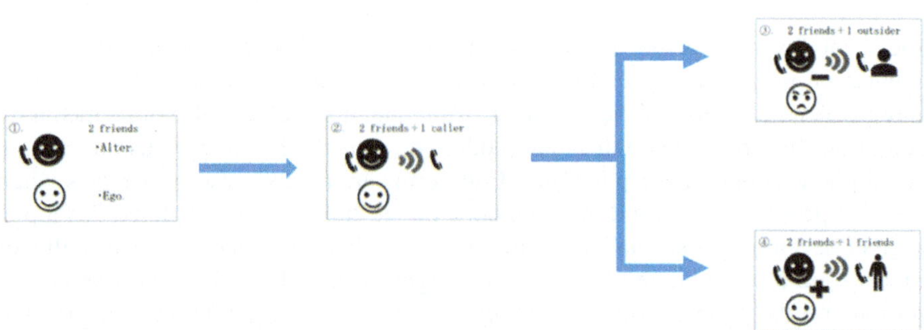


**Fig. 8** A model of emotional reactions of interlocutor when conversational partner accepts a mobile phone call

The negative emotions may not be severe, and may even be subliminal to Ego. However, they are likely to accrete over time, exacerbating negative moods and other sequela. One reason this process takes place is because Ego is being excluded from a group membership, ephemeral though it might be. As is demonstrated in social psychological experiments, triads quickly become dyads and monads. And, as argued at the beginning of this chapter, communication and inclusion are important for an individual's survival, including one's social identity; and exclusionary communication practices can threaten the individual's well-being.

Beyond the individual level, it's worth considering the accretive impact of all this phubbing and associated "mentally absent, physically present" engagement with our devices, that is our second offline. Arguably, there can be substantial downsides on an interpersonal and social level over a good number of years. That is the topic I would like to address next.

## 5 Socio-Psychological and Public Policy Ramifications of the Second Offline

In my final section, I would like to shift from commenting on the second offline in context, which has been the focus of my chapter thus far, to addressing some more subtle risks that the rise of the second offline poses. These risks are especially relevant to Japan which, more than any other country, has a culture that seems to readily adopt and innovate upon the fruits of the second offline format. This cultural characteristic has many advantages for the Japanese people and is integral to the nation's cultural and economic success story. Yet the second offline world may also be a source of societal problems, some of which seem readily apparent, but others may not be immediately causally linked.

On the one hand, the second offline brings people together, especially in ways that would otherwise not be possible. This is especially valuable during pandemics and other emergencies. But is it eroding face-to-face communication and other benefits that occur via non-mediated communication? Face-to-face communication may have benefits that simply cannot be replaced with contemporary communication, no matter how "visually rich" and authentic it may seem. That is, the gap between our sense of what is real and what is artificial cannot be overcome no matter how realistic the technology is that connects two physically distant people. There is something ineffable but nonetheless real about being in the physical presence of another human and technology, despite all its fantastic achievements, seems unable to reproduce that reality.

Assuming this line of reasoning is valid, it raises an important question about the effects of the second offline. Could it be that the ever-expanding embrace of the second offline is related to the (pre-pandemic) rise of loneliness? The second offline may be a factor that supports the formation of the single individual household, which would seem obviously related to loneliness. After all, single individual household units as a proportion of all living arrangements are at an all-time high in Japan (as, again, in many other countries). Second, and related, there seems to be decreasing relationship formation. Third, there appears to be deep pessimism about the future of Japan.[7] I would submit that these three are linked with each other, and are also linked with, and fed by, the rise of the second offline. We can expect virtual voice companions to proliferate, even as they are adumbrated in such gadgets as Amazon's Alexa, Google's Voice and Apple's Siri. And of course, these master trends seem to be manifesting themselves not only in Japan but in all developed countries.

What about robots and their role in the second offline? Robot and holographic companions are commercially available and are constantly improving in their capabilities. Will their easy access and frequent use further exacerbate loneliness and pessimism? My investigations, and those of many others, suggest the answer is yes, they will. Specifically, humans need challenges and demands placed on them in order to remain effective and fully operational in line with our biological heritage. Now I hasten to add that while we are not biologically determined in our behavior, still there are biological predicates to our behavior.

The second offline allows us to fulfill our desires in terms of entertainment, information, and amusement, as well as social relationships, including artificial relationships. However, the fact that they can do this with such ease and customization actually depletes or diminishes our social life's quality. Just as is the case with too much food, or the wrong types of food, our bodies become worse off due to our seemingly rational decisions. So as it is with too much of the wrong kind of food, it is likewise for too much of the wrong kinds of social or automated social interaction. They degrade aspects of our mental equilibrium, diminishing life quality.

Looking to the future, there are underlying risks with technological progress in terms of the second offline. This, surprisingly, is of not too many, but too few, psychological demands made upon people. This was not part of either the analog future imagined a century ago. But it was beginning to be seen in the concerns arising around the digital world 1.0.

Like other second-order effects of technologies, there are parallels here in that automobiles and mass transportation systems have robbed us of the health given by natural exercise such as walking. To put it puckishly, they have reconfigured our bodies even as they have reconfigured our built environments. Personal comfort, welfare and gratification are the manifest benefits of the second offline, but perhaps interpersonal diminishment is the latent cost that we, unaware, pay. However, awareness of this trap can provide us with an escape-hatch. Just as knowledge about the virtues of exercise have given rise to exercise studios, home treadmills, and jogging, the awareness of the social risks of what I might call "second offline laziness" will allow us to create affordances that will avoid such traps. This, I think,

[7]BBC NEWS, 26 July 2016, Japan knife attack: 19 killed at care centre in Sagamihara (Accessed on 27 November 2020). https://www.bbc.com/news/world-asia-36890655. Accessed 27 Dec 2020.

**Fig. 9** Children playing with mobile phones during Halloween festivities. *Source* James E. Katz

is the ultimate lesson for the next step in terms of applying an understanding of the second offline concept. The challenge before us is clear. First we need to do more research. This is especially the case with the second offline lifeworld of children, as metaphorically depicted in the photo (Fig. 9) of children using cell phones as they go about enjoying Halloween, a festival of fun and fright. Then, based on research findings, we should aim to inspire and direct technology designers to create the systems that will force us to leave our comfort zones and engage productively with other humans. And, once such technologies are identified, people should be urged to adopt them. Admittedly, this is not an easy task, but it is an important one.

Through research of people such as those who explore these topics in Japan and elsewhere, we can create a better life, a richer future, for the Japanese people and for those others around the world who are increasingly enthralled with the world of the second offline.

## References

Eksergian E (1902) Future possibilities of wireless telegraphy, *St Louis Star* (via 'Origins of the Sunday Comics'), February 20

Katz JE (1999) Connections: social and cultural studies of the telephone in American life. Transaction Publishers, Piscataway, NJ

Katz JE (2004) A nation of ghosts? Choreography of mobile communication in public spaces. In: Nyíri K (ed) Mobile democracy: essays on society, self and politics. Passagen Verlag, Vienna, pp 21–32

Katz JE, Aakhus M (eds) (2002) Perpetual contact: mobile communication, private talk, public performance. Cambridge University Press

Rice RE, Katz JE (eds) (2000) Internet and health communication: experience and expectations. Sage, Thousand Oaks, CA

Robida A (1883) Le vingtième siècle. Georges Decaux Editeur, Paris, p 71

Robida A (1893) Le vingtième siècle: la vie électrique. Librairie illustrée, Paris, pp 31, 187

Tomita H (ed) (2015) The post-mobile society: from the smart/mobile to second offline. Routledge, New York

Uzanne O, Robida A (1895) Contes pour les bibliophiles. May et Motteroz, Paris, p 142

**James E. Katz** is the Feld Professor of Emerging Media and also directs COM's Division of Emerging Media Studies. He recently concluded service as Distinguished Professor at Peking University's New Media School. His pioneering publications on the effects of artificial intelligence (AI), social media, mobile communication, robot-human interaction, have been internationally recognized and translated into many other languages, including Chinese and Japanese. His two most recent books, Journalism and the Search for Truth in an Age of Social Media, co-edited with Kate Mays, and Philosophy of Emerging Media, co-edited with Juliet Floyd, were published by Oxford University Press in 2019 and 2016, respectively. An earlier book, The Social Media President: Barack Obama and the Politics of Citizen Engagement, was published in 2013 by Macmillan. Other volumes include Social Consequences of Internet Use: Access, Involvement, Expression (with Ronald E. Rice) and Handbook of Mobile Communication Studies, both of which were published by MIT Press. According to Google Scholar, his work has been cited more than 16,000 times. Prior to his Boston University appointment, he was Board of Governors Distinguished Professor of Communication at Rutgers University (the title being the highest honor that Rutgers can bestow on one of its faculty) and served two terms as chair of its Department of Communication. Preceding his tenure at Rutgers, Katz was a Distinguished Member of Staff and director of the social science research unit at Bell Communications Research (Bellcore). In 2013, he received an honorary doctorate from Budapesti Műszaki és Gazdaságtudományi Egyetem (Budapest University of Technology and Economics, BME), the world's oldest technological university. Among his other awards are the Ogburn career achievement award from the American Sociological Association and the Fulbright Distinguished Chair in Twentieth Century Communications History. He is a Fellow of several professional societies, including the International Communication Association and the American Association for the Advancement Science (AAAS), America's most visible scientific society. I have spent time at other Boston area institutions, having been awarded fellowships at Harvard and MIT, and also at Princeton, where he was also awarded a fellowship. He holds two patents, one of which has been internationally licensed.

# Society Transformed through Mobile Media

# Merged Reality: A Second "Second Offline"

**Michael Björn**

**Abstract** This paper examines and expands upon the idea of a second offline from the perspective of market research carried out mainly between 2007 and 2018, primarily but not exclusively on early adopters of information and communication technology. Second offline is here taken to denote a situation where people are never completely offline anymore because the Internet has become so pervasive that it is used intermittently and without reflection, for example, in smartphones, also in situations that seemingly do not necessitate its use, creating an ever-present digital overlay of information on top of the physical world. We then conclude that there are two distinct types of second offline. In the first type, which many modern consumers currently experience, people can separate between physical and digital realities if they try. However in the second type, here called merged reality, people can no longer separate between physical and digital realities even if they try. Consumers do not experience merged reality today, but expect that to happen with AR/VR technology. Examples of consumer expectations from market research are given. Finally, ramifications of merged reality are discussed, including subjectification of reality, motion sickness, the importance of consumer imagination and the expectations on use of time.

## 1 Introduction: Offline and the Second Offline

Once there was a world without the Internet. And when the Internet was introduced, it divided the world into two halves; the part that had existed up to that point was now called "offline" and the new part was labeled "online".

But then, the Internet grew and people started taking it with them in their pockets wherever they went. Before long, they would use it hundreds of times every day without reflecting over it, and as a result, separating the world into offline and online parts no longer made sense to them.

M. Björn (✉)
Ericsson Consumer and IndustryLab, Stockholm, Sweden
e-mail: michael.bjorn@ericsson.com



H. Tomita (ed.), *The Second Offline*, Advances in Information and Communication Research 3, https://doi.org/10.1007/978-981-16-2425-4_3

Such unpremeditated use of the Internet in everyday situations could be described as a "second offline", since people were just acting out their lives in the world as they always had. In the second offline you cannot really be offline for a second—but you never think about that as being "online".

This paper is mainly an examination of the second offline concept, as proposed in the book "The Post Mobile Society: From the smart/mobile to the second offline" (Tomita 2016) from a consumer market research practitioner's perspective.

I start by examining the second offline from the perspective of consumer studies I have been driving or actively participating in over the last few years at Ericsson ConsumerLab. Based particularly on studies of early adopters of information and information technology, this gives reason to question the idea of the second offline as a single unified concept. Instead, we try to refine the second offline by talking about a first and a second generation of unpremeditated Internet use in everyday life. Here, the first generation will be called "second offline" as originally proposed by Tomita and the second generation will be called "merged reality" for reasons that will be explained in this paper.

I would like to stress that this proposal comes from a consumer market research perspective and would probably need further probing and theoretical enquiry.

## 2 The Basic Concept of Second Offline

According to Tomita (2016), second offline indicates a "context in which virtual information is superimposed onto real space". As a consequence, this leads to a discussion about the meaning of "virtual". This involves trying to distinguish between what is "supposed" in the sense of "not really possible" and "virtual" as "existing in essence or effect though not in actual fact or form".

However, to my understanding, the concept of second offline is not necessarily about virtual information per se, but rather about the integration of information and communications technology (ICT) into everyday life and, as an extension, the perception by consumers of digital information as a part of their reality. ICT can be described as an extensional term for information technology (IT) that stresses the role of unified communications and the integration of telecommunications (telephone lines and wireless signals), computers as well as necessary enterprise software, middleware, storage, and audio-visual systems, which enable users to access, store, transmit, and manipulate information. In other words, ICT combines the processing and management of digital information with its distribution over telecommunications networks. This latter part is crucial for a second offline because via such distribution, digital information becomes pervasively available throughout society at speeds which are perceived by the users of the information to be in real time, although from a technical perspective such distribution may only be near real time at best.

As a result, in the second offline, it is real information that forms the basis by being ubiquitously available through telecommunications networks, rather than virtual information. In fact, near-instant distribution of the information is more important for the forming of a second offline than the type of information itself. Hence, if we want to take the idea of a second offline as far back as the introduction of telephony and the first generation of cellular networks, we could also include analog information—as long as it is distributed by telecommunications networks.

However, as information density was lower back then, it is more productive to focus the discussion about a second offline on digital information. Thus, from an Internet user's point of view, the perception of physical reality has for all practical purposes merged with the perception of the Internet. Being offline is no longer an available or practical option to a person in such a situation, and hence we conceptualize this situation as a second offline.

For this merged perception to really arise, the Internet must be available at all points in time, which points to the centrality of information distribution, via the mobile phone in general and the smartphone in particular.

When is it then reasonable to assume that second offline situations as described above became commonplace? Based on a large data set, collected 2007–2014, consisting of mobile phone users in the Americas, Europe, and developed Asia, our analysis points to an accelerated increase in overall use of mobile social networking and mobile browsing from around 2011 onwards (Ericsson ConsumerLab 2016a). In other words, if we were to see this rise of mobile use of digital information as an indication of an everyday experience where digital data overlays are nearly always present, this started being commonplace around the year 2011 on a global scale (Fig. 1).

## 3 A Second Offline in Practice

What does it mean practically to experience a second offline? Here are some examples from our research that indicate actual shifts in consumer behaviors.

In a report called In-line Shopping (Ericsson ConsumerLab 2012) based on Internet users in the USA, we described how in-store and online shopping behaviors were merging to the point where they were no longer possible to separate. 32% of smartphone users in the survey were already shopping with smartphones. Furthermore, it turned out that they were simultaneously combining the benefits of shopping in-store and online, which is why the merged shopping phenomenon we witnessed would best be described as in-line shopping, or an interweaving of in-store and online.

Another example was put forth with the concept of social silos (Ericsson ConsumerLab 2016b). Here, we saw how people were willingly turning their social

---

[1]Base: Mobile phone users aged 15–69 in the Americas (Argentina, Brazil, Canada, USA), Europe (France, Germany, Italy, Spain, Sweden, UK), and Developed Asia (Australia, Japan, Korea). Mobile phone users aged 15–64 within tier 1–3 urban areas in Developing Asia (China, India, Indonesia). Source: Ericsson ConsumerLab Analytical Platform, 2007–2014.

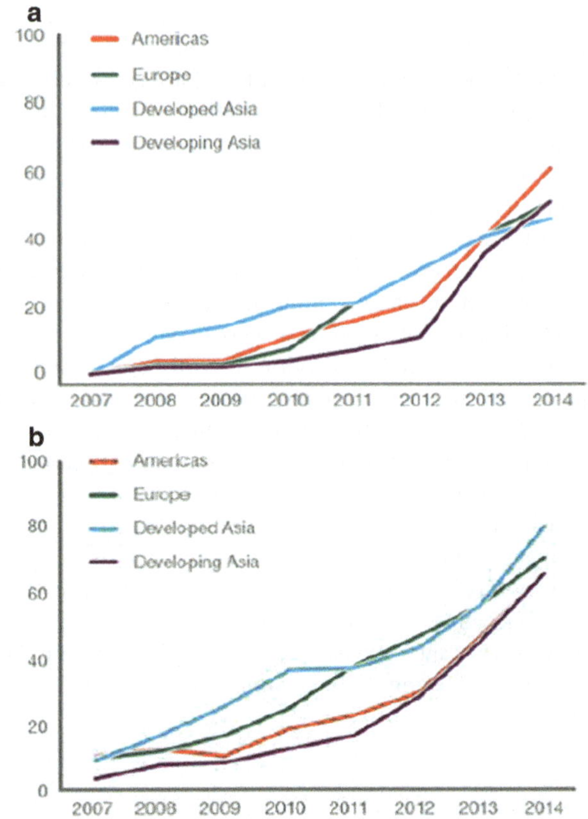


**Fig. 1** **a** Percentage of respondents who use social networking on mobile phone on a daily basis.[11] **b** Percentage of respondents who browse the Internet on mobile phones on a weekly basis

networks into silos and in a very concrete way superimposing information from their social network contacts over other sources of information in their physical environment. Based on early adopters from 14 major cities globally, respondents in the survey were in effect actively as well as consciously cutting out these other sources of information from their perception. For example, in this study one in three respondents said that social networks were their main source of news. They were in other words forming a digital silo around them that would render other sources less visible. More than one in four also valued their contacts' opinions more than politicians' viewpoints, meaning that the silo effect extended beyond personal relationships, influencing their perception of society and reality overall.

The final example comes from a report titled From Healthcare to Homecare (Ericsson ConsumerLab 2017a). In this case, the insights were based on a large online survey of smartphone/mobile broadband users in Germany, Japan, South Korea, the UK and the USA who had higher than average use of fitness trackers, smartwatches, and health apps to monitor their health. The analysis of their answers gave at hand that they wanted healthcare to become decentralized, moving from hospitals toward homes—and they could see this happening due to their previous experiences with the confluence of the digital and physical worlds. So, for example, 39% of patients with chronic ailments in the study preferred online consultations to face-to-face meetings. They did not see a digital consultation as "unreal" and a physical consultation as "real". Instead, they saw both types as simply a consultation. In addition, they saw substantial merits with a digital consultation as it would save them time and effort. Patients with chronic ailments need to visit hospitals regularly and not only does this take considerable time both for transportation and for wait time at the hospital, but it also disrupts other daily activities, such as work.

Furthermore, many were open to having patient data centralized, in effect turning hospitals into data centers. Specifically, 35% of respondents thought that an online central repository of medical records would improve healthcare management. Behind this is the expectation or even experience that what happens in the digital world happens in "reality", even when it comes to healthcare. Such expectations and experiences are truly of a second offline nature.

## 4 The Second "Second Offline"

Although we characterize the second offline as a situation where people's perceptions of reality have merged with the perception of the Internet, and we have given several examples of such behavior above, this is in fact only true on a generalized level. At any given moment, if you were to ask someone if his or her experience in that instant was primarily digital or primarily physical, you will likely get a clear-cut answer.

For example, if we go back to the in-line shopping case described above, although it would be true that consumers may no longer be able to disentangle all the steps that led to the purchase of a specific product or service into digital and physical experiential components a week after that purchase, they would still know things like "now I am doing price comparisons on my phone" or "I am talking to a sales representative in the store right now" if they were asked at the specific points in time of such activities occurring.

However, the Internet has shifted from being a predominately text-based source of information to one that is comprised of mainly video traffic. And video does no longer have to come with a TV sofa. Instead, video is viewed increasingly on the move and in real time. In fact, everything around us is increasingly being interpreted as moving images. And this digital imagery is improving quickly in quality, to the point where it becomes very realistic.

With the famous paper "Are you living in a computer simulation?" Nick Bostrom (Bostrom 2003) opened the perspective on a situation where consumers

[1] Base: Mobile phone users aged 15–69 in the Americas (Argentina, Brazil, Canada, USA), Europe (France, Germany, Italy, Spain, Sweden, UK), and Developed Asia (Australia, Japan, Korea). Mobile phone users aged 15–64 within tier 1–3 urban areas in Developing Asia (China, India, Indonesia). Source: Ericsson ConsumerLab Analytical Platform, 2007–2014.

would in fact not know if their experience was digital or physical, ever. This would be a situation where their perception of reality has fully merged with digital media itself. From an experiential perspective, we could call this a merged reality, and as such that would constitute a "second" second offline, because the confluence of the digital and the physical would no longer be possible to disentangle. A person experiencing a given situation would no longer be able to differ between the digital and physical components that make up the experience, even if she or he tried at the moment when the situation occurred.

Obviously, technologies like virtual reality (VR) and augmented reality (AR) are relevant to talk about as means that could potentially move consumer experiences to such a "second" second offline, or, merged reality as it will be referred to here. But it is also important to differentiate between technologies used and a person having an actual experience of such a merged reality.

A technology that further leads in this direction is so-called mixed reality (MR). But again, MR takes a technical rather than experiential approach. So, for example, whereas Wikipedia defines AR as a technology that "overlays virtual objects on the real-world environment",[2] it states that MR "not just overlays but anchors virtual objects to the real world and allows the user to interact with the virtual objects". Hence, MR could achieve an experience where the digital and physical become inseparable, but for someone with a vivid imagination, a good movie could potentially do that too.

Furthermore, a room-scale VR setup as offered by higher-end consumer VR headsets such as the HTC Vive (Vive: Roomscale 101) also both anchors virtual objects to the real world and allows for interaction. This means that VR is also an MR technology. The room can then be scaled up, such as is the case in many VR arcade setups, for example, Ghost In The Shell: Arise Stealth Hounds at VR Zone Shinjuku in Tokyo, which pitches two teams of up to four players to battle each other in a large room using physical gun mock-ups (VR Zone Shinjuku). In this setup, it should be noted that seen from one specific participant's perspective, the other players themselves are actually part of the real-world environment that virtual objects, such as bullets, are anchored to.

Room-scale can eventually also become world-scale. An example of world-scale oriented MR can be found at the K1 Speed go kart tracks in Pasadena, California, where visitors can drive real go karts around real race tracks while wearing a VR headset (Melnick 2018). More common, but less interactive examples of world-scale MR using VR are roller coasters that employ VR headsets, something which can be found in several amusement parks across the world (Louw 2018).

However, MR is not the same as a mixed reality experience. As an analogy, it is easy to mix any two liquids, such as oil and water, but it does not mean that they merge. Instead, MR is the technological combination of AR and VR to achieve more realistically anchored digital overlays and improved interaction across digital and physical boundaries.

---

[2]See https://en.wikipedia.org/wiki/Mixed_reality. Accessed 2018-12-02.

Importantly, consumers see AR and VR technologies as different sides of a related experience platform that will eventually become unified. As one of the Japanese respondents in one of our qualitative research sessions said: "Eventually VR and AR hardware will merge, and you will be able to do both from a single device" (Ericsson ConsumerLab 2017b). Furthermore, in our qualitative work, participants do not see AR as a digital overlay without interaction, so the difference between AR and MR would often not be recognized by consumers as even the well-known Pokémon GO game would qualify as a game that both anchors digital objects in the physical world and offers interaction.

The implication from consumer research is that if either VR or AR happens, the other technology happens too. From the consumer's perspective, they are just situational adaptations: "AR will be something you use more outside while VR will be something you use inside", as another respondent said.

It should also be pointed out that even in the case that Bostrom would be right and we are already living in a simulation, the distinction between digital and physical space is relevant. Also in the case that we are already living in a simulation, consumers would be able to differentiate between simulated physical and simulated digital experiences. However, in a merged reality situation, people would not be able to tell the difference even in a simulation, although, crucially, they could still know that the difference existed.

Furthermore, in merged reality, consumers could potentially still choose to turn off the digital part whenever they wanted to. There might be groups of people who for various reasons would choose to completely abstain from merged reality, whereas other groups might for other reasons choose to never leave such a merged reality.

## 5 Consumer Expectations of Merged Reality

Some early adopters of digital technology are already expecting merged reality to happen. As shown in our research (Ericsson ConsumerLab 2016b), almost four out of five of those respondents who used both fixed and mobile VR believed some virtual experiences would be indistinguishable from physical reality within the near future.

Indeed, some VR experiences lend themselves well to realistic simulation. In the case of table tennis, VR hand-controllers happen to weigh and balance roughly like a table tennis racket, and the haptic feedback they can produce allows for surprisingly realistic simulation of the impact of table tennis balls. Furthermore, the movement needed to play table tennis fits size requirements for first-generation room-scale VR headsets such as the HTC Vive mentioned above.

In extension, consumers expect that AR/VR will change daily life beyond recognition, as shown in (Ericsson ConsumerLab 2017b). More specifically, as many as 7 out of 10 early adopters we surveyed in this study expected six domains of everyday life to fundamentally change, namely: media, education, work, social interaction, tourism, and shopping.

The expected changes for media that consumers mention in focus group interviews include virtual live events, immersive movies and the ability to watch movies on big screens without having a big screen. For education, respondents expect textbook material through AR, field visits and experiments through VR, and virtual classrooms. Changes expected at workplaces include meetings, conferences, and shared workspaces in VR as well as private office rooms in VR, and AR replacements for desktops.

Social interaction is also expected to change fundamentally, with AR/VR becoming platforms for social hangouts, including mediating new shared experiences like playing music together. Similarly, tourism would benefit from using AR and VR as an easy way to experience places according to respondents, as well as providing additional support when traveling physically. Many also imagine a new kind of adventure tourism enabled by VR simulations to let them virtually travel to places they could not visit otherwise, such as space, animal worlds, points in history, and underwater.

Finally, AR and VR are expected to provide replacements for 2D online shopping and for example become more realistic by employing other senses that visual, such as haptic and or tactile feedback to let shoppers actually touch and feel products before purchasing. In our qualitative research, the expectations around shopping were particularly pronounced in Asia although less so elsewhere. This led us to continue exploring the future of shopping (Ericsson ConsumerLab 2018a). 64% of AR and VR users surveyed thought that, in 3 years' time, almost all shopping would take place through the smartphone, and physical stores would disappear, again with expectations being more forward leaning particularly in China. Furthermore, as many as 69% of current AR and VR users thought the technology would give smartphones all the benefits of stores in the same timeframe.

## 6 AR/VR Expected to Replace Physical Environments

As seen in the above examples, particularly for media and shopping, consumers are already today anticipating that technologies like AR and VR will decrease the need for physical environments. While this does not necessarily indicate a disregard for physical space itself, it does open the door for market acceptance of a merged reality situation where it no longer matters if a certain space is physical or simulated, and where these two aspects could eventually merge to the point where people neither know nor in fact care. Physical spaces that consumers say could be replaced by VR include movie theaters, classrooms and different kinds of stores (Fig. 2).

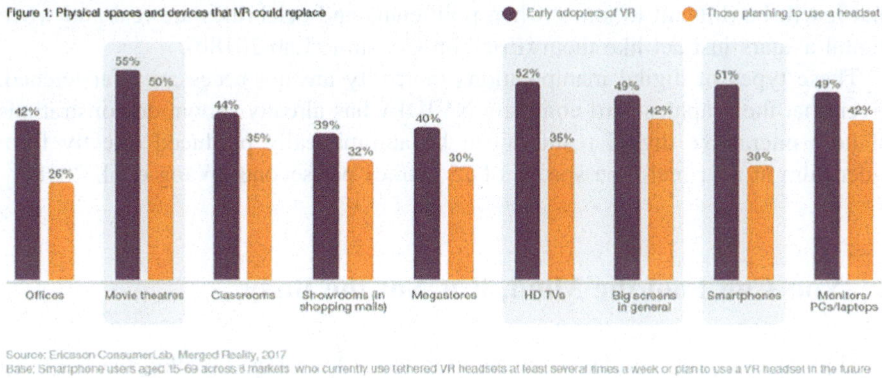


**Fig. 2** Physical spaces and devices that VR could replace[31]

## 7 Subjective Reality

Not only do AR and VR users agree that our view of the physicality of space itself will change, but they are also quite aware that anything that can be imagined—or at least visualized digitally—could potentially become part of reality.

So, for example, over half of respondents in our research would like to use augmented reality glasses to illuminate dark surroundings and highlight dangers. Furthermore, more than one in three would like to edit out disturbing elements around them, such as garbage or graffiti. Around 2 in 5 also wanted to change the way their surroundings look and even how people appeared to them (Ericsson ConsumerLab 2016b).

If and when such things not only become technically possible, but also part of everyday behaviors, reality will become a totally subjective experience. It may even be difficult to tell how much of reality is shared between two people witnessing the same scene, as they may use different digital overlays to make the situation suit their specific individual tastes.

Although the scenarios just mentioned may seem too extreme to be taken seriously by some readers, there are related examples that are already happening today. One such is the issue of so-called deepfakes where an artificial intelligence-based human image synthesis technique is used to combine and superimpose existing images and videos onto source images or videos. With this method, videos can today be produced where people have been replaced without viewers noticing the difference. Hence, in a 2018 study of AR/VR users based on early adopters in 10 major cities across the world, 47% of respondents predicted

[3]Base: Smartphone users aged 15–69 across 8 markets who currently use tethered VR headsets at least several times a week or plan to use a VR headset in the future. Source: Ericsson ConsumerLab (2017b).

that it will be difficult to know when politicians and celebrities are real and when digital avatars just act like them (Ericsson ConsumerLab 2018b).

These types of digital manipulations of reality are not necessarily far-fetched, given that the graphics card company NVIDIA has already shown demonstrations of how interactive digital realities can be automatically produced directly from video film at near real-time speeds of 25 frames per second (Wang et al. 2018).

## 8 You Can Fool the Mind, But Not the Body

Obviously, there are hurdles when moving toward a merged reality. On the most simplistic level, there are issues with current devices, with consumers complaining that VR headsets are too bulky, expensive, and have too many cables. "I have wires coming out of my head", as one early VR adopter told us (Ericsson ConsumerLab 2017b).

We have however uncovered more challenging hurdles in our research: First, there is the paradox of mobility: VR lets you virtually go anywhere, but since you are cut off from your surroundings you cannot currently physically go anywhere with it. Then, we have the paradox of isolation: VR lets you socialize remotely with others but isolates you from people standing next to you. Finally, there is also a social paradox of integration: Those who are socially challenged in the real world are more socially oriented in VR (Bjorn 2018). Although the first two paradoxes are likely technology-related, the paradox of integration points to a need for new social conventions.

But what has been discussed so far is mainly about convincing the mind—and stepping into the world of a novel or a movie is something we do with ease. There are numerous examples of fictions where the fictional world has a life independent of the will of the author, such as Flann O'Brien's At Swim-Two-Bird, where the characters of the book band together to overthrow their author. The novel was included in Time Magazine's list of the 100 best novels published in the English language between 1923 and 2005 (Grossman 2010), proving that it resonates with readers. In consequence, imagining a digital world as "real" in some sense and having characters with autonomy is not difficult for people.

The difficult challenge might instead be our bodies. We have been driving cars ever since Ford's Model T started being mass produced in the early twentieth century—and if we go back to trains, we have 200 years of motorized transportation. Yet, we are still getting motion sick in vehicles. In our research, one in five said they feel nausea in cars or buses every week also today (Ericsson ConsumerLab 2016b). Despite a 200-year history of motorized transportation, this

[3] Base: Smartphone users aged 15–69 across 8 markets who currently use tethered VR headsets at least several times a week or plan to use a VR headset in the future. Source: Ericsson ConsumerLab (2017b).

problem is not going away. If anything, the situation is getting worse, with 3 in 10 in the same study foreseeing needing car sickness pills when using autonomous cars.

Car sickness arises when the body is fed different motion stimuli through different senses, such as the eyes recording no movement while the body feels the impact of turns in the road (Nield 2016). And this is also the case with VR, as the eyes may register a lot of motion although the body is not sensing any impact from that motion. Hence, in our research, one in three also wants car sickness pills to combat motion sickness when using virtual and augmented reality technology (Ericsson ConsumerLab 2016b).

In qualitative research with employees in Ericsson, we set up an unpublished experiment where we had test subjects put on a VR headset and then asked them to do various tasks, while we increased delay gradually to see at what point motion sickness was induced. Three different levels of delay were simulated: No lag, medium lag and substantial lag. Although this was only a small qualitative study, the hypothesis we formed was what we internally called the "20–60-20 rule" for VR. It meant that 20% of the respondents would become motion sick even with no lag introduced whatsoever, 60% would gradually feel more nauseous the more lag we introduced, and the remaining 20% would not be affected regardless of how much lag we introduced (they were practically immune to motion sickness). This hypothetical rule is yet to be tested quantitatively and at this stage remains little more than an educated guess, but we can at least conclude that the human body will not easily adapt to immersive digital experiences with even small digital delays, even though we might not be conscious of these delays.

The implication is that even with near real-time implementation of digital overlays, substantial parts of the population would experience motion sickness, even though not consciously being aware of lag. On the other hand, given that an equally substantial part of the population suffering from car sickness has not stopped the car industry from booming for more than a century, maybe motion sickness will also not hamper the eventual mass-market acceptance of AR and VR.

## 9 The Importance of Consumer Imagination

In either case, with digital overlays now being ever-present in daily life, consumer markets have reached an important milestone: When digital information becomes the key component of any product or service, it is primarily the imagination (rather than the physical limitations of what can be produced at acceptable cost) of the consumer that sets the boundary for what she or he will demand. Although one common view of the consumer market is that it makes no sense to ask consumers about the future, because either they do not know, or they do not care, it may in fact be the other way around. Since the arrival of mass media, people have been trained in the consumption of fantasies, as provided to them in form of not only stories and movies but also advertising.

Our studies of gamers furthermore indicate that gaming culture is also very much about actively rather than passively placing oneself in such a fantasy and co-operating with the game developers in suspending disbelief in the game as mere fantasy. In this sense, consumers have been trained not only in imagining but also in assimilating fantasy worlds.

As digital overlays on top of reality become increasingly powerful and ubiquitous, any such fantasy could potentially not only be produced but also integrated with reality. Yuval Noah Harari says that if someone describes the future and it sounds like sci-fi, it is probably false. But Harari continues by pointing out that if a prediction does not sound like sci-fi, then it is certainly false (Harari 2018). If sci-fi is really what it is driving the future, that is essentially the same as saying that popular culture is driving the future. And popular culture is constantly increasing the capacity of consumers to imagine.

However, physical limitations remain. Specifically, AR/VR users across basically all studies we have performed have been imagining the arrival of glasses that are not bulky or "dorky" to better and more effortlessly display digital overlays either as AR or as VR. This has become almost a burden for us when doing market research, as it is making it increasingly difficult to produce results that are "new" in the sense that they take us beyond the discussion of glasses. The consumer expectations related to AR/VR glasses have truly become a glass wall that we hit in our projects, where we look at each other and realize that we are about to reproduce the same results that we already published in the previous study.

Simultaneously, Magic Leap in February 2016 received the greatest funding ever recorded for a company without a product (Page 2018), to bring their glasses to market. But they then received close to another $1 B in additional funding before eventually showing the first actual and concrete product demo in July of 2018. In other words, there seems to be high overlap between the imagination of the tech industry and that of early adopters of AR/VR.

However, just like the industry still might have some years to go before producing mature products suitable for the mass market, consumers also see this is as something that happens some years into the future. In our most recent study, we asked early adopters of ICT to pick the next product they thought would reach the mass market from a list of 12 future-oriented devices. They ranked smart glasses in 4th place after next generation AI-enabled phones, self-driving cars and AR phones in that order (Ericsson ConsumerLab 2018b).

## 10 Changing the Perception of Time

But maybe there is another new finding beyond glasses that is staring us so obviously in the eyes that we have overlooked it. In recent and as of this writing unpublished qualitative AR gaming research, expectations that a digital overlay on top of physical reality should also be able to change the perception of time are surfacing. "I would like games that slow down my perception of time", as one Japanese female participant in our study squarely put it.

Some of this slowing-down is related to reducing waste of time, such as being to be able to do other things in-game, such as studying and reading books while for example waiting for game teams to fill up with players. But other aspects are more focused on the fact that physical life is complex and many fantasy worlds that let you become a hero (or in some cases, a villain) are much simpler. So rather than facing the slowness of daily life, when entering game worlds, you get to go from one highlight to the next, without having to take on the drudgery in between.

As an example, rather than spending half a year taking a course to learn a new skill, in the game you might do something heroic. In reward, you receive a new spell, instantaneously, without having to go through years of training to master it. This creates an expectation that digital overlays on the physical world should be able to let users do much more per time unit, in effect stretching time to cover more experiences if not necessarily slowing time itself down.

As such, ability to experience more per given time unit, may itself be nothing more than an extension of the effects that mass media has already had previously on consumers. However, changing consumer perspectives on time as digital overlays on top of physical space is likely a very interesting area that needs much further study.

## 11 Concluding Discussion

This paper has tried to discuss what it means for people to be offline in a world where the Internet is everywhere. We have taken as a starting point the idea of a "second offline", a state where the Internet is used without conscious reflection as it has become an ever-present digital backdrop.

However, just like the online world to a large extent is a story of generations, in the form software version of everything from operating systems to Internet browsers to smartphone apps, and in the form of cellular connectivity generations such as 2G, 3G or 4G, we have here argued that the idea of generations should also be applied to the offline experience. So whereas the "second offline" describes the first generation of a reality that is no longer fully independent from Internet data flows, we have proposed the idea of a merged reality as a second generation "second offline" where physical and digital realities are have become experientially fully intertwined.

As humans, we base our expectations on how the world functions in everyday situations based on our experiences. We are already today starting to see how younger generations who have grown up experiencing the second offline turn their digital experiences into expectations on how the physical world should behave, such as swiping on flat surfaces of analog objects in the belief that they can be interacted with. One interesting thought could be how this might eventually even change our experience of time, and not only in the time-compression perspective discussed in this paper. Will we eventually experience Matrix movie-like bullet time as part of the physical world? Only time itself will tell.

## References

Bjorn M (2018) AR and VR: two sides of the same coin? AR-VR magazine. http://www.arvrmagazine.com/ar-and-vr-two-sides-of-the-same-coin/. Accessed 02 Dec 2018

Bostrom N (2003) Are you living in a computer simulation? vol 53, no 211. Philosophical Quarterly, Oxford, pp 243–255. https://www.simulation-argument.com/simulation.html. Accessed 02 Dec 2018

Ericsson ConsumerLab (2012) In-line shopping. Ericsson, Stockholm. https://www.ericsson.com/en/press-releases/2012/11/consumers-merge-in-store-and-online-shopping. Accessed 02 Dec 2018

Ericsson ConsumerLab (2016a) Interactivity beyond the screen. Ericsson, Stockholm. https://www.ericsson.com/assets/local/news/2014/6/interactivity-beyond-the-screen.pdf. Accessed 02 Dec 2018

Ericsson ConsumerLab (2016b) 10 hot consumer trends 2017. Ericsson, Stockholm. https://www.ericsson.com/49e93e/assets/local/reports-papers/consumerlab/reports/2017/ten-hot-consumer-trends-2017-ericsson-consumerlab.pdf. Accessed 02 Dec 2018

Ericsson ConsumerLab (2017a) From healthcare to homecare. Ericsson, Stockholm. https://www.ericsson.com/49e91e/assets/local/reports-papers/consumerlab/reports/2017/healthcare-to-homecare_screen_aw2.pdf. Accessed 02 Dec 2018

Ericsson ConsumerLab (2017b) Merged reality. Ericsson, Stockholm. https://www.ericsson.com/4a2c58/assets/local/reports-papers/consumerlab/reports/2017/ericsson_consumerlab_merged-reality_report_aw-screen.pdf. Accessed 02 Dec 2018

Ericsson ConsumerLab (2018a) Beyond smartphone shopping—the rise of smart assistants. Ericsson, Stockholm. https://www.ericsson.com/49ea09/assets/local/reports-papers/consumerlab/reports/2018/smartphone_shopping_consumerlab_rgb_screen_aw_10052018.pdf. Accessed 02 Dec 2018

Ericsson ConsumerLab (2018b) 10 hot consumer trends 2019. Ericsson, Stockholm. https://www.ericsson.com/4afb37/assets/local/reports-papers/consumerlab/reports/2019/10hctreport2019_screen_aw.pdf. Accessed 08 Jan 2021

Grossman L (2010) All-time 100 novels. In: Time magazine. http://entertainment.time.com/2005/10/16/all-time-100-novels/slide/at-swim-two-birds-1938-by-flann-obrien/. Accessed 02 Dec 2018

Harari NY (2018) 21 lessons for the twenty first century. Spiegel & Grau

Louw C (2018) How virtual reality is giving the world's roller coasters a new twist. Phys. Org, August 16, 2018. https://phys.org/news/2018-08-virtual-reality-world-roller-coasters.html. Accessed 02 Dec 2018

Melnick K (2018) Master of shapes combines VR racing with real go karts. VR scout, November 4, 2018. https://vrscout.com/news/master-of-shapes-vr-go-kart-racing/. Accessed 02 Dec 2018

Nield D (2016) Here's why you get car sick: your brain thinks it's being poisoned. Science alert. August 12, 2016. https://www.sciencealert.com/here-s-why-you-get-car-sick-your-brain-thinks-it-s-being-poisoned/. Accessed 02 Dec 2018

Page H (2018) A timeline of investor interest In: AR startup magic leap, which has raised $2.3 B. Crunchbase, August 27, 2018. https://news.crunchbase.com/news/a-timeline-of-investor-interest-in-ar-startup-magic-leap-which-has-raised-2-3b/. Accessed 02 Dec 2018

Tomita H (2016) What is second offline? In: Tomita H (ed) The post mobile society: from the smart/mobile to the second offline. Routledge, London/New York, pp 1–10

Vive Roomscale 101. HTC Vive. https://blog.vive.com/us/2017/10/25/roomscale-101/. Accessed 02 Dec 2018

VR Zone Shinjuku. Ghost in the shell: arise stealth hounds. https://vrzone-pic.com/shinjuku/en/activity/koukaku.html. Accessed 02 Dec 2018

Wang T-C et al (2018) Video to video synthesis presented. NIPS, Montreal. https://arxiv.org/pdf/1808.06601.pdf. Accessed 02 Dec 2018

**Michael Björn** is Head of Research Agenda at Ericsson Consumer & IndustryLab, and Research Fellow ICT Market Foresight at Ericsson Research. He has been driving the annual 10 Hot Consumer Trends report, now in its tenth year, since its inception. He joined Ericsson in 1997, after having completed his PhD in data modeling at the University of Tsukuba in Japan. Between 2000 and 2002, Michael Björn was responsible for mobile internet applications at Ericsson in Japan. Michael is also adjunct professor at the Lund University School of Economics and Management, a music journalist and a novelist with two published fiction books.

# Application of XR to Regional Development

**Yuichi Kogure**

**Abstract** Attempts have been made to apply XR technology that superimposes virtual information over real space to lead to regional development. In addition to the examples that the authors are currently working on, two examples are discussed that apply to the second offline theory attracting attention in Japan, and how these balance with the new theory of the second offline, "the doubling of place and time," is addressed. In addition to the relationship between the real and the virtual in the second offline theory, adding the overlap of time and place ("the doubling of time and place") to the point of view makes the theory more sophisticated. By superimposing content that transcends time and place in the most important space (real space), that is, the "here and now," the examples introduced in this chapter demonstrate the possibilities for new results and effects that have never been achieved before, such as evoking behavior that leads people to a place, creating novel, hitherto unknown tourist experiences, and, from there, bringing about new economic effects.

## 1 Spread of XR and Application to Regional Promotion

In this work, various scenarios related to the "Second Offline," which is defined here as an offline space where virtual information is superimposed on real space and in which references are constantly made to online information, are discussed. In recent years, situations as defined by the second offline have become more familiar as extended reality (XR) (Paradiso and Landay 2009)—augmented reality (AR), mixed reality (MR), and virtual reality (VR)—technology has come to be widely used. In brief, these three technologies can be explained as VR, which creates a virtual world, AR, which extends reality, and MR, which combines the virtual world and the real world.

---

Y. Kogure (✉)
Deputy Director, Digital Society Promotion Section, New Business Promotion Department, Regulatory Division, SoftBank Corp., Tokyo, Japan
e-mail: yu@kogure.jp



H. Tomita (ed.), *The Second Offline*, Advances in Information and Communication Research 3, https://doi.org/10.1007/978-981-16-2425-4_4

First, virtual reality (VR) is a technology that scientifically creates an environment that, although not the real thing, has in essence the same function, by stimulating the senses, including the five senses of the user. VR also includes the systems for this technology. The concept of VR is not new, and a goggles-type VR system appeared in the 1935 short novel "Pygmalion's Spectacles" (by Stanley Grauman Weinbaum, April 4, 1902, to December 14, 1935) (Weinbaum 2007). Such a system became a reality in 1968, when Ivan Sutherland developed the world's first head-mounted display. Much time has passed since then, and, in recent years, various elements came together such that, in 2016, a large number of companies released VR systems and content utilizing the systems, and the year was recognized as "a breakthrough year for virtual reality."

In contrast, AR is a variant of VR, which encompasses adding, deleting, emphasizing, and de-emphasizing information in relation to the real environment in the periphery at that time, and augmenting the real world as literally seen by humans (Azuma 1997). Although devices or techniques widely used in VR have been used for the presentation and acquisition of information in many systems, in recent years, smartphones have become widespread, and, because these are provided with a communication function on a standalone basis and a display capable of displaying additional information, AR content utilizing smartphones has spread from approximately 2009 and is now widely recognized by many people (Chen 2009).

As methods of presenting digital information in a space, a position-recognition-based method, a marker-based method, and a markerless method are used. Position-recognition-based AR causes additional information to be displayed over real space based on position information, such as the Global Positioning System. Marker-based AR displays information by reading specific marker figures not associated with a place. Markerless AR recognizes landscapes, actual things, and so on in order to display information. With these methods, because position-recognition-type AR and markerless AR can issue additional information when a user visits a specific spot, it is possible to induce certain behavior in a user, and attempts have been made to apply this to the promotion of tourism. The "Pokemon GO" craze is a typical example of position-recognition-type AR. In addition, the "rice-code" application introduced later in this chapter is an example in which guidance to a site is provided when a landscape is recognized.

Mixed reality (MR) (Freeman et al. 2005) is a technology that combines the virtual world and the real world by combining information on a virtual world artificially created with computer graphics and the like with the real world. In 2017, Microsoft developed the MR terminal "HoloLens" and launched it in the Japanese market. When the HoloLens is worn, computer images are displayed so as to overlap with the surrounding real landscape. The HoloLens is equipped with a sensor that senses hand movement, and various operations are also possible with the hand.

Attempts have been made to apply XR technology that superimposes virtual information over real space to lead to regional development. In addition to the examples that the authors are currently working on, two examples are discussed that apply to the second offline theory attracting attention in Japan, and how these balance with the new theory of the second offline, "the doubling of place and time," is addressed.

## 2 Example of Tourism Promotion Using VR

Owani town in Minamitsugaru-gun in Aomori Prefecture, where the authors carried out their research, is a town located at the southern tip of the Aomori-Tsugaru region and is a municipality with a history that became Owani town after being established as Owani village in 1889 and granted status as a town in 1923. The total population is 9064 people (estimated population in April 2018), and the town is known as a spa town, boasting a history of having hot springs open for 800 years and for prestigious competition skiing, which has been running there since the 1920s. In 2016, the authors started a local Web site, "Yu no Machi Owani Story" (the story of Owani, the hot springs town) (Yu no Machi Owani Story 2021), which publicizes information on this area in cooperation with the local government, along with social network service activities. In these efforts, as a means to broadcast the appeal of the region by a new method, it was decided to produce content to enable people to experience Owani using VR. Planning and data collection for the content was begun in April 2017 and, after undergoing editing work and other preparation, VR viewing equipment introducing regional attractions was set up in the Owani community exchange center, "Wanicome," and the Aomori Prefecture Tokyo tourist information office in Iidabashi, Tokyo, in the period from June 30, 2017, to December 25, 2017, and general users were encouraged to use the equipment (NTT Docomo press release presentation 2017).

As VR content for introducing the places of interest in the town through a 360-degree movie, the view from the driver's seat on the Konan Railway Owani line running in Owani, the interiors of the public baths located throughout Owani, the townscape, and other scenes were recorded. Wanicome, which set up the VR viewing equipment, has facilities, including hot spring facilities, restaurants, and local product shops, that are also symbols of the town, and there are many visitors from inside and outside the prefecture. In particular, because many visitors from outside the town come to Wanicome, they leave the town once their business is done. Therefore, VR was used to show that there are other attractive places in the town, with the aim of encouraging people to extend their stay in the town. In addition, the VR viewing equipment set up in Tokyo has content informing viewers of the hot springs and ski areas that are the features of Owani.

The results of installing the VR viewing equipment for approximately half a year are reported below.

The VR viewing equipment set up at Wanicome was installed on the path from the facility reception area to the hot spring facility, making it popular with passers-by who could stop and try it out at any time. Counting the number of viewers of the VR movies was not possible, because a counting function was not implemented. For this reason, questionnaire surveys and hearings with the visitors were used to measure the effects. The survey was conducted in early August 2017, and the number of valid responses was 28. By gender, the viewers were 32% male and 68% female, and, in terms of the age ratio, 47% were 10- to 29-year-olds, 32% 30- to 39-year-olds, and 14% 50- to 60-year-olds, with 7% not providing an answer.

The proportion that had watched a VR movie was 21%, and the proportion that had never watched a VR movie was 79%. As there were many people who answered "never," sightseeing PR using VR movies was thought to be effective in terms of being fresh and interesting. After seeing the "foot baths" and "public baths" in the VR movie, the number of people who actually wanted to stroll around Owani rose to 94%. In addition, 100% of people thought that seeing the "Konan Railway" would encourage use of the railway. Other comments on other freely written answers were "I felt a real feeling of speed," "there is a sense of presence," and "it felt just like actually being there."

In addition, the counter staff at the Aomori prefecture Tokyo tourist information office independently counted the number of viewers and kept a record. In the period from the launch on June 30 to the end of the installation on December 25, the total number of viewers reached 1075 (Figs. 1, 2, and 3).

Tourism promotion using this VR has continued to increase the number of users, even after the above period. Although an effect can be seen in that there is interest in the region, this may have much to do with attraction to the novelty. The tourism promotion using this VR goes no further than offering a virtual experience, and no superimposition is made on the real space in terms of the second offline theory.

**Fig. 1** A 360° camera was installed in a railcar and took photographs (Photo by Yuichi Kogure)

**Fig. 2** A 360° video (VR) viewing image (Photo by Yuichi Kogure)

**Fig. 3** Set to make VR viewing possible and installed for six months (Photo by Yuichi Kogure)

Regarding the application of XR to lead to further economic effects, it may be considered that superimposing the online on real places is important, as in the next example to be introduced.

## 3 Example Where a Rice Field Was Changed to a "Sales Point" Using AR

Inakadate village in Minamitsugaru-gun in Aomori Prefecture is known for its pioneering "rice field art" made by planting rice in rice fields. Rice field art is a project creating huge pictures and letters, using rice of different colors with the rice fields as the canvas (Inakadate village 2021). Inakadate village is a small municipality with a population of approximately 8000 people. Rice cultivation was the center of industry here, but due to Japanese people shifting away from rice in their dietary habits, in addition to aging and a declining population in recent years, sales of rice are decreasing year by year. Thus, work has been carried out on "rice field art" since 1993 as a regional effort to broaden the appeal of the "rice," which is a special product of this village. Currently, rice field art may be seen in various places in Japan, but the rice field art in Inakadate village was the original art. Using rice with different-colored leaves, magnificent pictures are made in rice fields. Although originally starting with rice of three colors, as technology improves year after year, now seven colors of rice are used to make delicate and precise art (Fig. 4).

Because of the scale, the precision, and the high artistic level of the art, the art has become a topic appearing in overseas media, and more than 300,000 tourists come every year to a village with a population of only 8000 people. From the tour fees from these tourists, the village office was collecting admission fee income for its observatory exceeding 90 million yen per year (2016) (Inakadate village 2017),

**Fig. 4** Rice field art in Inakadate village (Reproduced from rice-code project)

but this had not led to the crucial "increase in rice sales." Therefore, the "rice-code" application was invented to make a connection from the rice field art to a sales site using AR (Rice-code 2021). When the rice field art is photographed with a camera using an application, the application provides a link that enables the purchase of rice from Inakadate village (Fig. 5).

This rice-code application was set up by Japan's leading advertising agency, Hakuhodo Inc. According to Mr. Airo Takanohashi, senior creative director, the points for success are "creating a strong initial impression and a sharing window." The Internet, which is essential for solving social problems, was the focus. Thanks to the spread of the Internet, it has become possible in modern times to transmit information beyond regional boundaries. The further popularization of social networks has made it possible to share and spread information and to gain followers and friends easily.

When this is considered from the viewpoint of "creating a strong initial impression and a sharing window," the content of the "rice field art" had already made a strong initial impression when the rice field art in Inakadate village was viewed. The remaining question was how to make a "sharing window." There was a need to consider methods for making more people spread the information and to make a connection with the purchase of rice, which was the problem to be solved.

From this situation, Mr. Takanohashi thought about changing the location where the visits to the rice field art take place into a place for selling rice. It is said, in

**Fig. 5** Using the rice-code application with rice field art as a marker leading to rice sales Web site (Reproduced from Rice-code project)

human psychology, that the purse strings are loosest when someone is moved emotionally. During the busy season, the queues to view the rice field art are long lines lasting one to two hours. At the moment of finally arriving at the roof of the observatory after waiting and seeing the sight of the rice field art spreading in front of their eyes, visitors reach a peak of emotion and excitement. This timing is the moment at which they become liberal with their spending. Moreover, the visitors are all taking pictures of the wonderful art with their smartphones. When taking pictures with the rice-code application, it is possible to have rice delivered to your home as a souvenir at the same time. People were asked to download the "rice-code" application while waiting in line for the observation deck and at the moment when they were first beginning to enjoy the rice field art, in order to introduce them to the rice sales Web site by markerless AR for the rice field art. A link connected them to the sales of the local products, which was a great success.

## 4 Understanding Artworks Beyond Space and Time Using MR

Kennin-ji, which is known as the oldest Zen temple in Kyoto, was built in 1202 and has a long history going back more than 800 years. Tourists come here to visit the national treasure, the "Folding Screen of the Wind and Thunder Gods," invariably appearing in textbooks in Japan. This is a famous gold folding screen in which the wind god and the thunder god strike powerful poses on a sublimely beautiful gold folding screen painted by Tawaraya Sotatsu in the early Edo period.

In this gold folding screen, the thunder god is arranged on the left side and the wind god is arranged on the right side, but there is a "gap" in the center. These artworks were created with various backgrounds and world views, and there is an intended meaning in this gap, but few of the people viewing this art understand this. So, content was created that overlaid virtual information on this real-life folding screen, and a trial publicly opened, called the "Kyoto Mixed Reality Project," in February 2018 for a limited time only, in which it was possible to have an MR experience for approximately 10 min using the Microsoft HoloLens (National Treasure 2021). This product was launched jointly by Hakuhodo Inc. and Microsoft Japan.

With the aim of creating a new manner of appreciating cultural property and providing cultural education as well as a model for sightseeing, this case of combining a historical cultural property and MR is a world first (Hakuhodo press release 2018) (Fig. 6).

When the HoloLens is brought in front of the folding screen of the Wind and Thunder Gods, first, the monk of Kennin-ji, Mr. Shundo Asano, appears and begins to talk about this gold folding screen. Then, the Wind and Thunder Gods emerge in 3D and cause it to rain and thunder in front of your eyes. With approximately 10 min of content, the wish for a rich harvest contained in this gold folding screen

**Fig. 6** National treasure "folding screen of the wind and thunder gods" (Reproduced from Hakuhodo-VRAR, future of learning project)

is expressed by a movie that fills the room, making it possible to "experience art" with the whole body (Fig. 7).

The point of utilizing MR is to be able to experience 3D digital content superimposed on a particular place. MR gives us a time-traveling experience to a certain era, with the possibility of creating new innovations in the tourism sector, such as tours of historic places, in the future. Hakuhodo Inc. is also looking to

**Fig. 7** Experiencing an artistic view of the world with MR in front of the gold folding screen (Reproduced from Hakuhodo-VRAR, future of learning project)

utilize MR in educational activities in the future and will also try to enable learning based on "experience."

## 5 Relationship Between Second Offline Theory and XR for Regional Development

This chapter covers application examples of XR created for the purposes of regional development and how such contents and services fit in with the second offline theory.

In addition to the relationship between the real and the virtual in the second offline theory, adding the overlap of time and place ("the doubling of time and place") to the point of view makes the theory more sophisticated. By superimposing content that transcends time and place in the most important space (real space), that is, the "here and now," the examples introduced in this chapter demonstrate the possibilities for new results and effects that have never been achieved before, such as evoking behavior that leads people to a place, creating novel, hitherto unknown tourist experiences, and, from there, bringing about new economic effects.

When applying the three XR examples introduced in this chapter to the new second theory, the doubling of time and place, first, the example of using VR for tourism promotion does not relate to a real-time experience but to an experience of an aspect of a region that is undergone "now," regardless of the VR user's current location. This case is an example that is applicable to "the doubling of time," and a superimposition is not necessarily made on the "place." Also, the example of content for experiencing the historical background of artwork using MR is applicable to "the doubling of place" and is for understanding the historical background where the artwork was created beyond space and time at the place where the artwork exists. In this example, a superimposition is not made in terms of "time."

However, the example of the "rice-code application using AR makes a link to an online service from the experiences at that place and is an example of the doubling of time and place" (Fig. 8).

Regional development content using XR in this manner is still new and contributes to increased interest among tourists. Meanwhile, money for development and operation expenses is required to provide this content and these services. The issue is how all this will play out with local governments and the like with strict regional budgets. Although there have been cases where a set regional creation budget was used and development carried out as a trial experiment, no projects have subsequently succeeded in acquiring a stable operational budget. Nevertheless, if it is possible to make a link to the sale of goods, such as with the rice-code, it may be possible to continue the operations by charging a commission. Alternatively, in the case of content with the objective of tourism promotion, if the effects thereof are accurately measured through online means, the services may be established by

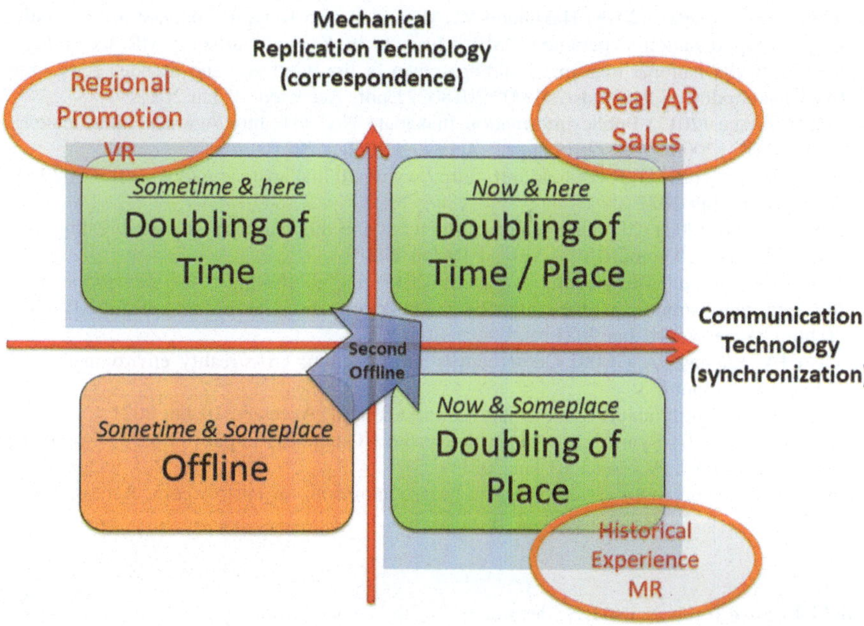


**Fig. 8** Relationship between the second offline and regional development XR

diverting a part of the tourism promotion budget toward content operation expenses based on such results.

There are also doubts about the verification of the effectiveness of traditional analog-based marketing in terms of its accuracy and validity. However, with digital marketing in which it is possible to trace user information and behavior, accurate effect measurement is possible to a certain extent.

Current XR content is of interest to viewers but is not yet something for which viewers will pay a viewing fee. To promote the utilization of XR as ubiquitous in society without it ending up a temporary fad, there is an urgent need to develop solutions considering how to monetize the development and operation of XR content and services.

## References

Azuma RT (1997) A survey of augmented reality. Teleoperators Virtual Environ 6(4):355–385

Chen BX (2009) If you see not seeing data, you're not seeing. WIRED. https://www.wired.com/2009/08/augmented-reality/. Accessed 10 Jan 2021

Freeman R, Steed A, Zhou B (2005) Rapid scene modelling, registration and specification for mixed reality systems. In: Proceedings of ACM virtual reality software and technology, pp 147–150

Hakuhodo press release (2018) Hakuhodo-VRAR and Kyoto Kennin-ji opened a novel cultural property appreciation experience, "MR Museum in Kyoto," utilizing MR technology in relation to the national treasure, "Folding screen of the wind god and thunder gods." http://www.hakuhodo.co.jp/uploads/2018/02/20180221.pdf. Accessed 10 Jan 2021

Inakadate village (2017) Public information Inakadate No. 741. http://www.vill.inakadate.lg.jp/docs/2017071200022/files/201711.pdf. Accessed 10 Jan 2021

Inakadate village (2021) Rice field art. http://www.vill.inakadate.lg.jp/docs/2013050200014/. Accessed 10 Jan 2021

National Treasure (2021) "Folding screen of the wind and thunder gods" x mixed reality. https://hakuhodo-vrar.jp/kyoto2018/. Accessed 10 Jan 2021

NTT Docomo press release presentation material 2017. Started offering "VR for everyone" service for corporations/municipalities. https://www.nttdocomo.co.jp/info/news_release/2017/06/14_00.html. Accessed 10 Jan 2021

Paradiso JA, Landay JA (2009) Guest editors' introduction: cross-reality environments. IEEE Pervasive Comput 8:3

Rice-code (2021) http://nature-barcode.jp/award/index.html. Accessed 10 Jan 2021

Weinbaum SG (2007) Pygmalion's spectacles, project Gutenberg (e-pub) http://www.gutenberg.org/ebooks/22893. Accessed 10 Jan 2021

Yu no Machi Owani Story (2021) Website http://yunomachi-owanistory.com. Accessed 10 Jan 2021

**Yuichi Kogure** received the B.S. degrees in health sciences from Kyorin University, Japan, in 1990, and Dr.Eng. degrees in functional systems engineering from Graduate School of Engineering, The University of Tokushima, Japan, in 2007. From 1990 to 1992, and from 2000 to 2002, he was a research student at School of Health Sciences, Faculty of Medicine, The University of Tokyo, Japan. From 2009, he was associate professor at Musashinogakuin University, and from 2013, he was a associate professor at Aomori Public University. From 2021, he joined SoftBank Corp. His research interest covers application of mobile terminal and network, and mobile interactions theory. He is director and member of Society of Mobile Interactions, and IT Healthcare Association.

# Media Mobilization and the Bricolage of Time and Place

**Kota Ito**

**Abstract** This paper identified that the digitalization and mobilization of media have been accompanied by a decreased amount of information that can be displayed on a device at one time, the fragmentation and miniaturization of content consumption time, and that the context of the content tends to be diluted. Then, based on the historical background in which the sense of time among poets centered on the "here and now" when the number of syllables decreased with the transition from tanka to haiku, a theory was established that media mobilization has had an effect on our sense of time and sense of place, and an analysis was conducted focusing on Skype and TikTok. The results showed that the rise of services and content in which neither the past nor the future but the "now" is enjoyed in "synchronicity" and that intentional mixing of different locations and times by users has formed a bricolage that produces a new sense of time and place centering on the "here and now." Such user behavior attempts to break up modern homogenous and absolute spatial awareness alongside homogenous and linear temporal awareness.

## 1 Introduction

This paper will focus on changes in the consumption of content and in the content itself that have accompanied the digitalization and mobilization of media. By analyzing various mobile contents and services that have appeared through these changes from the perspective of structure and user experience, we will discuss how our sense of time and sense of place is converging not on the past or future but on the "now" and the "here" that can be found nowhere else.

K. Ito (✉)
Faculty of Informatics, Kansai University, Osaka, Japan
e-mail: p085350@kansai-u.ac.jp



H. Tomita (ed.), *The Second Offline*, Advances in Information and Communication Research 3, https://doi.org/10.1007/978-981-16-2425-4_5

## 2 Spread of Mobile Technology and Decreasing Amounts of Information

As of 2018, the size of one page in the Asahi Shimbun, one of Japan's leading newspapers, is 21.50 in. (h) × 15.98 in. (w), which allows for up to 12,375 characters. On the other hand, the screen size of the iPhone X is 5.24 in. (h) × 2.4 in. (w) (Fig. 1). When reading a book on the Kindle app using font size 5, up to 407 characters can be displayed on the screen. This means that the amount of information that can be displayed at one time on a smartphone is only 3.3% of the text even when using a large smartphone such as the iPhone X. With such physical limitations on media, we are only able to convey messages of up to 140 characters using Twitter or one image and up to two lines of text using Instagram.

The very core of the media that we use to acquire information on a daily basis is changing from newspapers and publications using paper and ink to compact smartphones using LCD and OLED. One thing that this process has brought about is a decrease in the amount of information that can be displayed at a time.

Generally, the more we use the main forms of social media on our smartphones, such as Twitter, Facebook and Instagram, the more our followers and friends will increase and the more information will become accessible. If you acquire 1000 friends and each one of them publishes one post a day, you will be able to read posts from 1000 people in a day.

Yet our time is not without limit. Everyone has a limited life span with only 365 days per year and 24 h per day. Even if you only spend a total of one hour per

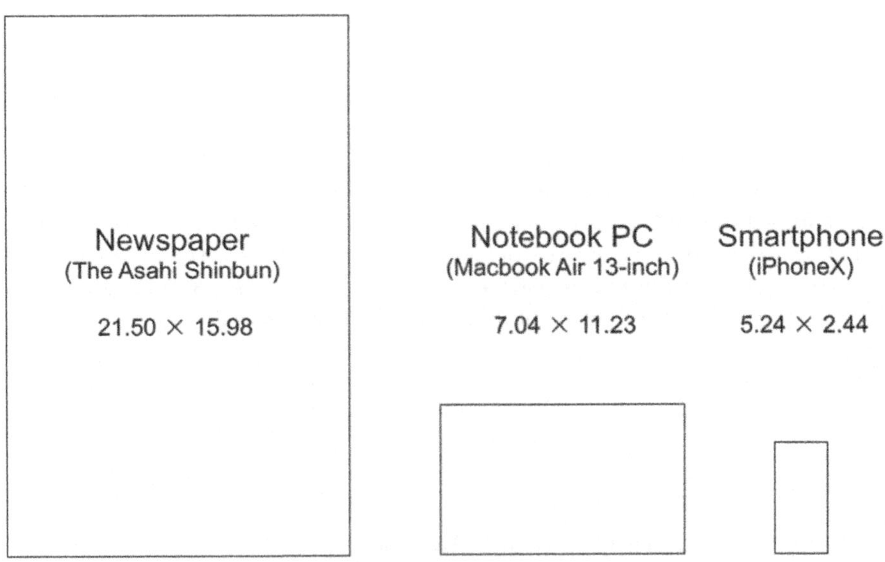


**Fig. 1** Comparison of screen sizes (inch)

day looking at your smartphone and read all of the updates from 1000 people, you will only have about 3.6 s per person. It is possible that you will miss important posts from your closest friends. In order to prevent such incidents, many forms of social media perform operations using an algorithm to prioritize the display of posts that can be considered important for each user, whereas content that is thought to be of low value decreases in priority or is even removed.

While our smartphones are certainly capable of accessing unlimited sources of information and have always-on connections, the amount of content taken in through the user interface has a limit in terms of physical and algorithmic restrictions.

## 3 Spread of Mobile Technology and the Fragmentation of Time

So far, we have considered the decrease in and limitations on the amount of information based on the characteristics of smartphones as a mobile media, but now we will consider it from the user's perspective. The following photograph (Fig. 2) shows a scene observed by the author when taking a taxi in Tokyo (photograph taken in April 2018). The truck driver took out his smartphone in the brief moments while waiting at the traffic lights and began playing a game. In terms of time, games can be played in just a few seconds, that is, in the time normally spent waiting at traffic lights. Similar scenes can be observed not only in vehicles waiting at traffic signals but also in locations such as in front of office building elevators and train station platforms.

**Fig. 2** A driver plays a game on his smartphone while waiting at a traffic light (*photo* Ito)

In order for such content consumption to be possible, the games and content must be designed so as to allow them to be played for just a few seconds. Rather than having long stories like movies, games involve individual operations that do not require thought. For example, with the free puzzle game "LINE: Disney Tsum Tsum" (offered via LINE, which is a major social media platform in Japan, and developed by NHN PlayArt Co., Ltd.—a subsidiary of LINE), players connect three or more of the same blocks in order to erase them within a time limit of one minute. The rule is that when the blocks are erased, they are replaced by the same number of blocks and "tsums," which descend from the top of the screen to the bottom. The time limit is only one minute, which is a small amount of time, but there is also a pause button that enables non-consecutive play in shorter amounts of time.

The fragmentation and reduction in the time taken to consume such mobile content is also occurring in relation to text content such as the news (Ito 2016). This phenomenon correlates with the rise in popularity of mobile media. As a result of smartphones becoming essential to our lives, content has been developed that is optimized for short periods of time, such as waiting for traffic lights or elevators. With this kind of content that, unlike movies, does not require continuous attention sitting down for two hours, it is difficult to win in the struggle for the customer's limited amount of disposable time. That is why the small gaps in our time are being filled with content that can be consumed in periods of time that can be subdivided into tens of seconds, such as 140-character content, single photograph content, or block games that can be paused.

## 4 Spread of Mobile Technology and the Dilution of Context and Its Production

In addition to the reduction in time, one other point can be made about the physical limitations of mobile media and mobile content that is optimized for a form of consumption in small amounts of time.

Compare the following two pictures (Figs. 3, 4). The first one (Fig. 3) was taken using an automatic film camera in the early 1980s and shows a child in a uniform in front of some pictures. From the fact that the pictures are in the background and the child is looking at the lens, it can be surmised that a parent is taking a picture of their child at a kindergarten art exhibition. Although the expression on the child's face may be a little difficult to read, we are quite able to make sense of the photograph, which is in the standard print size in Japan of $3.50 \times 5.00$ in.

In contrast, the second photograph (Fig. 4) is a selfie taken using the front camera of a smartphone. From the stance and gaze of the woman on the left, it can be surmised that she is stretching out her right arm to take the photograph, but there are almost no factors in this photograph that can be called a background. It is

**Fig. 3** A photo of a child and his drawing, taken by his parents (*photo* Ito)

**Fig. 4** A selfie taken by one of the group (*photo* Ito)

difficult to understand when and where this photograph was taken based only on the structures in the upper right.

In many of the selfies taken using the front cameras of smartphones that are distributed these days on the Internet, the photographer is close to the lens, which means that a large part of the screen is taken up with the upper half of people's bodies and the weighting given to the background tends to decrease. Of course, it is also possible to take a photograph from a greater distance using a selfie stick, etc., which gives more weighting to the background. However, the screen size of a smartphone such as an iPhone 7 is 2.32 × 4.09 in., which is smaller than the 3.50 × 5.00 inch-print size; thus, the relative area is only 55%. For this reason, people's facial expressions become more difficult to read the further one is from the lens or the wider the angle used.

We have already seen that news content intended to be browsed on mobile phones and social media such as Twitter poses difficulties in terms of understanding the background or context to news and comments, which arises from close control of the total amount of text. A similar phenomenon is happening in terms of image area. When communicating on a screen with a limited space of 2.32 × 4.09 in., the objects that the communicator wishes to photograph or to display are placed in close-up, and it is difficult to know the time or location in which the target object is set. That is, it is easy for certain contexts to become diluted.

However, attention must be given to one thing at this point. In the second picture, everyone is wearing a headband. The author states that it is difficult to understand the context from the background, but, in fact, it is possible to surmise that the photograph was probably taken at Disneyland because of the headbands. In a certain sense, then, the women themselves are producing the context.

Such contextual production can also be understood in the rooms of Internet celebrities during live streaming (e.g., SHOWROOM in Japan and YY LIVE in China, etc.). The user makes a real-time stream to the world with singing, dancing, cosplay, etc. via a camera or smartphone placed in a room in their home. Viewers are able to send messages to the streamer via a chat function, and the streamer can respond in real time. In such live streams, in many cases, characteristic stuffed toys and other objects are placed in a corner of the room that is half visible (not at the very front).

On the home pages of streaming sites, there are thumbnails showing the streamers that are currently online, and viewers are able to move to the page of specific streamers and can participate in the chat; however, many of these viewers may be participating at random. Streamers express their preferences by placing personal items in the field of view of "countless other people with whom they actually have no shared context" to produce and manage some small amount of context.

## 5 Decreasing Number of Syllables and a Changing Sense of Time: From Tanka to Haiku

Thus far, we have provided insights by looking at the phenomenon of the decreased amount of information in content, miniaturization of the time spent consuming it, and the dilution of context (and the production of context as a response to this dilution) that accompanies the ongoing spread of mobile media. Now, we will focus on another phenomenon: the changing sense of time.

We have gone from 21.50 × 15.98-in. newspapers that allow 12,375 characters to be read to 5.24 × 2.4-in. smartphones that only allow 407 characters. The transition from *tanka* (a 31-syllable poem) to *haiku* (a 17-syllable poem) can be cited as an example of a similar change in media size. *Tanka* was originally referred to as *waka*, which was a Japanese form of Chinese poetry established between the mid-seventh century and late eighth century. A *tanka* is a 31-syllable poem comprising five sections of lines consisting of 5, 7, 5, 7, and 7 syllables. Meanwhile, *haiku*, established in the seventeenth century, is a 17-syllable poem comprising lines of 5, 7, and 5 syllables and is considered to be the world's shortest form of poetry. Shuichi Kato, a critic, pointed out that the sense of time represented in the poems changed when the number of syllables decreased in the transition from *waka* to *haiku* (Kato 2007).

> I know so little of what is in a person's heart, but the fragrance of the blossoms remains as the scent of the past
>
> Ki no Tsurayuki "Kokin Wakashu" Vol. 1, Spring poem 42
>
> (I don't know what is in a person's heart. But in this familiar place, the scent of the plum blossoms is as beautiful as ever.)

This is a love poem written by Ki no Tsurayuki for a collection that was made in the eighth century. In this 31-syllable *tanka*, Kato identified that general reflections do not have any predictions or future references. Time does not look toward tomorrow, but rather it focuses on today while bringing up memories of yesterday. It does not flow from "past to present to future;" in fact, it does not go beyond "the current situation." In this poem, the word "past" is used, but it is used in the context of a fragrance that is the same as ever. Reflections on the past are made regarding current actions, so the past transformed into the present (Kato 2007, p. 74).

Although 31 syllables are by no means a long form of poetry; however, within that, it is possible to represent the process of time. At the very least, the past can be recollected and past experiences can be applied to the present. However, with the 17 syllable *haiku*, there is no room for reflection, and it is extremely difficult to show the passage of time within it (Kato 2007, p. 75). As a typical example, Kato cites some of the key poems written by Basho, who had a central role in establishing *haiku* in the seventeenth century. Three of the poems are shown below.

Rose petals fall every now and then to the sound of a waterfall

The burning red of the tireless sun, yet there is the autumn wind

A cicada cries out in the complete silence that cuts through stone

According to Kato, time has come to a stop in these poems. In order to capture the sense of a moment, Basho uses onomatopoeia and repeated syllables that represent not a continued state of mind but a momentary experience. Rather than emotions such as love that have highs and lows, he is capturing a momentary sensibility. As a result, in these poems, there is no past and no future, only a "here and now" in which the whole world is converged. It depicts no past and no future, only a "now" that stretches out like an elastic band. What is represented is "what appears in an instant and disappears in an instant" (Kato 2007, pp. 76–8). According to Kato, in the 17-syllable media size of *haiku*, the writers turn their emphasis to living in the "now."

In August 2016, Instagram began offering a new function called "Instagram Stories." According to the official press release (Instagram Web Site 2018), this "new function enables users to share moments from everyday life, while the images will be automatically deleted 24 h after posting."

Content that disappears after 24 h. The images and videos displayed will not appear as "past events" on the feed in the future but rather they are here "now, in this moment," and then they disappear. Paradoxically, in view of the name "Stories," continuous emotions and narrative elements are minimized; only momentary experiences can be shared before they disappear. We could say that there is something "haiku-esque" about this form of expression.

## 6 Content that Expresses the Sense of "Now"

In mobile media, even in content that itself forms a story, such as a novel, there may be a convergence on a certain kind of "now." One example of this is an iOS app called "Real Time Novel: Run, Melos!", released by Hiroki Kojima in 2016. "Run, Melos!", published in 1946, is classic work by Osamu Dazai (1909–1948), a major writer in Japan. It is based on an ancient Greek legend and a poem by Friedrich von Schiller from Germany. The following explanation is provided regarding this app based on Run, Melos! (Real-Time Moerus on Apple App Store 2016).

This is a novel app to enjoy the world of "Run, Melos!" in real time.

- Part of the novel is displayed in real time according to the time in the novel.
- Every time something happens in the novel, you will receive a notification.
- You can follow the story based on the notifications alone because they contain the beginning of the new part of the story.

(The story starts automatically at the appropriate time. Please close the app and wait for a while after starting it.)

In other words, the reader can only see the title and the name of the author at the time the app is downloaded. The text of the story is not displayed until the time points in the novel are synchronized with the time of the world in which you live, and even though it has started, you will not be able to move ahead of the time in the novel and read it through. You have to wait until the time in the novel and the time you live in overlap. For example, there is a sentence in the middle of the story that says, "His childhood friend, Selinuntius, was called to the castle late at night." You cannot read through this paragraph during the day, and the notification will be finally displayed on the iPhone lock screen at 10 PM, when you will be able to read it (Fig. 5).

As for the user experience of this app, readers cannot read the story at their own pace. Instead, it gives them a sense that the "now" in the novel and their "now" is always synchronized when reading. The value is, in fact, placed on sharing the "now" of the characters in the novel with your own "now" in synchronicity, rather than following the story diachronically.

## 7 Users Who Edit Space

There is a transition from the consumption of stories in which the various events in a story are followed diachronically to consumption that is shared synchronically through momentary experiences. Either way, it is a passive action in the sense that stories or phrases created by others are consumed. Now, we will consider the

**Fig. 5** Screenshot of real-time novel, *Run, Melos!*

possibility of active action. That is, the possibility that we ourselves create or edit the new meanings of "here and now" using mobile media.

Since the beginning of the 2010s, there have been cases in which free conference-calling services such as Skype are used for unique purposes. One such unique use of Skype is called "Sagyo-ype." "Sagyo" comes from "Sagyou," which means work in Japanese. It is a portmanteau of "work" and "Skype." "Sagyo-ype" refers to doing some kind of work that requires concentration, such as drawing illustrations, writing articles, and studying for exams, while keeping a conference call open with two or more people.

If a person wishes to do Sagyo-ype, he or she invites participants with a similar purpose by indicating the time and purpose on social media, such as Twitter or BBS. When the time comes, they connect to a call from their rooms and concentrate on their own work. However, although the workers are connected to a call, they do not necessarily talk all the time. For example, in the case of doing Sagyo-ype work in order to concentrate on drawing manga, although the workers may consult each other about composition, they talk to each other or to themselves only occasionally, and in some cases, they may be silent almost all the time.

It means that in Sagyo-ype work, the transmission and exchange of messages is a secondary factor and the main focus is on creating an environment in which there is the possibility of "being seen by someone" or "someone is watching." As there is mutual monitoring and recognition while sharing a "now" from each person's own room, which is a private space, they are creating a public "here" like a library or a cafe, in what has come to be viewed as the second offline (Tomita 2021). In a sense, it is very similar to the Panopticon mentioned by Michel Foucault (Foucault 1975).

The Panopticon is a circular institutional building devised by the English philosopher Jeremy Bentham. This facility consists of an inspection tower in the center, with prison cells arranged in a circle around the tower. Since there are two windows in a cell in total, one on the outside and the other on the inside facing the tower, the figure of prisoners appears in the backlight as you look from the tower. Meanwhile, the solitary guard in the tower cannot be seen by the prisoners. Similarly, Foucault considered that the structure of the Panopticon would internalize a consciousness of willing obedience to authority by placing those in custody in a condition in which they are aware of always "being watched," which would be the origin of a modern regulated society (Figs. 6 and 7).

However, the participants in Sagyo-ype work are not under observation because they are in the Panopticon because they are subordinate to authority but because they work together and create a voluntary Panopticon environment and manage their own motivation by intentionally being involved in the private spaces of others (Fig. 8).

More interestingly, as a result of the fact that there is an overlap (doubling of place) between different private places, which are participants' own rooms in this case, the second offline is manifested in a public place, such as a library. In other words, the private character of a person's own room is relativized through being synchronized, and it adopts the character of a public place.

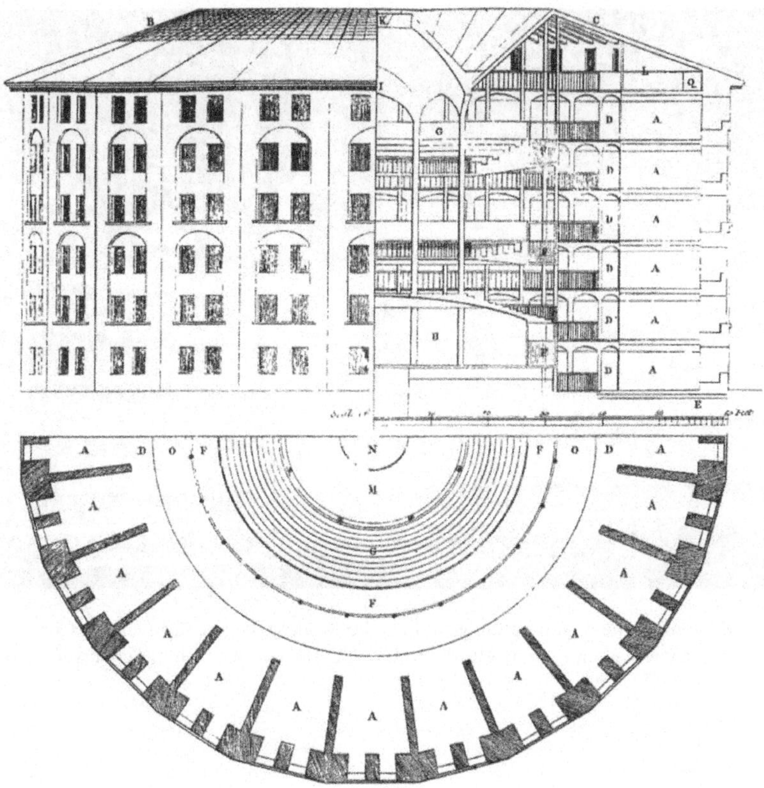

Fig. 6 Plan of the Panopticon by Jeremy Bentham

## 8 Users Who Edit Time

What about time, then? Is it possible for us to actively create a "now" rather than being passive?

A smartphone app "TikTok" from China released in 2016 is a lip-syncing video-sharing community app. Users who want to post a video choose a song from the list of songs offered by the app and record a 15-second video of themselves lip-syncing or dancing alongside the song. TikTok features advanced video editing functions, among which there is a unique function that speeds up or slows down the playback speed of the song being recorded.

However, when other users watch it after posting, playback will be at the original speed. That means that, if playback speeds up when the song is recorded, time is stretched out and played when watched and the motion of the object slows down. On the other hand, if playback slows down when the song is recorded, time is compressed when watched and the object is sped up. For example, a video taken in the latter method becomes somewhat comical and unrealistic as such fast

Fig. 7 Inside one of the prison buildings at Presidio Modelo, Isla de la Juventud, Cuba. I, Friman [GFDL (http://www.gnu.org/copyleft/fdl.html), CC-BY-SA-3.0 (http://creativecommons.org/licenses/by-sa/3.0/)]

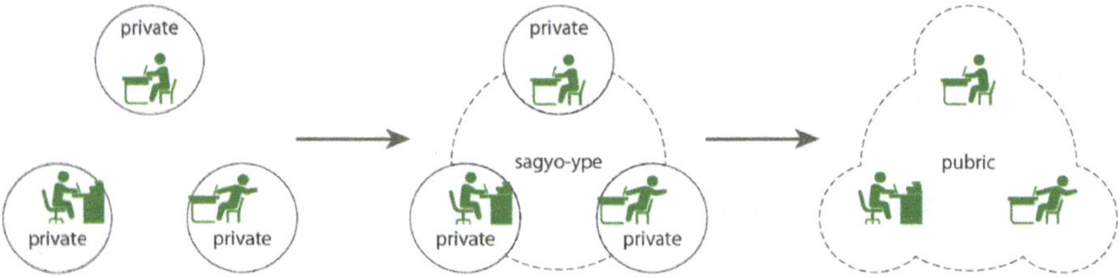


**Fig. 8** Sagyo-ype and voluntary Panopticon environment

movements are impossible for normal humans due to the limits of physical abilities and the effects of gravity.

The interesting thing here is that the audience will feel that time is elastic like rubber because of the change in playback speed. For the audience, time seems to go by faster for the poster when compared with the audience, whereas it seems to go by more slowly for other posters (Fig. 9). This strongly brings to mind the proposition from Albert Einstein's theory of special relativity that "different observers measure time or space differently."

Therefore, in user experiences of TikTok, the speed of time is not homogeneous and time at different speeds appears to synchronize (doubling of time), which goes beyond the difference in speed.

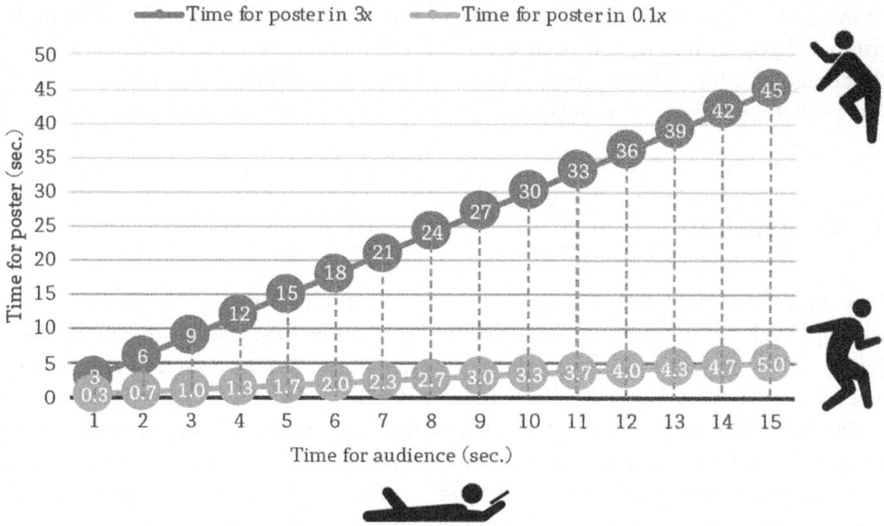


**Fig. 9** Time for audience and poster in TikTok

If these user experiences are understood using Hajime Maruta's concepts of synchronizing and coordinating (Maruta 2008, p. 188), the following can be said. In the act of Sagyo-ype work, users make it possible to intentionally mix the private spaces of each participant and manage their own concentration on a particular task through synchronization. In TikTok, users intentionally mix different speeds of time and enjoy a sense of time that expands and contracts through coordination.

In Sagyo-ype and TikTok, the time referred to as "now" and the place referred to as "here," which actually only exist in a single form, are mixed with another (or with multiple) "nows" and "heres."

The uniqueness of this becomes clear if you consider traditional photo album. For example, you go on a trip to Kyoto with your friend and take pictures at shrines and temples to preserve the memories. You develop them after returning to Tokyo and put them in an album to enjoy with others. This is an act of giving significance to the "place you have left" and "the days in the past." However, in Sagyo-ype and TikTok, a two-fold or three-fold level of new significance is conferred to the "place where you are now" and the "time you are experiencing at the moment."

Hidenori Tomita discusses the concept that our senses are given a "doubling of time" by a service called "live credits roll," which has been offered at wedding receptions in recent years (Tomita 2021). Live credits roll is a service to edit videos and pictures taken by photographers on the day of the wedding during the reception, which are shown as a video at the end of the reception like a movie credits roll. This is not the same as enjoying the pictures of wedding at a later date. It is used to "enrich the significance of the time you are experiencing right now."

Such multiplexing of time and place is realized using mobile media, in particular, to intentionally create a collage of different times and different places in the "now" and "here," which creates a sense of time and place that is different from the original. I would like to call such behavior a "bricolage of time to the 'now'" and "bricolage of place to the 'here,'" in line with the concept of bricolage (creating using whatever comes to hand), as propounded by Lévi-Strauss (1966).

## 9 Conclusion

This paper identified that the digitalization and mobilization of media have been accompanied by a decreased amount of information that can be displayed on a device at one time, the fragmentation and miniaturization of content consumption time, and that the context of the content tends to be diluted. Then, based on the historical background in which the sense of time among poets centered on the "here and now" when the number of syllables decreased with the transition from *tanka* to *haiku*, a theory was established that media mobilization has had an effect on our sense of time and sense of space, and an analysis was conducted focusing on a variety of mobile content. The results showed that the rise of services and content in which neither the past nor the future but the "now" is enjoyed in "synchronicity" and that intentional mixing of different locations and times by users has formed a bricolage that produces a new sense of time and place centering on the "here and now."

Such user behavior attempts to break up modern homogenous and absolute spatial awareness alongside homogenous and linear temporal awareness. The meaning of location is relativized and the new "here" is produced. "Now," which should be homogenous, has become elastic. If these things can bring about a second offline, there will be a continual growth of content and services that arouse and stimulate such a sense of time and place.

Why does our consciousness turn toward neither the past nor the future but the "here and now" when we have a mobile device? According to Munesuke Mita, the sense of history that was taken for granted by people until the 1970s was the sense that history was advancing and developing more rapidly. For example, this is supported by the accelerated increase in the amount of energy consumed worldwide. The present time is a period of rapid change that goes beyond ancient times or the middle ages, and even in modern times, changes were more severe in the nineteenth century than in the eighteenth century as well as in the twentieth century than in the nineteenth century. Even in the twentieth century, until about the 1970s, we have been in an era where changes have been more rapid in the last 10 years than the previous 10 years. Incidentally, in a survey of the awareness of Japanese people conducted every five years since 1973 by the NHK Broadcasting Culture Research Institute, when analyzing the changes in the awareness of each generation chronologically, the major generation gap that existed in the 1970s had decreased drastically by the end of the 1980s, and in this century, it has almost disappeared. Based on this, Mita stated that after the end of the 1970s, when there was a reversal of the rapid and consistent decrease in the global population, we entered an era in which the changes were small and steady, and the changes in awareness in the 30-year period since then have been "decelerating" or "stopping" (Mita 2018, pp. 2–10).

If we find the meaning of our lives not, as it once was, in the "future," which is an extension of current rapid changes, but in the "future ≒ now," which is not so different from the present as a result of a deceleration in changes, the derivation of unlimited time and unlimited place from the finite sense of "here and now" will produce a new practice of living.

## References


Foucault M (1975) *Surveiller et punir:* Naissance de la prison. Éditions Gallimard, Paris

Instagram Web Site (2018) https://ja.newsroom.fb.com/news/2016/08/instagram_instagramstories/. Accessed on 28 Nov 2018

Ito K (2016) Recreation and mobile content: the future of mobile content: a new "me" in rich context. In: Tomita H (ed) The post-mobile society: from the smart/mobile to second offline. Routlege, London

Kato S (2007) Time and space in Japanese culture (in Japanese). Iwanami Shoten, Publishers, Tokyo

Lévi-Strauss C (1966) The savage mind (nature of human society). University of Chicago Press, Chicago

Maruta H (2008) A theory of place: realism in the web, romanticism in the community (in Japanese). NTT Publishing, Tokyo

Mita M (2018) Where modern society is headed: carving out a view of the plateau (in Japanese). Iwanami Shoten Publishers, Tokyo

Real Time Moerus on Apple App Store (2016) https://itunes.apple.com/jp/app/%E5%AE%9F%E6%99%82%E9%96%93%E5%B0%8F%E8%AA%AC-%E8%B5%B0%E3%82%8C%E3%83%A1%E3%83%AD%E3%82%B9/id1082133515?mt=8. Accessed on 28 Nov 2018

Tomita H (2021) The doubling of time and place. In: Tomita T (ed) The second offline: doubling of time and place. Springer, Berlin


**Ito Kota** is a part-time lecturer at Kansai University and innovation planning director at the advertising agency in Tokyo, Japan. He completed the master's program at the Graduate School of Letters, Doshisha University in 2002. He develops marketing and branding strategies for Japanese and international corporations and local governments in Japan, acts as their futurist, and assists them with innovation. He is also an independent researcher in sociology and media studies and holds a master's degree in sociology. His paper "Digitalians Dreaming of Jomon Pottery: From Life information to Data Ethnography" was awarded the silver medal in the 2018 Japan Advertising Agencies Association treatise contest. He has been a lecturer of the Faculty of Informatics, Kansai University, since 2008. He has written about the rise of mobile media and acculturation as coauthor of the volume "Posuto mobairu shakai: Sekando ofurain no jidai e" (Sekaishisosha, 2016), edited by Hidenori Tomita, which is available in English under the title "The Post-Mobile Society: From the Smart /Mobile to Second Offline" (2016), published by Britain's Routledge.

# The Potential of the Participatory Design of Mobile Media in Post-mobile Society

**Tomoyuki Okada**

**Abstract** In relation to the kinds of devices and services that will be required and accepted in the 'post-mobile society' of mature mobile media, this study adopts a participatory design method and examines the methodology of proposing new media design.

## 1 Introduction

In their survey research of users and business operators, the development of the mobile phone and other mobile media was demonstrated by Okada et al. to have been greatly influenced by socio-cultural considerations, in contrast to the technological determinist media development model (e.g. Okada 2005, 2016). This research was located in the context of the innovation theory of scientific and technological history and technological society theory and responded to the social constructivist approach of Bijker, Low, and Fisher et al. (Bijker and Law 1992; Fisher 1992), and Latour's actor-network theory (Latour 2005). Thereafter, following the release of Apple's first iPhone in 2007, the smartphone's emergence as a mainstream mobile handset has greatly expanded the user-customisable domain and clearly defined the uniqueness of individual users. Meanwhile, smartphones feedback all kinds of new information on individuals' user behaviour, and such user data is utilised as a source of revenue whereby individuals are exploited as 'dividuals' (Mizushima 2019). Nevertheless, different from when the exclusively spoken media of the former mobile phone became equipped with text-messaging and camera features, this development could no longer be perceived as mobile phones' ongoing development into a media distant from its origins via a process involving general users. Further, it cannot be dismissed as a reduction of the diverse possibilities that had flourished until that point due to the commoditisation of media

T. Okada (✉)
Faculty of Informatics, Kansai University, Osaka, Japan
e-mail: okada@kansai-u.ac.jp



H. Tomita (ed.), *The Second Offline*, Advances in Information and Communication Research 3, https://doi.org/10.1007/978-981-16-2425-4_6

in the transition from the period of mobile phone proliferation and development to the mature period.

Mizukoshi (2007) highlighted the fact that the element of 'play' seen in the use of former media has contributed to the spread of the possible new modes of media and presented 'a critical media practice' that relies on workshop methodology as a way of locating new possibilities. Okada (2010) also responded to these prior studies and used the workshop method with users to locate a more specific and deeper level of utilisation and application of those possibilities that are difficult to imagine in everyday awareness. However, these previous studies were largely exploratory and experimental in nature and did not establish a design or technique for the methodology itself. Hence, the present study emphasises the verification of each process, such as the objective, exploration, and results of the design, and aims to refine a universally applicable design process. Similarly, there are as yet multiple unknowns in relation to how recent developments in wearable technology and augmented reality (AR) technology will be accepted at the consumer level of mobile media. For this domain to proliferate and transcend the imaginative capacity of the everyday user, a way of thinking about new media designs that is not restricted to technicians' ideas and involves users themselves will likely be required. Therefore, what follows is a consideration of the ideal design process for the introduction of new devices and services.

## 2 Research Methods

'Participatory design' is when users take part in the design process and, as Yutaka Yamauchi described, 'focusses on artefacts such as information systems, products, and structures, [although] the same framework can also often be used to discuss items of design that are not artefact-targeted, such as services, local communities, corporate strategies, learning curriculums, and policies' (Yamauchi 2012). One origin of participatory design is the arguments of Papanek, who is often referenced in discussions of design thought. In the 1960s, when environmental and climate issues came to the fore, Papanek was involved in design education with Richard Buckminster Fuller, who is known for advocating the concept of 'Spaceship Earth', and fiercely critiqued environmental destruction and any industrial design that lacks a human aspect. He believed the significance of design education lies in ordinary people 'being good consumers' and that the process of determining what constitutes sustainable design is the ideal form of participatory design (Papanek 1972).

Workshops occupy a major methodical position in this design process. According to Yuhei Yamauchi, workshops encompass the two respective aspects of a 'creative activity' and a 'learning activity' (Yamauchi 2013) because, by taking part in the design process through a workshop, users not only create new media but also improve their consumer literacy. Yutaka Yamauchi also cited the discussion that can take place creatively and outside of reality as another of a workshop's benefits, positing that the market opportunities for non-existent technology are underestimated (Yamauchi 2012). Hence, while novel and unknown technologies may be difficult to incorporate into designs, a workshop makes an escape from this limitation possible.

While forecasting may be based on the idea of prolonging current trends, it frequently misses the mark by a wide margin; for example, the 1994 prediction by the *Telecommunications Technology Council* of the former Ministry of Posts and Communication prediction that 'the number of radio pager (pocket beepers or pagers) users will increase to 34 million by 2010'. In the 1990s, pagers spread rapidly, primarily among young people, with the number of users reaching 10 million in 1996 and around half the high-school girls in metropolitan Tokyo possessing such a device. In these circumstances, this may have actually been a conservative prediction; however, the development of mobile phone functions exceeded previous expectations and replaced the pager, and the largest pager operator, NTT Docomo, discontinued the service in 2007. To overly fixate on the situation of media usage in the present is, unfortunately, to misjudge the reality of the future.

At this point, we introduce the method known as 'backcasting'. While also utilised in Okada's previous workshop practice, backcasting 'is a method of developing a roadmap by firstly depicting how the ideal future should be and what should be done to achieve that future image, and then setting the target by reflecting the future onto the present' (Okada 2010; Yuhashi 2005). Depicting the macro- and global situation of the world of that period and then applying a conceptual image to its specific systems of social life and media environment gives shape to the design results. In the workshop practice conducted previously by Okada (2010), the objective was established as designing potential modes of new media for a predicted future society; however, the present study aimed not only to design media devices and services based on the prediction of future social needs but also to implement a more specific approach by setting an objective of designing new media to solve these predicted issues.

## 3 Workshop Practice

### *3.1 'The Near Future of the News and Internet Media'*

I conducted my first survey on the workshop method in June 2017, focussing on the topic, 'Thinking about a new news ecosystem'. Alongside the development and proliferation of social networking services (SNS), major changes are occurring in the processes of generating, circulating, and consuming news. Problems such as the declining status of the existing mass-media and the deluge of fake news have emerged; thus, I presented the kind of models that can be drawn for the future of news and journalism. The workshop participants comprised 45 university students from the Kansai area who were divided into nine groups, with the survey taking place over nearly a whole day. During the session, the participants were firstly given approximately an hour's lecture on fake news and the problems it entails by a guest lecturer, Hiroyuki Fujishiro, who is a researcher of Internet journalism and a journalist himself. This was followed by individual groupwork in which the participants devised and developed proposals related to the ecosystem of 'new news'. This activity was interspersed with progress reports, breaks, and a short lecture from another guest speaker, Kota Ito, a marketing planner at an advertising agency, who described 'Pursuing the "What" not the "How"' when proposing designs. After a further few hours of group work, each group gave a final presentation.

Several ideas were raised in the presentations, including adding a verified mark from a public institution to circulating news to confirm its veracity and prevent fake news. Further, in relation to the algorithms that generate news rankings, a news distribution mechanism that works in the opposite direction to users' normal search behaviour and randomly selects the news we receive was also suggestions, as well as the distribution of news in a short video summary of the days' headlines. While no possibilities were found that were capable of overcoming the challenges to news that have occurred since the advent of the Internet, smartphones, and SNS (which were described in the first lecture), the attempt to communicate simply using short videos, as raised in the third example, is a phenomenon that has been spread by Youtubers and V-tubers, and maybe an interesting point to re-address at a later time.

In their post-workshop reflection sheets, the participants left many positive comments, stating that prolonging the initial schedule and redoing the groupwork upon instruction made the practice more valuable and that it was beneficial that students' own ideas and views could be changed by listening to other participants' and teachers' (facilitators) opinions. Example comments included, 'I was very stimulated by hearing the presentations of other teams' and, 'It was the first time I've engaged in protracted group work with people I've just met, and I was inspired by the final argumentative exchanges of opinions'. Conversely, issues were voiced by some participants for whom it was their first experience overall and who found themselves very confused and those who felt they let themselves down by not expressing their own opinion adequately. There were also complaints that the scheduling was tight and that 'the topics were too loose and difficult to understand'. Other comments criticised the lack of adequate management, indicating that future reflection is required, for example 'It felt as if the teachers (facilitators) were a little condescending towards students and lacked respect for them as people'. In the light of the fact that the worktables in the venue were too small and the worksheets had to be laid directly on the floor for the group work, one participant commented, 'On the ground? Don't be ridiculous!'

### 3.2 'Thinking About Mobile Life in Ten Years' Time'

Okada (2010) previously conducted a workshop considering mobile life and mobile media in 10 years' time; however, the present study's next workshop practice asked participants to produce proposals focussed on how to resolve anticipated issues (as also touched on in Sect. 2), and, as such, differed greatly from its predecessor. Participating students took intensive lectures at a women's college in the Kansai area, and the workshop was conducted as part of a course on mobile media and communication. At the end of August 2017, over a total of three days (in which two days equated to ten hours of lectures), 17 students were divided into four groups, and a workshop was conducted that lasted the entire final day.

This workshop proceeded in a similar fashion to Okada's (2010), whereby in Step 1, the macro-situation of society in ten years' time (i.e. in 2027) and the wider media environment was estimated, and the public's predicted values and awareness at that time were examined. The five areas of (1) politics and economics, (2) family life and local community, (3) education, (4) leisure and recreational culture, and (5) the media landscape were each expressed by a single phrase, and the items submitted by each group were summarised and used as a broad overview of the social situation. Next, based on the results examined in Step 1, aspects of specific mobile media use and the accompanying social life and interpersonal relations were discussed in Step 2, and there was an attempt to specifically depict the state of mobile media in ten years' time. Between Steps 1 and 2, the advertising planner who had given the short lecture on the ecosystem of news in the June workshop gave another lecture on ways of thinking when considering new media devices and services from a marketing perspective. Following the groupwork, the groups presented an external diagram of a handset, its features, and its available services, before each participant also completed a reflection sheet.

In Step 1, ideas such as the following were presented by each group in relation to society and life in 2027. (1) In terms of politics and economics, the groups predicted that social polarisation in, for example, information and poverty, would progress in various areas of society, that voting would become computerised, that the pension and taxation systems would be revolutionised, and that currency standardisation would advance with the introduction of global electronic money. (2) In family life, the groups said that the individual would be regarded as more important than the family; that ties between individuals would be ascribed greater importance; that technological advances would advance robotics, driverless vehicles, and self-checkout machines; and that as disconnectedness advances, more people would choose to live alone than with their families, local traditional events would also disappear, society would become a nation of AI, and that AI would come to permeate everyday life. (3) On the education front, the groups indicated that with greater developments in e-learning, studies would be conducted fully remotely through media such as virtual reality (VR); that studying without school registration would increase; that with the development and shift to ICT; every student would have an iPad, and the use of electronic blackboards would become standardised; that classes at cram schools would be conducted via video; that electronic devices would become standard; that paper-medium writing tools would cease to exist; and that teachers would be AI units. (4) In the area of leisure and recreation, participants forecasted a shift to indoor recreation that people enjoy alone at home; that VR would advance, and, consequently, physical exercise would also proliferate; that VR-driven 'experiencism' would progress; and that everyone would experience VR leisure activities at least once. (5) In media culture, a situation was envisaged in which media would become more centralised and only accessible via the Internet, that contemporary media would decline, that information would be acquired through familiar and accessible items with the spread of wearable devices, and that paper culture would decline.

Based on these predictions, the following proposals for mobile media were made by each of the four groups, A to D. Group A proposed a robotic device called the 'Family Guardian' that controls all communications related to the family, functioning like another member of the family and acquiring various data and detecting and notifying the family of potential risks. Group B proposed a device that uses VR to project ghosts and monsters in old local houses as a tourist attraction to make people more familiar with local areas and help save outlying settlements from crisis. Group C suggested a countermeasure to the stress of interpersonal relationships through the installation of an attraction that allows people to commune with nature. Finally, Group D's proposal encompassed a new business communication tool that uses a wearable device to scan brainwaves and enables people in various circumstances, such as those with serious disabilities, to work together by standing at the same starting line.

Among the comments received on the post-workshop reflection forms, some were positive:

> Envisaging the environment of the time point from several perspectives made it easy to consider the kind of problems there will be, as well as what will be needed. Similarly, envisaging the future in this workshop allowed me a glimpse into the way in which other members think and live on a daily basis, which was also stimulating.

> I learned how I had previously been ignoring the 'countermeasures that will be taken in future' when I thought about 'the future that will be derived from the present'. What will people need in a society that will 'become increasingly convenient as technology advances, even if left alone'? It may be direct communication with people, or irrational entertainment and pastimes. However, people's spirits will die if such activities are disregarded as irrational, and I believe there are already signs of this. I also learned a great deal from the point that even things that are not directly related and seem like they cannot resolve a problem can easily resolve it unexpectedly.

However, other comments emphasised problems in the design and facilitation of the workshop itself:

> The workshop was held in a single day, which was not enough time at all. If we'd had more time, we would've been able to fill it with more and achieved something better. Similarly,

> while I'm well aware this wasn't deliberate, the guest speaker's comments started by negating everything outright, which was very de-motivating, and from our perspective, the advice he gave us while we were working seemed more like simply pushing his own ideas rather than giving advice.

## 3.3 'The Post-mobile Society and Media in 2030'

In analysing the approach, what came to light was the challenge of how to shape the targets set for each workshop and how to evaluate the workshops at the interim and results stages. Similarly, there also remained the question of how to address the participants' feeling of a lack of completion after the workshops were conducted in the short, limited timeframe of a single day.

Therefore, we subsequently gave participants a certain amount of time to draw fully on their respective specialisations in their approaches. This time, the focus participants were 21 postgraduate students of a university master's programme who were organised into five groups. They comprised students from a socio-informatics major (Humanities) and a knowledge and informatics major (Engineering), and students from both majors were mixed evenly across the groups. In terms of the new technology on which the design work was to be based, we defined the round number of the year 2030 as the time point, rather than 'in ten years' time', and utilised the example of the high-speed, high-volume, and low-delay mobile communication technology of 5G with the aim of eliciting a specific future image. Since the participants included engineering postgraduates, we hoped that the approaches would draw fully on their particular specialist knowledge. We also invited business operators from the communications industry to give guest lectures and provide us with relevant information.

The workshops were conducted during graduate school classes and followed a process of firstly reading literature on the changes to various aspects of society that accompany the innovation of mobile technology. Thereafter, the participants split into groups and devised a general outline of society in 2030 (Step 1), then gave a specific form to the mobile media of that time (Step 2). In between the two steps, expert lectures were also given, in the same process recounted in Sect. 3.2; however, the implementation period took over a month in total, and the workshops were conducted in weekly classes.

Consequently, a vote was held to mutually assess the groups' final presentations, and the best proposal was selected. Though a physical experience VR cinema and a museum utilising VR were suggested, the results were unremarkable compared to the content that was hoped for.

Moreover, there were many negative opinions among the post-completion reflections, rather than a sense of accomplishment:

> When imagining 2030 and talking about the kinds of technology and services that will exist, everyone including myself unsurprisingly had ideas that were fairly confined to current technology and devices. We were unable to think up something completely different from what is available at present.

Since there was an overwhelming lack of presentation time given the content to be presented, I'd have preferred the workshop to have been divided over two sessions, for example. Likewise, because the groupwork was conducted with participants from other seminars and the activity times for each seminar were different, it was difficult to get together to refine the ideas, so, unfortunately, it ended up that a single person would summarise the materials, and someone who didn't understand them would be doing the presentation.

Regarding the limitations on presentation time, although the restricted number of classes was largely the result of several cancellations due to the frequent natural disasters (such as an earthquake and wind and flood damage) that affected the university's local area during this semester, upon reflection, we realised that the workshops should have been organised with slightly more leeway. Likewise, while it was unlikely that groupwork could have been conducted adequately in classes with a weekly timeslot, it was also problematic that we did not respond to this by providing venues and times for supplementary work but unfortunately left this organisation to the respective groups.

## 4 Introducing Field Research

### *4.1 Suggestions from Previous Studies*

Although some results had been achieved in both the workshop output and participants' reflections from participatory design implemented by this stage, issues persisted in relation to participants' sense of accomplishment and the long-term objectives of the design. To identify what was needed to overcome these issues, I referred to information on inclusive design and the approach of the Arki Research Group of Aalto University in Finland, which has been investigating the practice of participatory design for a long time.

Inclusive design aims to overcome the problem of exclusion arising from the design of products and services. Previously, certain senses and bodies (in other words, disabilities) have been excluded by designs, as have disparities, including economic disparities, due to digitalisation. Herein, an inclusive design is identified as 'an idea that aims for a design that includes previously excluded users and that constitutes a business' (Cassim et al. 2014). A project by the Kyushu University Graduate School of Design that has been achieving results in this field emphasised the importance of field research in practice (Kyushu University Graduate School of Design 2018). In Autumn 2018, a summary and report meeting for groupwork practice were held as part of the Kyushu University project, and a visit to its workshop was made by Kari-Hans Kommonen, the former leader of the Aalto

University Arki Research Group. Kommonen was interviewed and introduced the Arki Group's 'Future Media Home' Project (Arki Research Group 2000), in which he posited that when specifically presenting elements of new technology in the form of building blocks to general participants in design practice, these participants must be assisted in incorporating these new technology elements into their design work. Based on these results and interview outcomes, we conducted another workshop practice in September 2018.

### *4.2 Participatory Design with the Aim of Local Problem-Solving*

The subjects of the September 2018 workshop were undergraduate students of informatics at a women's university in the Kansai area who were taking intensive lectures. The participatory design was conducted as part of their lectures on mobile media and communication, and after a total of 10 h of lectures over two days, a one-day workshop was held. Taking the theme of 'The Post-Mobile Society and Media in Nara Machi (the old downtown of Nara) in 2030', the workshop encouraged students to devise specific ideas related to developing mobile media in the former town centre of the municipality of Nara-shi, close to their campus. We organised eight students into two groups of four, and, as with the earlier workshop, in Step 1, the groups envisaged the macro-situation and media environment of society in 2030. The workshop then proceeded by examining the values and awareness of people at that time and, based on that, imagining ideas for mobile media in 2030, in the same progression as previous workshops. The images of society that the participants depicted in Step 1 and the envisaged social changes were as follows:

1. In politics and economics:
    - Paper currency will cease to have value, banks will cease to exist, and consumer taxes will rise as social insurance expenditure becomes necessary. Internet-enabled elections will be possible.
    - Cashless transactions will proliferate. Election campaigning will take place via the Internet.
    - Political activity will be more Internet-based and will be open to participation for all. Social control will advance with the evolution of the 'My Number System' (a 12-digit ID number issued to all citizens and residents of Japan used for taxation, social security, and disaster response purposes).
2. In family life and local community:
    - All shopping will become possible from the home. Common-law marriages will increase.
    - Housework will be automated.

- It will be possible to do anything and everything from the home. Individuals' actions will be monitored by surveillance cameras.

3. Education:

- Distance learning will become mainstream. It will no longer be necessary to learn English.
- High-school and university study will become Internet-based. Teaching materials will be electronic.
- It will be possible to attend classes from anywhere without going to a physical school. Paper textbooks will decrease. Virtual-experience studies will become possible.

4. Leisure and recreational culture:

- Developments in VR will render it possible to enjoy virtual travel and live performances. Zoos will cease to exist.
- Developments in VR and AR will allow for yoga and other lessons at home.
- With the over-development of VR, more attention will be directed to analogue experiences, such as farming.

5. Media landscape:

- Chips implanted in the body will enable telepathic communication via brainwaves.
- TV will become 4-dimensional. It will be possible to experience TV and media through the tactile and olfactory senses as with a theme-park attraction, and there will be an increase in information that utilises the five senses.

In response to this, and based on suggestions from the abovementioned extant studies, field research was established as a new element in Step 2, entitled, 'Nara Machi 2020'. Therein, the groups were asked to develop either, (1) ideas to encourage people to want to visit Nara, that is, the leisure domain, or (2) encourage people to want to continue to live in Nara, in other words, the domain of everyday life. To help them consider media in central Nara Town in 2030, we asked each group to walk around the town for 1–2 h. Similarly, within the fieldwork, the groups were required to interview a minimum of two people and, based on the results, deduce the issues related to points (1) and (2) that required a resolution.

Based on the field research results, what had previously been defined as Step 2 was this time set as Step 3, which specifically included the process of devising ideas for media devices and services. During the process of designing the 2030 'Mobile Media in Nara Town', and considering the results examined in Step 1 and Step 2, we considered the situations of specific mobile and media use and the accompanying social life and interpersonal relationships and attempted to portray the exact state of mobile media in 12 years' time. Here, based on suggestions obtained from the earlier interview with Kommonen, we predicted the elements of the new technology as follows: (1) It will be equipped with features related to the olfactory and tactile senses and can be enjoyed with the five senses; (2) It will also be equipped with VR and AR features, encouraging the inclination to seek analogue senses; and (3) It will incorporate the sharing of users' brainwave data. We set the prerequisite that new media must be equipped with one of these items.

In an interim lecture, we invited Makiko Ogita (then Associate Professor at the Hokkaido University of Education Iwamizawa Campus), who specialises in visual communication design and information design, to discuss the ways of thinking about design with a focus on the theme of ideas related to designs incorporating 'the benefit of inconvenience'.

The progress and results presented by the ensuing groupwork were as follows. Firstly, the group that opted to focus on leisure, namely, inspiring the desire to visit Nara, conducted their fieldwork interviews at private museums and tourist offices in the town and observed issues that included the townspeople's desire for more young people to visit without spoiling the area's tranquil atmosphere and the challenge of coping with multiple languages due to the increase in international tourists. Since mobile media could resolve this, the group designed wearable media for use on group study visits in the form of GPS-equipped goggles that would give people a guided tour of ancient sites through which they could relive the experience of the historic events shown via AR on their displays (Fig. 1). At each checkpoint, a historic event would occur; for example, during a visit to the Great Buddha at Todaiji in Nara, the Great Buddha's eye-drawing ceremony of 752 would be replayed, in which the goggle wearers would become the Emperor Shomu as he draws on the eyes of the Great Buddha. Audio guides and commentaries would be provided via automated translation, which, in emergencies such as a natural disaster, would be able to address the wearers directly in the voice of their supervising teacher and relate the escape route. Similarly, in situations such as where a member of the group wanted to go to the toilet but was hesitant to interrupt the tour, a brainwave scanning system would detect the urinary urge, and the AI guide would insert a toilet break for them.

Meanwhile, the group that opted to focus on everyday life, namely on encouraging people to want to continue to live in Nara, conducted their fieldwork interviews with female customers who visit nearby supermarkets to do their shopping. In so doing, they collated views such as that living in the centre of Nara provide access to few nearby parks in which young children can play. Although the Nara Park at the centre of the city is huge and has abundant nature, interviewees were hesitant to let young children play there freely or take a bento lunch box for a picnic as many suspicious people frequent the park, and it is sullied by widespread deer droppings. Based on these views, the group developed the idea for a cleaning robot in the shape of a deer called 'Ayumu-kun' (Fig. 2). With two modes—Mode 1: Transit and Mode 2: cleaning—Ayumu-kun would walk around the park on four legs in Mode 1, and when it reached a place in which there were scattered deer droppings, it would enter Mode 2 and go about cleaning in a sitting position. The robot was also intended to bring enjoyment to the public via a camera in its head, which would photograph tourists who approach it and send the images to their devices. If people came to pet the robot, its head and facial expression would change. It would also have a display on its back showing the distribution of the

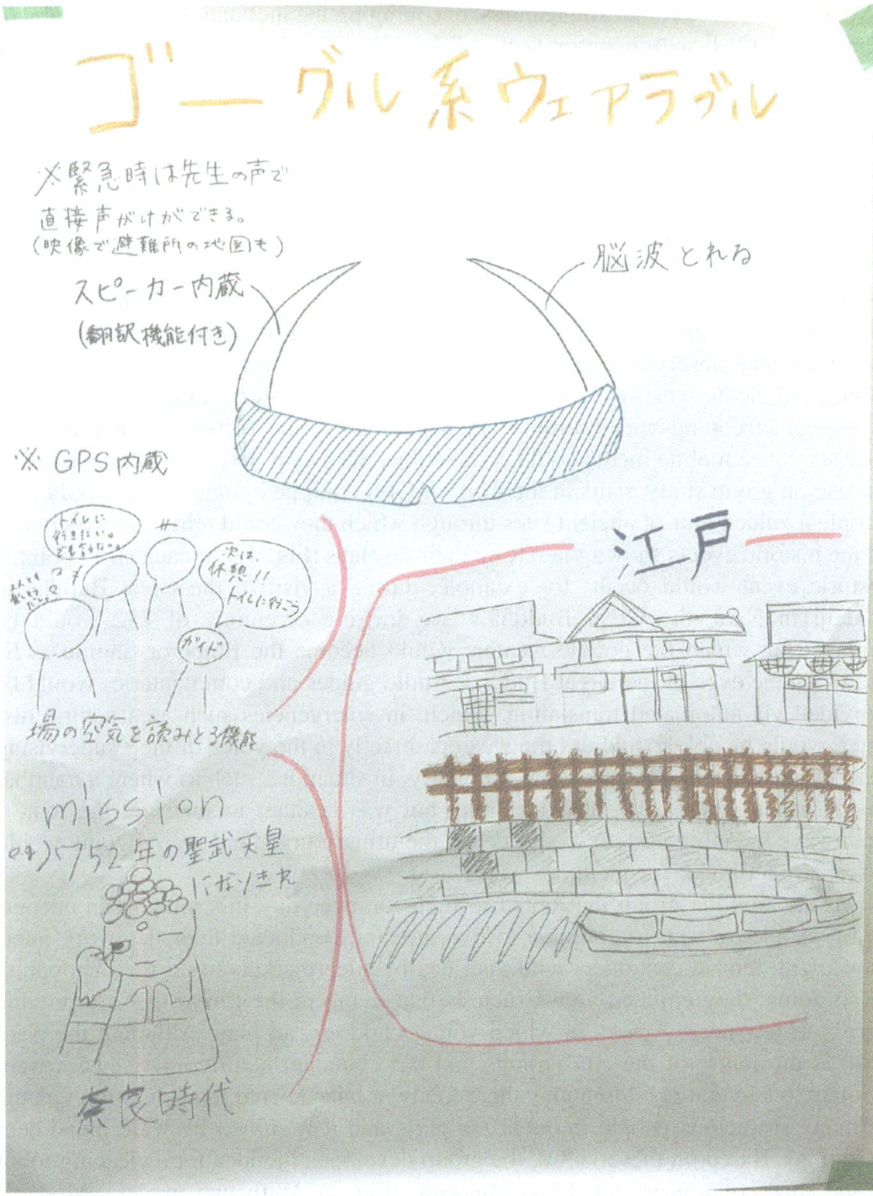


**Fig. 1** Wearable media for use on group study visits

nearby area and would be able to go and view places in which people are gathered and any works that are in progress to see how they look. It would also be possible to check this distribution data on the Internet so it could be enjoyed by tourists and other viewers.

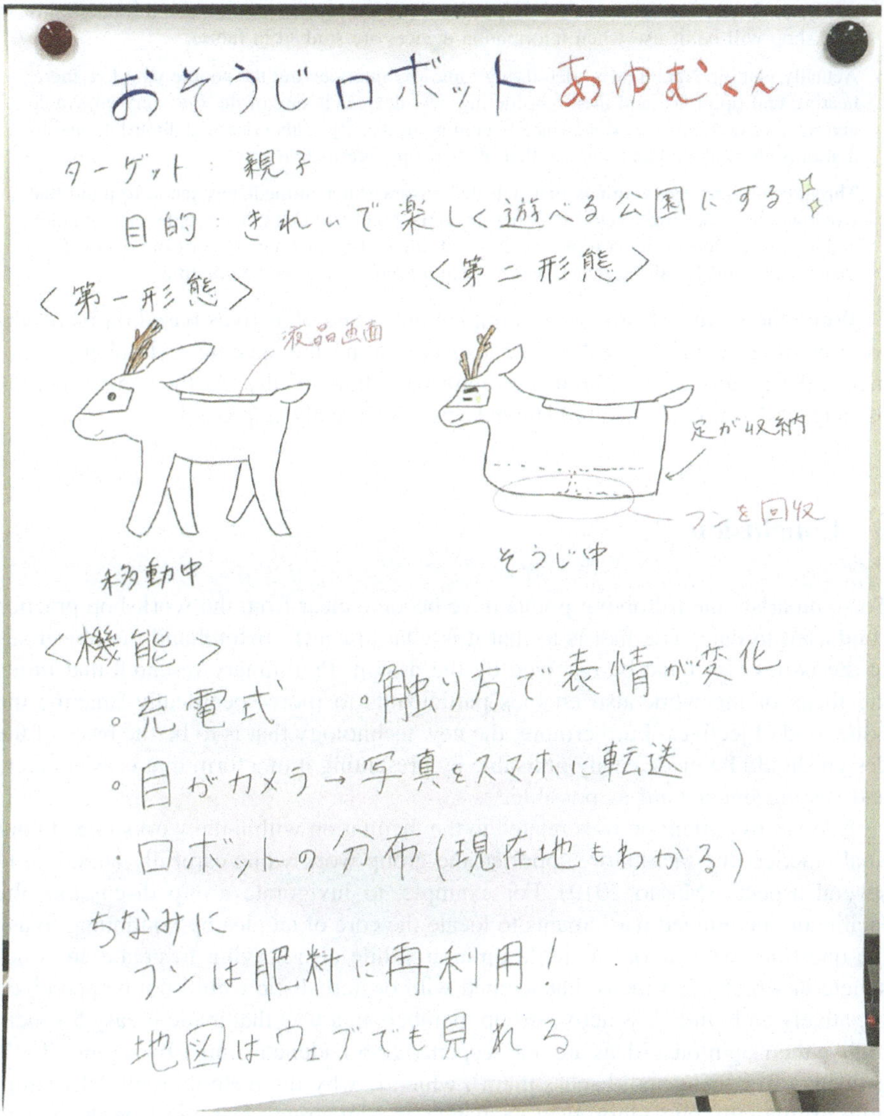


**Fig. 2** A cleaning robot in the shape of a deer called 'Ayumu-kun'

To summarise, the products of the workshop were all unprecedentedly groundbreaking and very well suited to the needs of the local area. Further, the comments in the post-completion reflections were all very positive:

> By trying to imagine the future in ten years' time as a group, it was helpful that there were opinions on a [more] convenient world that would not have occurred to me and opinions on things we have now that will cease to be. Without this opportunity, I wouldn't think so

much about how my future world will be, so I hope that the views obtained through this workshop will be of use when information devices are studied in future.

Actually visiting Nara Town, identifying topics by interviewing the people who live there, hearing real opinions, and then considering new devices is one of the first very enjoyable and refreshing things I've done since beginning university. I also [learned about] the issues that only the stakeholders can see that other people are unable to.

Through the interviews, things that will make Nara better immediately came to mind that would not have occurred to me at all before, and while I feel that other people's imagination and local experiences are completely different things, I got a keen sense of my own lack of imagination and I realised that I need to acquire more imaginative potential.

While the fieldwork survey was implemented and objectives based on its results were clarified in this workshop, by also presenting the specific technological elements, the quality of the output was improved dramatically. At the same time, the participants' sense of accomplishment was also greatly improved.

## 5 Conclusion

To summarise, the following points have become clear from the workshop practice conducted to date. The first is to that it is vital to clarify beforehand the objectives of the issues that must be resolved by the design. Preliminary research that limits the focus of the work also enables participants to more specifically imagine the issues and objectives. Furthermore, the new technology that is to be the basis of the design should be made easily utilisable by presenting it in a form that is as concrete and easy to understand as possible.

Another important point is related to the facilitation within the workshops. In our final practice, the facilitator supported the group work while carefully attending to several aspects (Maruo 2019). For example, to invigorate group discussion, the facilitator encouraged participants to locate the core of an idea by continuing to ask the question 'why' about a single opinion, while also striving to create an atmosphere in which even ideas that seemed wild or unrealistic would not be perceived negatively and guide less active group members in a way that made it easy for them to give their opinions. Ideas are not deepened or broadened simply by saying, 'Let's exchange free ideas and discuss them', which is why the methodology delineating how to mutually and vigorously exchange and integrate ideas must be developed into something more refined.

In terms of future challenges, we highlight that the field research methods used in this practice could not be followed up to a great extent. It is also undoubtedly necessary to continue to examine the problem of facilitation that was ultimately indicated. To construct a participatory design with general users with no prior specialist knowledge and a process that encourages reflection on the development of mobile media services and devices, in future, more venues for practice must be acquired, and while being aware of the abovementioned challenges, studies must be advanced to establish a new methodology.

## References


Arki Research Group (2000) Future media home. http://fmh.uiah.fi

Bijker WE, Law J (1992) Shaping technology/building society: studies in sociotechnical change. The MIT Press

Cassim J et al (eds) (2014) Inclusive design: participatory design solves social issues (in Japanese). Gakugei Shuppansha

Fisher CS (1992) America calling: a social history of the telephone to 1940. University of California Press

Kyushu University, School of Design (2018) Societal design fiction family friendly Japan 2040: redesign of society, vol 4. Kyushu University

Latour B (2005) Reassembling the social: an introduction to actor-network-theory. Oxford University Press, Oxford

Maruo K (2019) What Maruo is careful about when working as a facilitator (in Private note)

Mizushima K (2019) Beyond capitalism of communication and accelerationism: for politics of transindividuality. Revue de la Pansèe d'Aujord'hui 47(1):171–182 (in Japanese)

Mizukoshi S (2007) MoDe and Critical Media Practices. In: Mizukoshi S (ed) Communal Keitai: re-weaving the mobile media society. Iwanami Publishing, pp 46-68 (in Japanese)

Okada T (2005) Youth culture and the shaping of Japanese mobile media: personalization and the Keitai internet as multimedia. In: Ito M et al (eds) Personal, portable, pedestrian: mobile phones in Japanese life. MIT Press, pp 41–60

Okada T (2010) An examination of possible media form through a workshop method. J Informatics 32:1–16 (in Japanese)

Okada T (2016) Development of mobile handsets and services on the supplier's side. In: Tomita H (ed) Post-mobile society: from the smart/mobile to second offline. Routledge, London, pp 24–34

Papanek V (1972) Design for the real world: human ecology and social change. Pantheon Books, New York

Yamauchi Y (2012) Participatory design and its new developments. Systems, Control and Information 56(2):57–64 (in Japanese)

Yamauchi Y (2013) Workshops and learning. In: Yamauchi Y et al (eds) Workshop design. Keio Univ. Press, pp 1–39 (in Japanese)

Yuhashi H (2005) Mobile society visions in 2030. Mobile Soc Rev 4:70 (in Japanese)


**Tomoyuki Okada** is a professor of the Faculty of Informatics at Kansai University, Japan. He has been working on media studies and sociology of culture. During 2015–2016, he was a visiting professor of the Department of Media in the School of Art, Design and Architecture at Aalto University, Finland. His publications include The Post-Mobile Society: From the smart/mobile to second offline (as contributor of a chapter, Routledge, 2016), Understanding Keitai Society: Mobile Communication and Society (in Japanese, as co-editor, Yuhikaku, 2012) and The EXPO What I Loved: Unofficial documents of EXPO 2005, Aichi, Japan (in Japanese, as co-editor, Liberta pubishing, 2006), Personal, Portable, Pedestrian: Mobile Phones in Japanese Life (as contributor of a chapter, MIT press, 2005).

# Workation and the Doubling of Time and Place

## —Topophilia and Nowstalgia—

**Keita Matsushita**

**Abstract** This chapter examines the relationship between workation and second offline, based on field work undertaken in workation places: Hida City, Japan; Bali Island, Indonesia; Tarifa, Spain; and New York, USA. Workation is a work style that involves staying in a resort area and working at a local coworking space on a weekly or monthly basis. Communication technologies such as telephone and email have made it possible to connect with someone in another place, but the boundary between 'connecting' and 'superimposing' is gradually beginning to blur as a result of mobile media. Furthermore, the meaning of 'mobile' is also changing. Results of field work demonstrate that workation is a work style in which 'kairological time,' 'clock time' and 'instantaneous time' are simultaneously superimposed. Furthermore, coworking spaces situated in resort areas where workation takes place are a hybrid collect-if of people and materials that enable the superimposing of time and bridge the online and offline worlds.

## 1 Introduction

The transformation of how we perceive time and space brought about by the spread of mobile media including smartphones and tablet devices is closely related to both the places where we work that account for so much of our time, including offices and coworking spaces, and work styles, in other words, the way we work.

First, we briefly look at the spread of mobile media in Japan. From the mid-1990's, Personal Handyphone System (PHS) mobile phones began to spread rapidly. In 1999 NTT DoCoMo's i-mode was launched and more and more people began to access the Internet from mobile devices. In 2000, for the first time, the number of contracts for PHS and cellular phones exceeded that of fixed phones. Media research centered around mass media had hitherto overlooked mobile media, but during this period it began to grow as a field of research.

K. Matsushita (✉)
Faculty of Sociology, Kansai University, Osaka, Japan
e-mail: keita-m@kansai-u.ac.jp

 
H. Tomita (ed.), *The Second Offline*, Advances in Information and Communication Research 3, https://doi.org/10.1007/978-981-16-2425-4_7

Around the year 2000, research began to emerge that discussed communication, human relations, and societal transformation brought about by the spread of mobile media. This is considered to be the first generation of mobile research (Kopomaa 2000; Katz and Aakhus 2002; Ling 2004; Rheingold 2002, Ito et al. 2005, etc.).

In 2004, Facebook launched in the United States, and mixi started in Japan. This was followed by the launch and subsequent spread of social media networks YouTube in 2005 and Twitter in 2006. In addition, in 2007 the first iPhone was released, and since then there has been a shift from mobile phones to smart phones. Around 2010, more studies that focused in particular on the separation and fusion of the real and the virtual began to attract attention, based on the research done by the first generation. These studies have been called the second generation of mobile research (Hjorth 2007, 2011; de Souza e Silva 2006; Gordon and de Souza e Silva 2011; Farman 2012; Goggin 2007, 2012; Okada and Matsuda 2012; Moores 2012, etc.). The third generation of mobile research appeared around 2015 and included the concepts of second offline and Non-Media-Centric Media Studies. This generation of research focuses on the offline world created by the process of being constantly connected online (Tomita 2016; Moores 2017; Farman 2018, etc.).

How can the topics of work place and work style covered in this chapter be positioned in the context of research into second offline, as generated by mobile media? Work places and work styles are also undergoing a redesign process with regard to the act of work or the place where the act of work is performed. In the past, blue-collar and white-collar work referred to receiving compensation for work done for a fixed amount of time (work hours) at a fixed place (such as an office or factory). In particular, the wage was determined by how much time workers had worked, as typified by words such as hourly wage, daily salary, and overtime. Accordingly, the measurement of time was emphasized. The time recorder introduced in the United States in the latter half of the nineteenth century was a piece of technology aimed at optimizing the management of employee attendance and calculating wages.

In recent years, as the emphasis has shifted toward performance-based systems, creativity, and innovation, the series of information processing and communication systems that were formerly embedded in 'place' have been replaced with online-based systems such as SaaS, email, Slack, and Zoom. As a result, work hours are no longer the only factor used to determine wages. The motivation of workers and the growing interest in health management also indicate this change.

The changes that second offline has brought to work places and work styles have been wide-reaching. Among them, in this chapter, we will focus on situations where labor and leisure, ordinary (daily life) and extraordinary life (for example, vacations), concepts that were formerly diametrically opposed in modern society, are being mixed and edited together through the use of mobile media. In the first half, we will look at an overview of office, coworking, and the expansion of workplaces in urban areas. In the latter half, the topic of workation will be explored. This newly coined word is used to describe a combination of work and vacation. The changes occurring to our sense of time and space as a result of circumstances brought about by second offline including the concept of the doubling of time and place—will also be discussed.

## 2 The Doubling of Place: Extension and Diffusion of Work Places

### *2.1 From Office as Connecting Place to Office as Superimposed Place*

As white-collar workers became mainstream, the office became synonymous with the workplace. How have these offices been designed until now? Myerson and Bichard (2010) classified offices into three categories from a historical point of view. The first was the Taylorist Office, an office that applied scientific management methods developed in order to efficiently manage workers, the so-called "Taylor system." These methods were used mainly in the early twentieth century, in order to improve the productivity of factories. The second was the "Social Democratic Office." From the middle of the twentieth century in Europe, a labor shortage occurred during the Post World War II economic recovery. Companies tried to attract employees by offering a better work environment, that is, a sense of comfort. This design of space focused on wellbeing and the identity of workers, while also considering efficiency and the budding service economy. The third office was the "Networked Office." Globalization of business rapidly advanced around the year 2000, and the development of the Internet and mobile media promoted office design that combined offline space and online space as necessary. Flexibility and connectivity were essential elements of this design type.

How does the transformation of the office relate to informationization? From the beginning of twentieth century, from photographic transmission systems (modern-day faxes) to mainframe computers, many of the information devices introduced were large or very expensive and therefore not practical for personal use. From the 1970s to the 1980s, small personal computers started to be introduced and their use steadily increased. The rationalization and efficiency improvements made to work as a result of introducing information devices such as small computers, word processors, and faxes are collectively referred to as "Office Automation (OA)."

Office Automation was focused on automating the processing and exchange of information and improving efficiency and productivity. The offices that existed under OA progressed from the 1970s to the 2000s and could be perceived as metaphorical "factories" aimed at improving productivity. From the 1970s to the 1980s, attempts were made with satellite offices and teleworking, connecting the office with various other places through networks and concentrating work in the office. Throughout the 1950s and 1960s pagers appeared and their use spread, although initially it was only possible to receive calls. As a result, pagers were predominantly used by medical professionals who needed to be called urgently, or outsourced salespeople who were connected to the office unidirectionally. The office of this era can be regarded as a 'connecting place'. And the office as connecting place reflects the "anytime, anywhere" work style of membership-type organizations, as observed in Japanese companies and typified by the bulk-hiring of new graduates, promotion by seniority, and lifetime employment. It could be called a community rather than an association, one that is formed on the basis of mutual common values and objectives.

From the 1990s when pagers became interactive, through the introduction and popularization of PHS and mobile phones, until the latter half of the 2000s when PCs further downsized and mobile phones and tablet devices were introduced, the development of mobile media has had a significant influence on the office. In addition to the development and diffusion of mobile devices, business tools such as Chatwork and Slack have enabled the sharing of information and improved communication efficiency. In business, knowledge creation and innovation through collaboration occupied a more important position, and the demand has increased for snap judgments of markets that are constantly changing. Also, the organization and work style known as Job Type/Project Type has increased, in which the expertise of various employees is deployed for the implementation of one project, and some work is carried out in collaboration with external parties.

Both time and space were required to be personalized to allow workers to work flexibly and to accommodate different family circumstances and time zones. Information technology also adapted to fit these work styles. In the office, the offline focus was on the 'here and now', while presupposing online sharing of information and communication. Along with this, the idea of being an association has again strengthened in relation to the concept of 'connection in the office', as opposed to the sense of community created by sharing time and place for a long time. Office design styles that can be seen to reflect this orientation have increased in popularity since the 2010s and include Activity Based Workplaces (ABW) and creative offices, in which workers are able to move around freely depending on their work activities. In this way, the work place that has emerged from the second half of the 2000s can be positioned as a place in which various situations and activities are superimposed in one place, a so-called "Superimposed Place" (see Table 1).

## 2.2 *Coworking Space*

In recent years, coworking spaces such as WeWork are becoming commonplace. Starting with the advent of coworking spaces in 2005, their increase in numbers from around 2010 can be linked to the development and diffusion of mobile media. Teleworking and remote work become more common due to the use of mobile media such as smart phones and laptop computers for work, and constant connection to the Internet. As more workers have been released from the restrictions of the office, the number of freelancers has also increased. Johns and Gratton (2013)

**Table 1** From office as connecting place to office as superimposed place

| As Connecting Place | | As Superimposed Place |
|---|---|---|
| Fax, PC, mobile, email, etc | Media tool | Smart phone, social media, chat, cloud, etc |
| Improve productivity communication stock | Purpose | Knowledge creation, innovation collaboration share |
| Membership | Organization, member | Job, project |
| Anytime/anywhere | Mode | Here and now |
| Expansion of office | Direction | Personalized work place |
| Community | Place for | Association |
| OA, satellite office, telework | Practice | ABW (Activity Based Working), creative office |

describe the transformation of work styles on the Internet as having undergone "three waves." The first, "virtual freelance" appeared as a result of computer communication tools, as typified by email in the early 1980s. In the early 2000s, the September 11 terrorist attacks in the USA and the SARS outbreak increased the need for Business Continuity Plans (BCP). At the same time, remote working to maintaining productivity and increased globalization led to the rise of "virtual corporate colleagues". In the 2010s it was observed that corporations that fostered remote work lacked the collaboration that occurs when colleagues meet by accident in the corridor. At the same time, workers themselves perceived a lack of community feeling and collaboration in remote work as a problem. In response to this, the use of coworking spaces was explored, and the era of "virtual coworkers" began.

The first coworking space is said to be C-base which was established as a hacker space in Berlin in 1995. Coworking in the contemporary sense is said to have started at Spiral Muse (later Hat Factory), which was founded in San Francisco by software engineer Brad Neuberg. After that, coworking spaces appeared all over the world. According to a survey by Deskmag (2017), the number of coworking spaces increased from 1130 in 2011 to 13,800 in 2017, and the number of coworkers increased from 43,000 in 2011 to 1,180,000 in 2017. In addition, 32% of the members responded that they work overseas for at least three weeks of the year, and 44% (14% of the total) described themselves as "digital nomads".

The first coworking space, Spiral Muse, began as a self-help mechanism to enable freelancers to work together in a shared space. At the same time in Berlin, the Sankt Oberholz coworking space was established, providing WiFi and the kind of large tables normally seen in cafes. Around 2005, the spread of smartphones and social media increased the need for cafes and spaces to be equipped with power supplies and WiFi, and such cafes and spaces become an "oasis" for remote workers.

Business-oriented Coworking spaces were aimed less at the formation of community and more at inducing accidental collaboration and the possibility of building business connections. For example, at Seats2Meet in the Netherlands, the users' 'social capital' fee is visualized in a display at the entrance. This allows visitors to see the skillset of users currently in the space, assisting with introductions and leading to business connections. This design creates an environment where serendipity is inevitable, making it a 'Serendipity Machine'. In contrast, serendipity does not automatically occur when mobile media or social media are used. A survey of the Repubulikken coworking space in Copenhagen, Denmark showed that the incorporation of social media into communication by community managers in order to create realistic situations is an important factor in community formation and collaboration in such spaces (Matsushita 2016, 2019). 'Serendipity' occurs not by the community manager controlling the situation, but by careful facilitation of a communication environment that entrusts the management to its participants.

In this way, mobile media not only expanded the work styles of coworking spaces, it also had a significant influence on design and facilitation in relation to community formation and collaboration, by creating a second offline situation that referred seamlessly to online information.

## 2.3 The 'Office-Ization' of Interim Time and Space in Cities

Separate from the coworking spaces discussed above, a trend toward 'office-ization' has progressed in the area of individual work. For example, in 2016 the karaoke box company Big Echo founded by Daiichi Kosho began a trial collaboration with NTT Communications, and in 2017 it started to offer 'business plans' in metropolitan areas that made its spaces available to individual workers until evening. In September of the same year, the areas covered expanded to include urban areas of the country. The plan includes free access to WiFi, power supply, HDMI cables, and desktop whiteboards. According to a user survey of NTT DoCoMo's car-sharing service, 12.5% used it for purposes other than mobility: 64% to take a nap or break; 40% to call friends or family; and 38% to make work phone calls. When asked if they would like to use the car for purposes other than transport, 6.5% of respondents said they were keen to try it, and 34% said they would use it if the opportunity arose—a total of more than 40%.

In June 2018 Tokyo Metro collaborated with Fuji Xerox to trial providing satellite offices at subway stations, setting up work booths for personal use. Stations are key locations for movement including commuting, sales, and business trips. In addition to being used frequently, they are also places we tend to spend more time in than planned, waiting for connecting transport. These attempts to fill vacant transit time with work, and carve out spaces in the city for working indicate an increase in the intensity of work, both for individual workers and cities as a whole.

This trend is not limited to Japan. Manhattan, New York is said to have more than 2000 restaurants, but these restaurants have idle time after lunch and before dinner. Spacious is a service that rents out vacant time at these restaurants to remote workers. It is cheaper than the monthly charges of coworking spaces, and users are free to select and use the registered spaces. Today, this service is deployed not only in New York but also in San Francisco.

Having been formed by mobility and media, places such as stations, airports, expressways, hotels, and shopping malls have been positioned as homogeneous and uniform "inter space" (Urry 2007) or "non-places" (Augé 1995). What is interesting is the fact that at the same time that karaoke boxes, cars and train stations fall under the category of city 'inter space' and 'non-place', 'alone space' in cities (Nango 2018) are simultaneously being 'office-ized'. What makes this office-ized 'alone space' possible is the constant connection with mobile media. At the same time as if functions as a communication medium that connects us with other people, mobile media can also be seen as a "territory machine" (Fujimoto 2005). This machine allows users to create their own personal 'territory', and can also convert any space in the city into an office. In addition, the smartphone application Timee released in 2018 is a service that matches the time when students are free and available for work with the time that shops or stores need staff. In this way, the progress of the sharing economy has enabled people and organizations to finely-tune or micro-coordinate the interim times that arise as we move from one work place to another.

As we have seen, mobile media has created a situation in which rather than simply 'connecting *to* the office', it is as if we are bringing the office *with* us to different spaces across the city—in other words, a *doubling of place* is occurring. The office has been reconstructed as a place in which offline places are designed based on the assumption of online information. At the same time, many places in the city including coworking spaces have been 'office-ized'. So, what of the *doubling of time*, another element of second offline? The above-mentioned examples in which *inter space* and *non-place* are being office-ized as 'alone space' against the backdrop of the sharing economy show that architecture designed to 'convert' the interim time of workers and service providers into work through the use of micro-coordination is spreading, yet by no means can we say that time is doubling or superimposing in such cases.

It is, therefore, necessary to explore further whether it is possible to superimpose time spent *doing* work over time spent *not doing* work—that is, to do both things concurrently. In the next section, I will discuss how the *doubling of time* relates to the *doubling of place* by taking up the topic of Workation (a combination of work and vacation) as a case study.

# 3 Workation as Second Offline

## *3.1 Working in the 'Garden'*

The diffusion of coworking spaces is not restricted to urban areas, where technology is most concentrated. It has also recently spread to tourist destinations such as resorts. The background to this trend is the emergence of the digital nomad, a person who works while traveling around the world, and workation, a combination of work and vacation that has gained popularity in recent years, mainly in Europe and the United States.[1] Workation is a work style that involves staying in a resort area and working at a local coworking space on a weekly or monthly basis. An internet search for the term workation returns images of workers in beach and forest settings working on laptop computers. This use of the laptop to represent work shows the close connection between mobile media and the development of the workation work style.

In this section, the relationship between workation and second offline will be examined, based on field work undertaken in workation places. For the field work, I spent at least one week at a coworking space at the following locations: Hida City, Japan (November 2016); Bali Island, Indonesia (February–March 2017); Tarifa in Spain (June 2018); and New York, USA (July 2018). I conducted interviews with workers and managers and recorded observations at each coworking space. First, let us look at the characteristics of each region.

Hida City is located in a mountainous region of central Japan. Hardwood tree forests are plentiful, and historically wood-related industries such as furniture manufacturing have made use of traditional woodwork techniques. More than three hours from Tokyo or Nagoya, it is not a location easily accessed from large cities. However, inbound tourism has grown in recent years, and the historic townscape preserved in the Hida area attracts more than 500,000 foreign visitors annually. The FabCafe Hida coworking space in Furukawa town here opened in 2016 on a site that was previously used as a brewery and woodwork studio. It has a café and provides a variety of digital production tools including a 3D printer, 3D scanner, and laser cutter. Accommodation is provided on the second floor to allow longer stays by designers and artists.

Ubud is situated on Bali island in Indonesia, and is a good base for Asia. It is two and a half hours by plane from Singapore, four hours from Bangkok, six hours from Sydney, and seven hours from Tokyo. Ubud is located inland on Bali island, surrounded by forest and countryside. While Islam is the dominant religion on Jawa island and in the capital city Jakarta, Hinduism is active in Bali. Accordingly, there are many Hindu temples and associated crafts, music, paintings, and dances. In the early twentieth century, a number of painters moved from Europe, particularly the

[1]"Workcation" is often used in English-speaking countries, but "workcation" is used more often in Japan. In this paper, unless it is a proper noun, we use "workation".

Netherlands. For these reasons, Ubud is blessed with tourism resources and is visited by a large number of tourists.

Ubud also attracts a large number of digital nomads, and there are many cafes, coworking spaces, and places where English is the main spoken language. The Hubud coworking space was established in March 2013 and has been a pioneer location for workation in Ubud. Hubud is based on the concept of four types of 'Co-': (1) Coworking; (2) Coliving; (3) Colearning; and (4) Cogiving.

Tarifa is located at the southernmost tip of the Iberian Peninsula in Spain. Visited by over 80 million tourists annually, the country has many resort areas, especially on the Mediterranean coast. While Tarifa's population is below 20,000, it is only about an hour by ferry to Morocco, and it therefore has a large transient population as people pass through on their way to or from Morocco and the African continent.

At the same time, the Old Town of Tarifa is home to white buildings that are peculiar to the Andalusian region, and the beaches along its extensive coastline make it a Mecca for kite surfing, and popular with European tourists. Also, despite not being so far from Andalusian tourist cities such as Granada, Seville, Málaga, Cádiz, prices are comparatively low because it is not on the tourist trail and is yet to be gentrified. Devoid of famous hotel chains and fast food restaurants such as McDonald's, the old town has retained its regional charm and is instead home to local cafes, bars, and small-scale hotels. The transport system is also convenient and efficient. These factors combine to make Tarifa a workation hub for Europeans. The CocoTela coworking space and hostel (the name indicates that it is smaller than a hotel) is located in the center of the Tarifa Old Town.

New York is well known for having some of the highest rents in the United States. Famous for the financial and insurance industries centered around Wall Street, in recent years other industries including IT/FinTech, fashion and design have become more grown here, with many associated startups hailing from the city. New York is the birthplace of global coworking space franchise WeWork, and home to nearly 60 WeWork workspaces. In addition to WeWork, a large number of coworking spaces can be found to suit a variety of tastes. In addition to coworking spaces, outsite offers co-living spaces, and has expanded beyond New York to 15 locations including California, Hawaii, Austin, Costa Rica, Lisbon, Portugal, and Bali, Indonesia.

In *Topophilia*, Tuan (1974) presents three types of environments: wilderness, garden, and city. Tuan pointed out that while the city was formerly a symbol of order, freedom, and oppression, its image reversed post-eighteenth century romanticism and the industrial revolution. The city came to be seen as a chaotic place, a jungle dominated by people who had been abandoned by society. The garden is a place where people can escape from city life, and in that sense, garden and city tend to be referred to as opposite sides of a country-city dichotomy. However, Tuan points out that the garden is an artificial construct distinct from "untouched nature" because of the input of human hands, and that a better dichotomy is wilderness-city. The garden is an intermediate landscape, and since at least the eighteenth century it has been viewed as an "Edenic existence" or an ideal human world.

I would like to apply Tuan's viewpoint to the topic of workation. Workation involves a departure from cities and offices, often to places rich in nature such as Hida, Ubud, and Tarifa. These places are not only abundant in nature but also have rich cultural backgrounds. The low cost of living in these places makes it easy for people from developed countries such as Europe and the United States to stay long term. Coworking spaces provide WiFi and fully developed meeting spaces, and FabCafe Hida provides equipment necessary for experts including 3D printers and laser cutters. There are also modern accommodation facilities, cafés, and restaurants in the surroundings, without losing the features of the land. Although coworking spaces in Hida, Ubud, and Tarifa are not within cities, these locales are not wilderness, but at the very least should be termed 'the garden'. This is what makes them attractive as a workplace, and for workation. In that sense, workation can be said to be a work style in which the work place is an 'Edenic Garden' made possible by opening up a 'wilderness' resort area and portraying it as the opposite of the office. In a contemporary sense, it is WiFi and mobile media, not axes and farm tools, that have transformed the 'wilderness' into a workplace and 'the garden'.

### 3.2 Pop-Up Community

Other than some managers, coworking spaces used for workation have no regular long-term members who stay for several years. The workers who arrive are mostly workation workers returning for a stay of from one week to several months, or digital nomads moving on to the next place. They are not seeking a community of regular members or one connected to a particular business or startup. However, this does not mean that no community exists. As one of the managers at FabCafe Hida put it, "People who make things can talk to each other naturally, regardless of where they are from. It starts when one asks another, 'What are you making?' Whether that person is from Tokyo, Israel or Hida, they can make a connection based on manufacturing". As she said, communication is born through the things that are being produced. In co-living spaces such as Coco Tela in Tarifa and Outsite in New York, for example, there are no explicit instructions on what to do with the contents of the refrigerator, how to use kitchen appliances, where the detergent is or how the coworking space printer works. Therefore, many cases were observed in which users consulted with one other on these topics. As a result, each such 'inconvenience' functioned as a 'communication trigger' that promoted cooperation and involvement among workers.

In addition to Coco Tela, Tarifa also has several similar coworking spaces/ hostels. An interesting aspect of the Tarifa community is the formation of an online community of workation workers throughout the region. "Tarifa Digital Nomads" is a Facebook group that exchanges information on digital nomads in the Tarifa area, and as of August 2018, it had 3724 registered members. At Tarifa Digital Nomads, people currently staying in Tarifa, or about to arrive post a variety of questions and suggestions. In August 2018 there were 21 posts, with a new question post or reply almost every day. The posts can be classified into five categories: (1) the provision of lifestyle information; (2) requests for such lifestyle-related information; (3) the provision of specialized skills; (4) requests for specialized skills; and (5) information on events. In addition to these categories, local recommendations and Tarifa-related news can be found.

Since the guidelines prohibit advertisement and promotion, there are not many posts regarding the provision of specialized skills. Instead, this information tends to be included within user self-introductions in the form of work history and skills. The most frequent posts are requests for lifestyle-related information (room sharing/renting, goods sales, etc.) or professional skills (languages, programming, design, etc.), followed by information on events.

Lesette, a writer from the Netherlands who often stays in Tarifa, has spent much of her working time at Coco Tela. Although not an operator of the coworking space, as a moderator of the Tarifa Digital Nomads group she plans meet-ups and posts information on various events. At the same time, she often responds to posts with her own knowledge of the area. In other words, Lesette is not only a 'hub' of the network of digital nomads in Tarifa, but also fulfills the function of a 'hub' connecting online and offline worlds. In this sense, lifestyle and event information is being exchanged not just offline but also online, with a seamless connection between the two worlds. This community is not simply an accumulation of lifestyle and regional information, but could be said to be a 'flow architecture' that emphasizes the 'here and now'.

As we have seen above, the movement of digital nomads and workation workers means that the loose ties formed in order to realize the workation lifestyle are in constant flux. This leads to the formation of a 'pop-up community' based on temporary, loose connections, rather than a permanent community. A 'pop-up community' is not an online community, nor is it one strongly connected to a particular place. It is a community based on the sense of unity shared by members who all have loose ties to a certain place, on a temporary basis.

Other forms of pop-up community in recent times include flash mobs, the Shibuya street crossing scramble in Tokyo at Halloween and music festivals. These events are closely related to the idea of the 'value of the ephemeral', a concept that gained popularity with the emergence of ephemeral social media networks in the latter half of the 2010s. Examples include Instagram's Story and Snap Chat, in which content disappears after a certain time period has passed.

This ephemeral value can also be said to reflect values that are important to digital nomads, namely mobility and freedom. It also reflects the desire of workation workers to avoid committing to a community on a permanent basis, while also desiring a "sense of community" during their stay. From the viewpoint of actor-network theory, a pop-up community can be seen as a *hybrid collectif* that includes not only goods to create cooperation or involvement, but also people such as digital nomads, workation workers, and managers, and immaterial aspects such as insufficient explanation of lifestyle procedures and management systems (Callon and Law 1995).

### 3.3 Sense of Time in Workation

Workation refers to working while on vacation, as opposed to zero-sum practices such as work-life balance. The situation of work superimposing with vacation results in a vacation style or a work style that can only be realized by being always online using mobile media. The coworking space used for workation is both a resort (vacation place) and an office (workplace). Many of the coworking spaces in resort areas used for workation have been designed to emphasize the sense of the local surrounds. For example, FabCafe Hida is a refurbished Japanese brewery and Hubud is a Balinese-style building that features bamboo. The Coco Tela design features the distinctive white walls of the Andalusian region and Outsite in New York incorporates design features distinctive to Brooklyn.

Design that gives members a sense of local color contrasts with the design of global coworking spaces like WeWork and Mind Space, which have been designed to give workers a sense of familiarity and therefore look the same all over the world. Design and interiors that give a 'regional flavor' (heavy-handed though it may be) enable the 'extra-ordinary (vacation)' to be superimposed on the 'ordinary (work)'.

From this viewpoint, Workation seems to be based on the sense of the *doubling of place*, with the office and the resort superimposing in the coworking space, however, that is not the only point. Workation workers feel that they are doing work while enjoying leisure at the resort, or working in situations where they are spending their leisure time. In other words, they feel like they are superimposing time that should not be superimposed. This idea of the *doubling of time* is an essential element of workation.

Because we can continuously refer to online information through mobile media, the superimposing of vacation and work can be seen not only as a superimposing of *place* but also of *time*. The industrial revolution of the nineteenth century and the accompanying railroad developments brought about a vastly different sense of time. Until then, daily life had passed at different times in different regions. This has been referred to as subjective 'kairological time'. However, with the expansion of railway operation in the 1840s and the global adoption of Greenwich Mean Time in 1884, 'kairological time' was gradually replaced by 'clock time', a homogenized and abstracted construct, through the use of clocks and architecture based on them. In other words, time separated from place (Lefébvre 1991).

From the era when communication pointed to transportation, the conquest of space progressed according to 'clock time' as it became possible to connect instantaneously across the world with the appearance of telephone, radio, and television. However, the development of these communication technologies led to the further expansion of the concept of 'instantaneous time' which consists of: (1) instantaneously connected communication technology; (2) the simultaneous existence of social/technical relations; and (3) a metaphor based on the importance of short-term/fragmentary time, instead of linear logic such as 'clock time'(Urry 2000).

In Workation, workers are living on "kairological time" in the sense that they can enjoy leisure time while living in Hida, Ubud, Tarifa, and New York. At the same time, the workers are spending "clock time" in the sense that they are placing orders and doing work in the coworking spaces. In other words, workers were often editing the time in the work that adjusts the time difference, setting meetings in real time using video conferencing software or the like, or using the time difference to progress work during the night of another time zone. Design that features a space for online meetings right next to offline meetings as seen in Hubud is symbolic of this. The time difference between Ubud and Japan is just one hour, but there is a 12 h time difference with New York, and a seven-hour time difference with London. This means that if work is requested in the evening, New York time, the work can be done in Ubud and delivered by the next day in New York time. In this way, it is possible to appear to be working continuously for 24 h of "abstract time" by taking advantage of the time difference in different areas.

At the same time, it is also possible to make meetings in 'real time' with Skype, telephone, video conferencing and so on. In that sense, when working in a global team, it is possible to work while adjusting two types of times: 'abstract time' and 'real time'. Workation can therefore be said to be a work style in which 'kairological time' based on perpetual online connection via mobile media, 'clock time' and 'instantaneous time' are simultaneously superimposed in parallel.

## 4 Conclusion: Topophilia and Nowstalgia

In this chapter, I started by pointing out that in recent years, Activity-Based Workplaces (ABW) and creative offices can be regarded as *superimposed places*, and that coworking spaces and "office-ized" places in cities are part of an architecture being used to 'convert' interim time into work time. In addition, the topic of workation was discussed and analyzed in terms of the superimposing of time in workplaces and work styles. I have demonstrated that workation is a work style in which 'kairological time', 'clock time' and 'instantaneous time' are simultaneously superimposed. Furthermore, coworking spaces situated in resort areas where workation takes place are a *hybrid collectif* of people and materials that enable the superimposing of time, and bridge the online and offline worlds.

Tuan distinguishes *space* and *place* thus: *space* corresponds to freedom and yearning; *place* corresponds to safety and attachment (Tuan 1977). *Space* is open, evoked by images that suggest expansion and intervals. In that sense, it can be said to be abstract and homogeneous. *Place*, on the other hand, is represented by images such as houses and rooms. These are objects that are closed and partitioned, with a stable value, hence they are sentimental and safe. When we have experiences and spend time in a *space*, meaning is attached to it and the *space* becomes a *place*. In this sense, *place* exists in a variety of scales: region, town, house, and room.

When we first move to a new town or house, we feel like a stranger there. But after living there for a while we get used to it, and feeling ourselves accepted there we gradually form an emotional attachment to it. Tuan (1974) expressed the affection that arises as a result of the emotional connection between a person and a place or environment as *topophilia*. *Attachment* arises and transforms a *space* into someone's home or *place* as a function of experience—that is, a superimposing of meaningful time related to that place. In other words, topophilia can be said to be caused by the superimposing of information from different times in the same place. Topophilia is therefore a kind of *doubling of time*, and *space* converts to *place* through the *doubling of time*. As seen in the pop-up community, mobile media can be regarded as a tool that facilitates this attachment instantaneously.

If the *doubling of time* produces topophilia, what on earth will the *doubling of place* produce? It will be a sense of attachment to that moment, or *Nowstalgia*. *Nowstalgia* is not an abstract time, it is an attachment caused by an emotional connection with the 'now'. And it is caused by superimposing different places at the same time.

Video conferences are becoming commonplace, but in recent years Virtual Reality (VR) conference gatherings have begun to appear, as seen in rumii and NEUTRANS BIZ. In these meetings, users meet virtually in an online conference room, rather than simply seeing one other on their screen as in traditional video conferencing. In addition, the North American real estate company eXp Realty has an office online and no offline office, and workers 'go to' the office virtually. In doing so, workers are connected by a shared emotional attachment (in business-speak, a "value") to the 'now', the time spent in business meetings or at the virtual office. In these cases, meaning is to be found not because it is convenient to use various functions such as screen sharing, but because it visualizes a gathering of people in different locations at one 'now'. And not only does it connect people at the same time, but it also implies the value of superimposing the place where participants are 'now', even if it only takes place virtually.

These technologies were almost realized even in Second Life, but the difference here is that participants share a context—they work in the same company or are working together on a project, both online and offline. As Tomita (2016) points out, the information that is superimposed in second offline cannot be any old information, but it must be meaningful information in that place. Therefore it is essential to share a certain context between offline and online.

Communication technology such as telephone and email has made it possible to connect with someone in another place, but the boundary between 'connecting' and 'superimposing' is gradually beginning to blur as a result of mobile media. Furthermore, the meaning of 'mobile' is also changing. For example, the OriHime robot developed by the Ory laboratory aims to be a 'second body' that goes places where its owner cannot. Operated by smartphone and equipped with a camera, microphone, and speaker, it is possible to see OriHime's surroundings and have a conversation with someone through the robot as if you were really there. It is currently being used not only for childcare and aged care, but also by people with disabilities who are in hospital, who can use it to do telework. In 2018 it was announced that OriHime-D can now be moved remotely, and is capable of simple manual labor.

So far mobile and other media such as smart phones have provided mobility on the 'user side', but robots like OriHime are enabling mobility on the 'other side' of the user connection. The sense of time and place these new mobile environments create will no doubt become a topic of future study.

## References

Augé M (1995) Non-places: introduction to an anthropology of supermodernity. Verso, New York
Callon M, Law J (1995) Agency and the Hybrid Collectif. S Atl Q 94:481–507
de Souza e Silva A (2006) From cyber to hybrid: mobile technologies as interfaces of hybrid spaces. Space Cult 9(3):261–278
Deskmag (2017) First Results of the 2017 global coworking survey. Retrieved June 20, 2021 from https://www.deskmag.com/en/background-of-the-2017-global-coworking-survey
Farman J (2012) Mobile interface theory: embodied space and locative media. Routledge, New York
Farman J (2018) Delayed response: the art of waiting from the ancient to the instant world. Yale University Press, New Haven
Fujimoto K (2005) The anti-ubiquitous "territory machine"—The third period paradigm: from "girls' pager revolution" to "mobile aesthetics." In: Ito M, Okabe D, Matsuda M (eds) Personal, Portable, Pedestrian: Mobile Phones in Japanese Life. MIT Press, Cambridge, MA, pp 77–101
Goggin G (2007) Cell phone culture: mobile technology in everyday life. Routledge, London
Goggin G (2012) The evolution of Australian mobile screens: new technology, new formats, new business models. Stud Australas Cine 6(3):263–277
Gordon E, de Souza e Silva A (2011) Net locality: why location matters in a networked world. Wiley-Blackwell, Chichester
Hjorth L (2007) The game of being mobile: one media history of gaming and mobile technologies in Asia-Pacific. Convergence 13(4):369–381
Hjorth L (2011) Locating the online: creativity and user-created content in Seoul. Media Int Aust 141(1):118–127
Ito M, Okabe D, Matsuda M (eds) (2005) Personal, portable, pedestrian: mobile phones in Japanese life. MIT Press, Cambridge, MA
Johns T, Gratton L (2013) The third wave of virtual work. Harvard Bus Rev 91(1): 66–73
Katz JE, Aakhus MA (2002) Perpetual contact: mobile communication, private talk, public performance. Cambridge University Press, Cambridge
Kopomaa T (2000) The city in your pocket: birth of the mobile information society. Gaudeamus, Helsinki
Lefebvre H (1991) The production of space. Blackwell, Malden, MA
Ling R (2004) Mobile connection: the cell phones impact on society (Morgan Kaufmann series in interactive technologies). Morgan Kaufmann Publishers, San Francisco
Matsushita K (2016) Mediated workplaces and work styles as second offline. In: Tomita H (ed) The post-mobile society: from the smart/mobile to second offline. Routledge, New York, pp 37–46
Matsushita K (2019) Workstyles in mobile media society. Keisoshobo, Tokyo
Moores S (2012) Media, place and mobility. Palgrave Macmillan, Houndmills

Moores S (2017) Digital orientations: non-media-centric media studies and non-representational theories of practice. Peter Lang, New York

Myerson J, Bichard J-A (2010) New demographics, new workspace: office design for the changing workforce. Routledge, London

Nango Y (2018) Hitori kuan no toshiron. Chikuma Shobo, Tokyo (in Japanese)

Okada T, Matsuda M (2012) Mobile society. Yuhikaku, Tokyo (in Japanese)

Rheingold H (2002) Smart mobs: the next social revolution. Perseus, Cambridge, MA

Tomita H (ed) (2016) The post-mobile society: from the smart/mobile to second offline. Routledge, New York

Tuan Y (1974) Topophilia: a study of environmental perception, attitudes, and values. Prentice-Hall, Englewood Cliffs, N.J.

Tuan Y (1977) Space and place: the perspective of experience. University of Minnesota Press, Minneapolis

Urry J (2000) Sociology beyond societies: mobilities for the twenty-first century. Routledge, New York

Urry J (2007) Mobilities. Polity Press, Cambridge

**Keita Matsushita** is a Professor at Kansai University in the Faculty of Sociology, Japan. He received his Ph. D. from Kyoto University for his study of the impact of new media technology on school education. His main research interests are workstyle, workplace, and media communication. He has conducted several research projects and workshops for social innovation with major Japanese companies. His publications include "Workstyles in Mobile Media Society" (Keisoshobo, 2019), "Various Phases of Internet Society" (Gakubunsya, 2015), "Career Education for University Students" (Keio University Press, 2015), "Digital Natives and Social Media" (Kyoiku Hyoronsya, 2012).

# Mobile Media As a Cultural Milieu

# Ambient Play: Understanding Mobile Games in Everyday Life

**Larissa Hjorth and Ingrid Richardson**

**Abstract** In this chapter, we seek to conceptualize the shifts in mobile gaming through two key rubrics – ambient play and digital wayfaring—to coalesce the multiple forms of domestic, casual and urban play that constitute mobile gaming. This chapter begins with a contextualization through a short history followed by a discussion of pervasive games as vehicles for transforming urban environments into playspaces. We finish with a brief discussion of the *Pokémon Go* phenomenon as exemplary of both the possibilities and limits of contemporary mobile gaming. The chapter brings together three areas often disconnected—pervasive urban games, casual mobile games and domestic gameplay on mobile devices—to think about how mobile play has become ubiquitous and diversified.

## 1 Introduction

For 12-year-old Esther Madison, mobile games encapsulate everything from the digital urban wayfaring of *Pokémon Go* to the creative world-building of *Minecraft*. For Esther, play in and around mobile devices is a key part of her everyday rhythms, both inside and outside the home. Mobile devices accompany Esther everywhere—at home, at school, on public transport, or hanging out with her friends. In these various forms of mobility and stillness, she plays with her parents and animals physically co-present, as well as friends and strangers virtually co-present via games such as *Minecraft*. Esther's experiences of mobile games echo those participants in many of the sixty Australian households we followed ethnographically over three years.

The Madison family's media practices are indicative of the multiple ways in which mobile games inhabit our everyday lives. As Dean Chan (2008) noted in his study of mobile games in Japan, most mobile games are played in domestic con-

L. Hjorth (✉) · I. Richardson
School of Media and Communication, Royal Melbourne Institute of Technology University, Melbourne, Australia
e-mail: larissa.hjorth@rmit.edu.au



H. Tomita (ed.), *The Second Offline*, Advances in Information and Communication Research 3, https://doi.org/10.1007/978-981-16-2425-4_8

texts—especially bedrooms. However, with the rise in accessibility of augmented reality (AR) functionality on smartphones, mobile games such as *Pokémon Go* have become increasingly visible and mainstream in urban spaces. Mobile game revenue now accounts for $41 billion of the $91 billion in-game revenue worldwide.

As we will discuss, *Pokémon Go* is one of the most popular mobile games; even though its peak has passed, the game still has 5 million daily active users, has been downloaded 750 million times, generating a total revenue of over $1.2 billion, and accruing $2 million daily. As now "old" and mundane media, *Pokémon Go* has now developed different features to enhance social engagement with place through Raid Boss meet-ups coordinated by Telegram or WhatsApp. This has seen a rapid take up by the elderly in Japan, Singapore and Spain to encourage ageing well attributes in the form of social engagement and exercise.

In this chapter, we seek to conceptualize the shifts in mobile gaming through two key rubrics—ambient play and digital wayfaring—to coalesce the multiple forms of domestic, casual and urban play that constitute mobile gaming. In the first two sections, we provide a definition of these two terms, and then a short history of mobile casual gaming in terms of the mobilization of private space. This is followed by a discussion of pervasive games as vehicles for transforming urban environments into playspaces. We finish with a brief discussion of the *Pokémon Go* phenomenon in terms of what constitutes mobile gaming today (Fig. 1).

**Fig. 1** Understanding haptic screens and mobile games (*Photo* Hjorth)

## 2 Locating Ambient Play

Understanding play—mobile, haptic, ubiquitous and ambient—is central to understanding contemporary forms of mobile gaming. Play and playfulness have attracted much-needed attention in recent research (Frissen et al. 2015). In *Play Matters*, Miguel Sicart (2014) fleshes out the multiple dimensions of play as an activity, and playfulness as an attitude. Through a variety of tropes derived from politics and architecture, Sicart maps how play and playfulness migrate across all facets of contemporary life. Given the broadness of play as a category that spans cultural practice (Sutton-Smith 1997), animal play to current do-it-yourself (DIY) strategies (Gauntlett 2011), Sicart explores "playfulness" as the key characteristic of contemporary media.

Similarly, Kerr identifies play as a "key concept for understanding the interaction of users with new media" (2006, 69), in which all media interfaces could be said to be part of the "collective playful media landscape" (Frissen et al. 2015, 29). Within this context, we suggest that mobile media and mobile games engender a mode of ambient play, or play that traverses multiple contexts and diffuses throughout daily life. The ambience of mobile media is also deeply entangled within practices of wayfaring across online and offline spaces.

Wayfaring describes the way that knowledge and meaning are produced through walking, movement and traversal. As we move from place to place, we develop an embodied sense of knowing and being in the world. As explored by Hjorth and Pink (2014), contemporary entanglements between the online and offline can be interpreted through the conceptual and embodied metaphor of digital wayfaring. Hjorth and Pink (2014) further revise Tim Ingold's notion of wayfaring as a type of embodied mobility that is both routine and familiar (e.g. commuting) in which knowledge is produced through repetitive movement. Hjorth and Pink repurposed this notion to reflect upon the way in which the digital entangles itself in our everyday practices and movements, especially through mobile media. As we will discuss below, the experience of digital wayfaring is further complicated within a hybrid reality game.

Notions of ambience, as well as atmosphere (Böhme 1993), have taken on a certain currency in recent scholarship, as a way to understand the increased digital mediation of everyday life and how this is reshaping the relation between embodiment and modes of attention. From Malcolm McCullough's *Ambient Commons: Attention in the Age of Embodied Information* (2013) to Paul Roquet's *Ambient Media* (2016), the ambient has been used as a lens that can reveal how contemporary media moves in and out of different forms of engagement with spaces, places, bodies, practices and performances. Here, the notion of ambient play considers how the increasing popularity of mobile gaming lies in its capacity to move between and across co-located and networked spaces, adapting or fitting into the patterns of quotidian life. While ambience has been given significant attention in human–computer interaction (HCI) and the study of urban environments—exemplified by McCullough's aforementioned *Ambient Commons*—it is the bringing together of ambience and play that can help us to understand the embodied, intimate and affective relations of media in the home.

As we argue elsewhere (Hjorth and Richardson 2016), ambience is about the sensorial and affective texture or atmosphere of a place. As McCullough suggests, ambient awareness reflects "a more general mindfulness", a social and embodied sensibility of one's immediate and mediated surroundings (2013, 13). There are many features of gameplay that are ambient—most explicitly the soundtracks that play a pivotal role in developing the mood, genre, and emotional cues for the player. Without their soundscapes, many games would fail, and yet, like ambience, the importance of sound is also relatively overlooked in game studies despite its pivotal role in player embodiment. Ambience is about the "game feel"—that is, the often-tacit affects and relative "stickiness" of the play (Swink 2008; Isbister 2011).

In a more expansive textural sense, what constitutes ambience within the context of mobile gameplay—especially as it moves across different modes of mediated and co-located presence, and thus different experiences of emplacement—needs to be more robustly developed and articulated. In mobile games, audiovisual ambience is augmented by the haptic, social, networked and locative elements of the game experience. As we have suggested, interpreting mobile gaming as ambient play "contextualizes the game within broader processes of sociality and embodied media practices", and defines play as something that takes place both in and out of games, reflecting broader shifts in everyday cultural practices and phenomena (Hjorth and Richardson 2014, 60).

In this chapter, we bring together three areas often disconnected—pervasive urban games, casual mobile games and domestic gameplay on mobile devices—to think about how mobile play has become ubiquitous and diversified. It is the productive tensions between mobile play in public spaces and domestic spaces that we argue need reconciling if we are to have a nuanced and resilient definition of mobile games. Indeed, understanding mobile games as both ambient play and digital wayfaring requires us to recalibrate notions of engagement beyond dichotomous interpretations of attention and distraction. It enables us to locate play as part of everyday practices which are messy and always in flux, and to comprehend the complex and contested ways play and the playful are activated and practiced across different modalities, spaces and places and forms of embodiment (Fig. 2).

Play is a much contested, interdisciplinary and complex term, especially in the context of contemporary media cultures (Malaby 2009; Sicart 2014; Flanagan 2009). While the cultural dimensions of play have been discussed in detail by Sutton-Smith (1997) and in the context of games by Salen and Zimmerman (2003) who draw upon Huizinga (1955) and Callois, urban play has a long history that can be linked to historical motifs like the flâneur and the 1960s movement Situational International (de Souza e Silva and Hjorth 2009; Montola 2010). In keeping with these historical and socio-cultural dimensions of play, we argue that mobile games have emerged from these earlier phenomena, yet also suggest that place has always involved variable modes of co-presence and ambient play. As Sicart points out (2014), play is increasingly becoming recognized as an integral part of all facets of

**Fig. 2** Waiting and Playing: Oscillating between background, middle and foreground (*Photo* Hjorth)

life and not confined to specific contexts. Play is fundamental to being human and has multiple cultural, social, historical and emotional entanglements.

Ambient play suggests a need for nuanced and dynamic readings of mobile media as it moves in and through place. As Paul Dourish argues, "ambience draws our attention to distractions between focus and periphery… and different ways in which information can be incorporated into an environment" (Dourish 2005, 25). Dourish et al. (2005) encourage us to understand information, ambience and intelligence as cultural categories that are continually contested and reimagined. Ambience, along with interaction, has become a key cornerstone in HCI and especially ubiquitous computing; moreover, both are modes of engagement that are culturally specific and locally informed. For Kjeldskov et al. (2013) the term "digital urban ambience" is a more refined lens for interpreting the role of mobile devices mediating urban contexts.

In the following sections, we first outline how mobile casual games deploy a form of ambient play through the mobilization of private space into urban environments, and then turn to hybrid reality play as a form of digital wayfaring.

## 3 Casual Gaming in Public: The Mobilization of Private Space

Genealogically, we can trace the roots of mobile play to the late nineteenth century. As Parikka and Suominen (2006) identify, the various situational contexts of modernization at that time—including industrialization, transportation, and urbanization—enabled particular forms of mobility and movement. These processes entangled changing notions of leisure, spectatorship, and the rise of personalization and individualization. From playing cards to portable chess and the stereoscope, games were part of the Victorian mediascape, which emphasized mechanization, consumption, and mobility. For Parikka and Suominen the mobile phone reenacts a "third place" between public and private space. It is a new form of an old habitual practice already common in the nineteenth century:

> [W]hat is new in this division of space and creation of a place of one's own? Instead of seeing this solely as a trend of digital mobile culture, we argue that this is more a phenomenon that took off with the creation of modern urban space and the new paradigms of media consumption… [T]he pattern of mobile entertainment usage as the creation of a private sphere was already part of the railway culture of the nineteenth century—even if people consumed such media content as newspapers and books instead of digital entertainment. (Parikka and Suominen 2006, n.p)

This mediated closing-off is perhaps more common with the ubiquity of mobile interfaces, prompting Groening to comment that a society of "portable personal electronics is a society in which private space is as physically mobile as the populace and privacy itself is radically mobile" (Groening 2010). For Hjorth, the mobile phone is frequently used as a micro-mobile home or metaphoric caravan, allowing us to carry private space in our pockets and activate it when needed (Hjorth 2012).

Mobile games also exemplify and extend Raymond William's (1975) notion of mobile privatization. Williams coined the term in the 1970s to highlight the deep contradictions around domestic television which traversed and provided access to the public domain but made users feel more "at home". Mobile privatization has been heightened within the rise of mobile media, which has seen a further tethering to notions of the home (i.e. the containment of familiar content and services, and provision of familial connectivity enabled by the mobile device) whilst also setting the user "free" to roam (Morley 2003).

Domestication approaches to technology acknowledge the blurring distinctions between work and leisure with mobile media (Ling and Haddon 2003). One way of understanding this entanglement between work and leisure in terms of contemporary mobile media is through Sicart's notion of "playfulness". Many of the affordances of mobile media apps draw on users' playful engagement with media, and frequently employ gamification strategies, as in the case of productivity, self-monitoring and fitness apps that reward the user with game-like digital objects such as badges, icons and virtual currency.

Wilmott et al. (2017) argue GPS (global positioning systems) enabled smart-watches and smart-bands invite us to redefine our quotidian environments as playful labourious playgrounds where leisure activities are redefined in terms of work and quantifiable data. This blurring of work and leisure practices by mobile media has been highlighted by many cultural scholars (Gregg 2013; Wajcman 1991) and is also encapsulated by Kücklich's (2005) term playbour, which describes how various player practices (such as modding, remixing, sharing and liking) produce social, creative and cultural capital. In these terms, mobile media can be mutually characterized by both ambient play and soft labour (Hjorth 2017).

Mobile media practices are often characterized by paradoxes. They allow us to roam physically but oblige us to be constantly on-call. Yet despite this tethering, our use of mobile screens is quite different to the dedicated attentiveness we give to other screens such as television, cinema and even home computers. We often 'turn towards' them momentarily and for minutes at a time (checking for messages, social media posts or a missed call, playing a level of *Kick the Buddy* while waiting for the bus). Mobile phone engagement is characterized by interruption, and sporadic or split attention betwixt other activities.

This has been recognized by mobile phone game developers who have labelled the mobile player a "casual gamer"; casual mobile games are typically interruptible, allowing play to become intertwined with everyday routines and the existing patterns of daily life. Within the game literature, casual games are often described in terms of their properties; that is, they are designed for casual use, are easy to learn (such as simple puzzle, card, and word games), offer quick rewards and consist of levels of short duration. Thus, casual gaming is often understood as a mode of engagement that requires relatively low-level skills and only sporadic attention up to a threshold of around five minutes. When we ask our research participants to describe their mobile game play, they often pass it off as an incidental distraction, a peripheral and unimportant activity. Some are even embarrassed to admit they play such trivial games.

Yet the pejorative term "casual" actually disguises the substantial investments made by some casual gamers, and oversimplifies an increasingly diverse and rapidly developing mode of gameplay (Taylor 2012). As Mia Consalvo notes, smartphones and mobile touchscreens have put mobile gaming platforms "in the hands of millions of people who would never consider themselves gamers" (Consalvo 2012, 184). Like being "online", games have become normalized, embedded in the many other navigational, informational, productivity and social media apps within our mobile mediascape, all of which change the way we move through and experience the urban environment. It is this normalization of mobile games, together with their mode of perpetual availability, which renders mobile play ambient, as it increasingly infiltrates our habitudes and routines.

It has been argued that portable music devices such as the Walkman, iPod, mp3 player and mobile phone provide us with a kind of "auditory privatization" of urban space, transforming how we behave in public (Helyer 2007). As Michael Bull has commented: "Mediated isolation itself becomes a form of control over spaces of urban culture in which we withdraw into a world small enough to control" (Bull 2005, 169). For Amparo Lásen (2017), mobile listening also can be understood as a form of public engagement with urban spaces, which has a long history of portable media including the transistor radio, boom boxes, personal stereos (Bull 2000) and the boom car (Bull 2007).

Yet while music players provide discrete sound bubbles or "sonorous envelopes" that allow us to shut out the bustling noise of urban life, the mobile phone is also a communicative and networked device. It is unpredictable and disruptive, puncturing the soundscape as users pepper urban space with their own "noises" of familiarity and intimacy, irruptions of personal ringtones, bleeps and one-sided conversations. Nevertheless, a number of studies have found that much like listening to music, mobile phone use and casual gaming are often used as a proxy "do not disturb" sign when we are alone in public. This kind of behaviour is now one that we all recognize, a mode of media distraction similar to book- or newspaper-reading on public transport, an indicator of privacy well understood by those around us.

When gameplay is mobile and situated in public places, the particular way we engage with the game is determined by the motility and mobility of the pedestrian body, taking place in the interstices of productive and goal-oriented activity. We play casual mobile games while waiting (for a friend, at a bus stop, or for a journey to end), and use our mobile devices as a means managing the bodily agitation of impatience, aloneness and boredom in public, enabling a mobilization of personal entertainment while "being-with-others" (Hjorth and Richardson 2010). In this way the mobile device becomes co-opted into the labour of waiting, filling and suturing the "dead" or "fractured" times and spaces that are part of everyday urban life (Bissell 2007).

Here, the activity of casual gaming enacts a particular kind of "face-work" in Goffman's sense—the deliberate posture we present to the public—yet at the same time it permits an "environmental knowing", or a peripheral awareness of our surroundings in readiness for the busy-ness of life to resume (Goffman 1972). This transient and non-dedicated attentiveness to the small screen—you can "switch off" but "not totally"—allows us to remain alert to the "arrival" which marks the end of waiting, yet also able to cooperate in a kind of tacit social agreement of non-interaction among strangers. For many of our research participants, this kind of engagement with the mobile screen provides safe seclusion from unwelcome interaction in potentially risky situations of co-present waiting, while still remaining "open" or attentive to the proximity of that risk.

As we will explore below, mobile location-based gaming enacts and enables a quite different experience of space and place in urban environments, opening up a hybrid space that coalesces physical location and online networks, transforming urban spaces into ambient and collaborative playgrounds.

## 4 Location-Based Mobile Games: Transforming Urban Environments into Playspaces

Over the past decade, we have seen a proliferation of location-based games and playful apps that invite us to upload and share our personal and local content in-the-moment. In this way, we enact a hybrid, layered and multifaceted experience of place, presence and communication.

Location-based services typically provide situational information about the urban environment via online databases and media libraries, such that informational changes on the mobile screen change both our navigation and experience of physical space. In this way 'being online' becomes enfolded inside present contexts and activities, as we find our way through the city, search for a good place to eat, drive to a friend's house for the first time, or tag our location on location-based apps such as Foursquare. Location-based mobile gaming is a particularly robust example of this emergent hybrid experience.

Historically, location-based games—referred to as urban games, big games, pervasive games and mixed reality games—emerged out of avant-garde new media art, and involved creative experimentation with new media interfaces, platforms and networks. In the 70s and 80s the New Games Movement, currently experiencing a revival, sought to popularize cooperative and creative urban play, and deliberatively challenged and disrupted the mundane and familiar by transforming public spaces into playful places. Yet although location-based social games were once considered experimental, they have more recently been mainstreamed and commodified, and part of the more general cultural shift towards gamification, where game techniques are embedded into non-game activities. For example, the playful app-based service Foursquare, (with a purported 30 million users) invites users to share first-hand recommendations of 'the best places to go', integrates the tagging of places visited into friend-networks, and offers consumer rewards for the most prolific taggers.

Against this turn towards gamification and commodification, creators of urban and community games such as UK new media group Blast Theory continue to deliberately 'hack' public space, inviting players to experience a de-familiarization of their everyday perceptions of the urban environment. In this way, location-aware and hybrid reality mobile games can transform urban spaces into participatory gameworlds. This potential can be seen in "sandbox" games that encourage an emergent mode of play that often embeds player-centred design and relies on community feedback and content contribution. New York game designer Frank Lantz, who has been involved in such pivotal projects as Pac-Manhattan, argues that big urban games will play a significant role in the future of gaming. Big games are, for Lantz, "large-scale, real-world games that occupy urban streets and other public spaces and combine the richness, complexity, and procedural depth of digital media with physical activity and face-to-face social interaction" (Lantz 2006).

In his analysis of geocaching, Jason Farman describes the mixed or augmented realities of pervasive location-based games where bodies, networks and material space converge (Farman 2009). Played in over 200 countries, Geocaching is treasure hunt game requiring game players to hide "geocache containers" marked with GPS data in public places; players then "use their mobile devices (from GPS receivers to iPhones) to track down the container, sign the log, and leave tradable and trackable items in the cache" (Farman 2009). In such games, we must seamlessly combine and accommodate both immediate and mediated experience of the world.

In an early incarnation of location-based gaming, the game Mogi, launched in 2003, represented the city of Tokyo both as a map on players' mobile phones and on the web, the latter of which provided computer players with an expanded view of the gamespace overlaying the city, along with both the geographic and gameworld location of all players. Mobile and computer players both accessed different views of the gamespace, and collaborated to collect virtual objects and creatures at various locations throughout the city. It is this collaboration that worked to "construct" the hybrid space. Licoppe and Inada described players of the game Mogi as "hybrid beings" who are able to "smoothly integrate the embodied lived experience of the body and the mediated perception of oneself and of the environment" (Licoppe and Inada 2006).

Location-based mobile games generate hybrid experiences of place and presence, requiring the player to integrate their own situated and embodied perception of the world with dynamic GPS-enabled information, embedded within an augmented and networked game reality. As Farman notes, this is one of the characteristics of mobile technologies, which have effectively transformed our experience of presence and absence into perpetual co-presence (Farman 2012, 108). Indeed, we would suggest that mobile media users experience different kinds of presence: co-located presence (while in the same physical space as others), telepresence (while talking on the phone), absent presence (viewing blog or Facebook posts), distributed presence (online multiplayer gaming) and ambient presence (the perpetual sense of others in the network) (Okabe and Ito 2005; Hjorth and Richardson 2014). In this way, location-based mobile games and applications can be said to add a complex dimensionality to place and space.

The consequence of this is that we need to rethink the spatial and place-based experience of being-in-public, as we increasingly integrate online information about our immediate environment into the patterns of urban life and pedestrian movement. Gordon and de Souza e Silva have argued that such hybrid practices generate what they term net-local public space, which describes our movement between "the immediately proximate and the mediately distant" (Gordon and de Souza e Silva 2011). Net-local public space includes those engaging in location-based activities with mobile devices, those (both co-present and online) participating in this network activity, and those non-participants who are co-located in the urban setting.

For Pellegrino, hybridity is the keyword that describes this "co-constructed dimension of participation" in contemporary media culture (Pellegrino 2010). De Souza e Silva (2006) and Pellegrino use the term hybridity to refer to the way our experience of presence and participation have been transformed in contemporary life, through multiple forms of proximity, both physical and virtual" (Pellegrino 2010, 99). We used to clearly differentiate between the actual and the virtual, and the online and offline, but now these dichotomies have collapsed, such that our attention and sense of presence has become ambient and dispersed.

In what follows we discuss one recent example of location-based augmented reality mobile gaming, *Pokémon GO*, to highlight the hybrid and contextual nature of mobile play as it transforms the urban environment into a ludic or playful space.

## 5 Pokémon GO

Within the first weeks of its launch in July 2016, millions of people across several countries downloaded the *Pokémon GO* app onto their iOS and Android devices, and entered an augmented reality, wandering their neighbourhoods and public spaces in search of Pokémon and PokéStops, and competing with other players at virtual Pokémon gyms. In this location-based hybrid reality, users are required to move through physical space as they tag, collect, trade, and battle for digital artefacts and player achievements. Effectively, they access a game microworld through their smartphone via the digital overlay of game objects and virtual locations across the actual environment.

Through this augmented layering of the digital onto place, banal and familiar surroundings are transformed to become significant game locations. A Pokémon can be found and caught in one's own bathroom, a gym or PokéStop might be situated at the local library, cafe, or graveyard. The popularity of *Pokémon GO*—touted as the first ever really successful location-based game—has already been the subject of much criticism and celebration. The unprecedented success of *Pokémon GO* in the first months of its release, provides us as urban media researchers with an opportunity to explore and document the experience of *en masse* location-based mobile gameplay. It is clear that the game and its uptake is situated within historical, social, and cultural contexts. It brings together decades of mobile media use, locative arts, gaming practices, and Japanese culture.

For some, *Pokémon GO* is a positive experience—the gameplay evokes twenty-something nostalgia (McCrea 2017; Surman 2009) encouraging physical exercise, facilitating "genuine human-to-human interaction," (Wawro 2016) and effectively enhancing our sense of wellbeing and belonging (Vella et al. 2017) Yet as with mobile media and mobile games more generally, *Pokémon GO* can be flexibly deployed by users as a way to facilitate social interaction, or as a "shield" to avoid engagement with others in public spaces.

For others, the game forces us to reflect on the ongoing gendered, racial, socioeconomic, age-based, and bodily inequities of urban mobility that affect many of us on a daily basis (Isbister 2016). Jordan Frith explores the "commercial potential of augmented reality," and how *Pokémon GO* can be used by businesses to attract foot traffic through the placement of "lures," revealing how digital "objects" can influence our movement and behaviour in the physical world (Frith 2017). As we enact the pedestrian labour of location-based gaming, and interweave digital and physical information, the "spatial legibility" of urban space—or the way urban environments appear as coherent and recognizable patterns—is transformed (Frith 2013) Yet as Miguel Sicart warns, while *Pokémon GO* may open up new possibilities for design and play in augmented reality, we should be wary of the potential for corporate appropriation of public spaces enabled by the game (2017).

*Pokémon GO* is manifestly ambient, as the game becomes diffused throughout our daily routines, pedestrian movement, and interaction with the familiar strangers populating our neighbourhoods and urban spaces. As we have suggested, in a very fundamental way the mobile interface changes what we pay attention to, and the modalities and duration of that attentiveness. This is clearly evidenced by the wide-scale integration of casual mobile games such as Candy Crush and Angry Birds into our daily lives (Keogh and Richardson 2017). Yet even more significantly and poignantly, our involvement with location-based hybrid reality games such as *Pokémon GO* require us to adopt an "as-if" structure of experience, moving through the environment "as if" it were game terrain or an urban playground. That is, *Pokémon GO* is not just a casual mobile game, for while we might play it in the midst of other daily activities, it also explicitly intervenes with and modifies those activities and relations.

As some media theorists have suggested, there is evidence that games such as *Pokémon GO* may act as catalysts for large-scale changes in people's "destination choice" or "trip distribution" (Colley et al. 2017). In other words, such games have the potential to incentivize "people to do something they rarely do: substantially change where they choose to go" (Colley et al. 2017). Although it is just a game, *Pokémon GO* reveals how our experience of public space is mediated by networked connectivity and increasingly "transformed through collisions of the digital and the urban" (Iveson 2016).

As media become more mobile and playful, and games embed geo-locative data, our everyday experience of place is interwoven with playful virtual environments. Familiar neighbourhoods and urban environments are transformed into ludic spaces. Lammes (2016) has explored the way location-based games (such as RunZombieRun and others) effectively turn maps into "navigational interfaces and gameboards", a description that can equally be applied to *Pokémon GO*. With developments in mobile technologies and the rise of collaborative platforms, making and sharing maps has taken on new playful, ambient, and co-present dimensions.

Yet we are also reminded of the inherently spatial and mobile nature of popular culture and media more generally, and how popular culture forms have always been part of our everyday geographies (Horton 2012, pp 11–12). In bringing together childhood and play studies with human geography, for example, Horton documents how his young research participants integrated Pokémon play into the structure of their mundane spatial practices and daily space–time routines, effectively remaking their homes, local shops, and neighbourhoods as part of the Pokémon universe (Horton 2012).

In the context of location-based AR games, it is important to highlight the uneven ways players come to the game space and how gameplay is interwoven with our own culture and location. These uneven attributes of PokeStops and Gyms are more of a reflection of the advanced players of Niantic's original AR game, *Ingress*, than the discriminatory intents of Niantic. As Salen Tekinbaş (2017) argues, certain bodies have more latitude to deviate from normalized practices, while others don't. Salen turns to the potential disempowerment and marginalization that affects players of augmented reality games and mobile location-based apps such as *Pokémon GO*. That is, *Pokémon GO* requires users to explore their (sub)urban environment, a form of gameplay that is underscored by issues of racial inequity and the relative freedom people have to move playfully through their neighbourhoods and cities.

Salen asks, what can *Pokémon GO* teach us about mobility, accessibility, race, and privilege? It is clearly more dangerous for some bodies to be in some places at certain times, and there is undoubtedly a hierarchy of risk at work that acts upon our bodies differently, depending on our age, gender, ethnicity, or social milieu. In their study of the racial and ethnic bias of *Pokémon GO*, Colley et al. examine how the game's data and code that "augments" reality often "reinforces preexisting power structures" and "geographic contours of advantage and disadvantage", as PokéStops and game resources are distributed more densely in wealthier areas with predominantly white non-minority populations (Colley et al. 2017).

Since its highly successful launch in mid-2016, *Pokémon GO* has gone through a few iterations. As noted in the introduction, elderly players in Japan, Singapore and Spain to name a few are using the game to combat social isolation and develop healthy exercise routines. Moreover, some of the features of the original *Pokémon GO* have been revised to enhance social meet-ups in urban spaces. Features like Raid Boss battles, coordinated through applications like Telegram and WhatsApp, create improvised events for people to meet-up physically and work together. Some of these Raid Boss battles can have up to 500 people meeting at a physical place (Fig. 3).

*Pokémon GO* highlights the paradoxical and dynamic role of mobile games in contemporary society. On the one hand, it points to the power of play in contemporary media cultures, and consolidates decades of urban and hybrid reality gaming and place-making experimentation. On the other hand, we might argue that *Pokémon GO* players are narrowly goal-oriented, driven to collect and compete for virtual items as they engage in what is essentially a gamified activity. That is, *Pokémon GO* could be seen as a simplified reduction of a popular but fairly complex trading game that was originally targeted at preteens.

In this view, as appealing as it may be to contain and control an imaginary microworld, *Pokémon GO* is not an open-ended playground full of creative

**Fig. 3** *Pokémon Go* Raid Battle meet up in Badalona, Spain (*Photo* Hjorth)

possibility, but rather a transformation of the local environment into a game resource, where urban loci are literally made relevant by the extent to which they are populated by virtual currency, game objects, and rewards.

## 6 Conclusion

As noted in the introduction, in everyday contexts from homes to public spaces an assemblage of mobile devices and play practices can be found. Far from being mere casual games on mobile phones, what constitutes mobile gaming is as ubiquitous as it is divergent. In this chapter, we have considered the informal and formal practices of intentional and unintentional mobile game play in everyday life through two tropes—ambient play and digital wayfaring.

In the first sections, we have conceptually sketched the burgeoning and dynamic field of mobile gaming in the context of broader cultural and historical trends. As a way of capturing the various worlds of mobile play—domestic, casual and urban—

we brought together two modalities of media practice: ambient play and digital wayfaring. As we have argued, mobile games extend and transform earlier patterns of media use that saw the increasing mobilization of private space. As a casual form of gaming, they have become infused into our daily routines and habitudes.

Finally, we traced the emergence of augmented or hybrid reality gaming, culminating in the mainstream popularity of *Pokémon Go*. In each of these instances of mobile gaming, we can see the coalescence of ambient play—the diffusion of gameplay across temporal and spatial dimensions of everyday life, and digital wayfaring—the incursion of digital information into our experience of place and our movement through the urban environment.

Along with contextualizing mobile gaming historically, we can also see a few emerging fields for the future of mobile gaming research. With global phenomenon such as ageing societies, the demographics and types of games are changing. *Pokémon Go* is one example where it is increasingly being used by the elderly as a means to counteract social isolation and also as a form of exercise. As the future of society moves towards aged communities, the power of mobile games could be used to fuel innovative forms of care, engagement and sociality. In the convergence of technology with future imaginaries, it is perhaps the older examples like *Pokémon Go* or *Minecraft* that could provide solutions in the designing for socially active and more mindful futures.

**Acknowledgements** This chapter draws from our previous publication "Pokémon GO: Mobile media play, place-making, and the digital wayfarer". *Mobile Media & Communication*, 5 (1): 4–14.

## References

Bissell D (2007) Animating suspension: waiting for mobilities. Mobilities 2(2):277–298

Böhme G (1993) Atmosphere as the fundamental concept of a new aesthetics. Thesis Eleven 36:113–126

Bull M (2000) Sounding out the city. Personal stereos and the management of everyday life. Berg Publishers, Oxford

Bull M (2005) The intimate sounds of urban experience: an auditory epistemology of everyday mobility. In: Nyíri K (ed) A sense of place: the global and the local in mobile communication. Passagen, Vienna, pp 169–178

Bull M (2007) Sound moves. iPod culture and urban experience. Routledge, London

Chan D (2008) Convergence, connectivity, and the case of Japanese mobile gaming. Games Cult 3 (1):13–25

Colley A, Thebault-Spieker J, Lin AY, Degraen D, Fischman B, Hakkila J, Kuehl K, Nisi V, Nunes NJ, Wenig N, Wenig D, Hecht B, Schoning J (2017) The geography of Pokémon GO: beneficial and problematic effects on places and movement. CHI 2017, May 6–11, 2017, Denver, CO, USA

Consalvo M (2012) Slingshot to victory: games, play and the iPhone. In: Snickars P, Vonderau P (eds) Moving data: the iPhone and the future of media. Columbia University Press, New York

De Souza e Silva A (2006) From cyber to hybrid: Mobile technologies as interfaces of hybrid spaces. Space Cult 3:261–278

De Souza e Silva A, Hjorth L (2009) Urban spaces as playful spaces: a historical approach to mobile urban games. Simul Gaming 40(5):602–625
Dourish P (2005) The culture of information: ubiquitous computing and representations of reality. Design Ubiquitous Inf Environ 185:23–26
Dourish P, Brewer J, Bell G (2005) Ambient intelligence—information as a cultural category. Interactions 12(4):31–33
Flanagan M (2009) Critical play. MIT Press, Cambridge, Mass
Farman J (2009) Locative life: geocaching, mobile gaming, and embodiment. In: Proceedings of the digital arts and culture conference—after media: embodiment and context, University of California, Irvine, 12–15 December 2009
Farman J (2012) Mobile interface theory: embodied space and locative media. Routledge, New York
Frissen V, Lammes S, de Lange M, de Mul J, Raessens J (2015) Playful identities: the ludification of digital media cultures. Amsterdam University Press, Amsterdam
Frith J (2013) Turning Life into a game: foursquare, gamification, and personal mobility. Mobile Media Commun 1(2):248–262
Frith J (2017) The digital 'lure': small businesses and Pokémon Go. Mobile Media Commun 5 (1):51–54
Gauntlett D (2011) Making is connecting. Polity, London
Gaver B, Dunne T, Pacnti E (1999) Design: cultural probes. Interactions 6 (1). http://dl.acm.org/citation.cfm?id=291235
Goffman E (1972) Relations in public: microstudies of the public order. Penguin Books, Middlesex
Gordon E, de Souza e Silva A (2011) Net locality. Wiley-Blackwell, London
Gregg M (2013) Work's intimacy. Polity, Cambridge, UK
Groening S (2010) From 'a box in the theater of the world' to 'the world as your living room': cellular phones, television and mobile privatization. New Media Soc 12(8):1331–1347
Helyer N (2007) The sonic commons: embrace or retreat? Scan J 4(3)
Hjorth L (2012) iPersonal: a case study of the politics of the personal. In: Hjorth L, Burgess J, Richardson I (eds) Studying mobile media: cultural technologies, mobile communication and the iPhone. Routledge, New York, pp 190–212
Hjorth L (2017) Ambient and soft play: play, labour and the digital in everyday life. Eur J Cult Stud 21(1):3–12
Hjorth L, Richardson I (2010) Playing the waiting game: casual mobile gaming. In: Greif H, Hjorth L, Lasén A, Lobet-Maris C (eds) Cultures of participation: media practices, politics and literacy. Peter Lang, Berlin, pp 111–125
Hjorth L, Pink S (2014) New visualities and the digital wayfarer: re conceptualizing camera phone photography and locative media. Mobile Media Commun 2(1):40–57
Hjorth L, Richardson I (2014) Gaming in social, locative and mobile media. Palgrave, London
Hjorth L, Richardson I (2016) Mobile games and ambient play. In: Leaver T, Willson M (eds) Social, casual and mobile games: the changing gaming landscape. Bloomsbury, New York, pp 105–116
Hjorth L, Richardson I (2017) Pokémon GO: mobile media play, place-making, and the digital wayfarer. Mobile Media Commun 5(1):4–14
Horton J (2012) 'Got my shoes, got my Pokémon': everyday geogrpahies of children's popular culture. Geoforum 43:4–13
Huizinga J (1955) Homo Ludens: a study of the play element in culture. The Beacon Press, Boston
Isbister K (2011) Emotion and motion: games as inspiration for shaping the future of interface. Interactions Sept-October: 24–27
Isbister K (2016) Why Pokemon go became an instant phenomenon. In: The conversation, July 16. Accessed 5 August 2016. http://theconversation.com/why-pokemon-go-became-an-instant-phenomenon-62412
Iveson K (2016) "Pokémon GO and public space, cities and Citizenship Blog. http://citiesandcitizenship.blogspot.com.au/2016/08/pokemon-go-and-public-space.html

Keogh B, Richardson I (2017) Waiting to play: the labour of back ground games. Eur J Cult Stud 21(1):13–25
Kerr A (2006) The business and culture of digital games. Sage, London
Kücklich J (2005) Precarious playbour: modders and the digital games industry. Fibreculture 5. http://five.fibreculturejournal.org/fcj-025-precarious-playbour-modders-and-the-digital-games-industry/
Kjeldskov J, Skov MB, Nielsen GW, Thorup S, Vestergaard M (2013) Digital urban ambience: Mediating context on mobiledevices in a City. Pervasive Mob Comput 9(5):738–749
Lammes S (2016) The map as playground: location-based games as cartographical practices. Convergence (online First). https://doi.org/10.1177/1354856516679596
Lantz F (2006) Big games and the porous border between the real and the mediated. Receiver 16. Retrieved February 7, 2007, from http://www.receiver.vodafone.com/16/articles/index07.html
Lasén A (2017) Disruptive ambient music: mobile phone music listening as portable urbanism. Eur J Cult Stud 21(1):96–110. https://doi.org/10.1177/1367549417705607
Licoppe C, Inada Y (2006) Emergent uses of a multiplayer location-aware mobile game: the interactional consequences of mediated encounters. Mobilities 1(1):39–61
Ling R, Haddon L (2003) Mobile telephony, mobility, and the coordination of everyday life. In: Katz JE (ed) Machines that become us: the social context of personal communication technology. Transaction Publishers, New Brunswick, NJ, pp 245–265
Malaby TM (2009) Anthropology and play: the contours of playful experience. New Lit Hist 40 (1):205–218
McCrea C (2017) Pokémon's progressive revelation: notes on 20 years of game design. Mobile Media Commun 5(1):42–46
McCullough M (2013) Ambient commons: attention in the age of embodied information. MIT Press, Cambridge
Montola M (2010) Flâneurs and Phoneurs. In: Pervasive games: theory and design blog, March 4. Accessed 5 August 2016. https://pervasivegames.wordpress.com/2010/03/04/flaneurs-and-phoneurs/
Morley D (2003) What's home got to do with it? Eur J Cult Stud 6(4):435–458
Neff G, Nafus D (2016) Self-Tracking. MIT Press, Cambridge, MA
Okabe D, Ito M (2005) Personal, portable, pedestrian images. Receiver 13. http://www.receiver.vodafone.com/13/
Parikka J, Suominen J (2006) Victorian snakes? Towards a cultural history of mobile games and the experience of movement. Game Stud 6(1)
Pellegrino G (2010) Mediated bodies in saturated environments: participation as co-construction. In: Fortunati L, Vincent J, Gebhardt J, Petrovcic A, Vershinskaya O (eds) Interacting with broadband society. Frankfurt am Main, Peter Lang, pp 93–105
Roquet P (2016) Ambient media: Japanese atmospheres of self. Minnesota UP, Minnesota
Salen Tekinbaş K (2017) Afraid to roam: the unlevel playing field of Pokémon GO. Mobile Media Commun 5(1):34–37
Salen K, Zimmerman E (2003) Rules of Play: Game Design Fundamentals. MIT Press, Cambridge, Mass
Sicart M (2014) Play matters. MIT Press, Cambridge, Mass
Sicart M (2017) Reality has always been augmented: Play and the promises of Pokémon GO. Mob Media Commun 5(1):30–33. https://doi.org/10.1177/2050157916677863
Sutton-Smith B (1997) The ambiguity of play. Routledge, London
Surman D (2009) Complicating Kawaii. In: Hjorth L, Chan D (eds) Gaming cultures and place. Routledge, London
Swink S (2008) Game feel. Morgan Kaufmann, New York
Taylor TL (2012) Raising the stakes. MIT Press, Cambridge, Mass
Vella K, Johnson D, Wan Sze Cheng V, Davenport T, Mitchell J, Klarkowski M, Phillips C (2017) A sense of belonging: Pokémon GO and social connectedness. Games Cult (Online First) 1–21. https://doi.org/10.1177/1555412017719973

Wawro A (2016) How did Pokémon GO conquer the planet in less than a week. Gamasutra, July 13 2016. http://www.gamasutra.com/view/news/276955/How_did_Pokemon_Go_conquer_the_planet_in_less_than_a_week.php
Wajcman J (1991) Feminism confronts technology. Polity Press, Cambridge
Williams R (1975) Television: technology and cultural form. Schocken Books, New York
Wilmott C, Fraser E, Lammes S (2017) 'I am he. I am he. Siri rules': work and play with the apple watch. Eur J Cult Stud. https://doi.org/10.1177/1367549417705605

**Larissa Hjorth** is a digital ethnographer, socially-engaged artist, Distinguished Professor and director of the Design & Creative Practice (DCP) research platform at RMIT University (see http://dcp-ecp.com). Hjorth has two decades experience leading interdisciplinary and collaborative digital and mobile media projects that innovative methods to understand intergenerational relationships. She has lead 20 national and international research projects in locations such as Japan, South Korea, China and Australia. Hjorth explores the role of mobile media for play, grief and sociality. Hjorth has published over 100 publications on the topic—recent publications include Haunting Hands (with Cumiskey, Oxford Uni Press), Understanding Social Media (with Hinton, 2nd Edition, Sage), Creative Practice Ethnographies (with Harris, Jungnickel and Coombs, Rowman & Littlefield) and Ambient Play (with Richardson, MIT Press).

**Ingrid Richardson** is Professor of Digital Media in the School of Media & Communication at RMIT University. She is a digital ethnographer and phenomenologist with a broad interest in the human–technology relation, mediated embodiment and the wellbeing effects of networked interfaces. She has published on topics such as scientific technovision, virtual and augmented reality, games, mobile media and small-screen practices, urban screens, remix culture and web-based content creation and distribution. She is co-author of Gaming in Social, Locative and Mobile Media (with Hjorth, 2014), Ambient Play (with Hjorth, MIT Press), and Mobile Media and the Urban Night (with Hardley, Palgrave Macmillan, forthcoming). Over the past ten years she has taken a particular research interest in games and play as integral and significant aspects of contemporary media ecologies.

# Re-Genesis of 'Now' by Parasites' Interruptions/Advents: Mobile Media Solipsist and the Re-Enchanted 'Possible Worlds'

**Kenichi Fujimoto**

> "The storm irresistibly propels him into the future to which his back is turned, while the pile of debris before him grows skyward. The storm is what we call progress."
> "Dieser Sturm treibt ihn unaufhaltsam in die Zukunft, der er den Rücken kehrt, während der Trümmerhaufen vor ihm zum Himmel wächst. Das, was wir den Fortschritt nennen, ist dieser Sturm."
> (W. Benjamin, the ninth thesis in "Theses on the Philosophy of History")

**Abstract** I have proposed a 'triple junction model' that replaces the communication dogma. In accordance with M. Serres (La Parasite, Bernard Grasset, Paris, 1980), we call the third parties who observe, intercept, hear, interfere, obstruct, and intervene as 'parasites' I have applied the 'triple junction model' to these sense of time of 'mobile media solipsists' in the 'Possible Worlds', by means of five senses of '*Nagara*' (in Japanese), Our lives in the twenty-first century are re-enchanted as a whole "because of" the popularity of advanced technologies. This re-enchantment drastically changes the relationship between individuals. Instead, a super-subjective, transcendental, and solipsistic world view—individual (I) with a sense of omnipotence versus a group of anonymous characters. I would like to describe a subjective model that is temporalized according to an icon of 'non-history angel of amnesia'. As W. Benjamin once told a poet, Ch. Baudelaire, modern humans have the strong desire for *nouveauté* (novelty), replacing gods and faith. As novelty is valued as the only absolute value instead of gods, 'mobile media solipsists' are obsessed with the "now" and experience amnesia. A wonderful "future" arrives every moment, immediately as if intending to 'interrupt' each "next moment."

---

The epigraph is from Benjamin (1940). https://www.versobooks.com/blogs/2791-the-storm-blowing-from-paradise-walter-benjamin-and-klee-s-angelus-novus

---

K. Fujimoto (✉)
Faculty of Human Environmental Sciences, Mukogawa Women's University, Hyogo, Japan
e-mail: sonntag@mukogawa-u.ac.jp



H. Tomita (ed.), *The Second Offline*, Advances in Information and Communication Research 3, https://doi.org/10.1007/978-981-16-2425-4_9

## 1 Introduction: "Territory Machine," Dialectical Logic "Re-Enchantment"

Unlike desktop computers, mobile media can be freely switched on and off owing to its nature of being a "Territory Machine" (a characteristic of being constrained by location while being able to create its own place or territory); it can be transparent or opaque, or even semi-transparent.[1]

When the concept of "involvement shields" by E. Goffman was relevant, face-to-face interaction and encounters between people appeared to be transparent two-way traffic even before the appearance of mobile media; therefore in practice, they were only dogmas.[2]

Furthermore, by applying the philosophical insight of M. Serres, although face-to-face interaction appears to be one-on-one communication at all times, it was found to be only an illusion. There always exist third parties with good intentions or malice who observe, intercept, hear, interfere, obstruct, and intervene in the immediate vicinity of the interacting parties, both online and offline.[3]

Thus, I proposed a three-branch theoretical model ('triple junction model') that replaces the "communication dogma". Currently, "three-branch" information traffic associated with mobile media has become not only theoretical but also actual routine communication. In accordance with Serres, we call the third parties who observe, intercept, hear, interfere, obstruct, and intervene as "parasites." The origin of the word parasite comes from standing next to someone/something (para-site = stand beside).

Ideological and philosophical anti-rationalism, anti-scientism, anti-positivism, and anti-humanism, that began in the early twentieth century, gradually gained momentum with the overall trends of the twentieth century. However, in the twenty-first century, information technologies, such as computers and smartphones, and advanced technologies, such as artificial intelligence (AI), bioengineering, and financial engineering, became deeply ingrained in our daily lives. In this manner, humans smoothly adapted to scientific technologies and accepted them with great affinity.

Does this mean that ideological and philosophical concepts such as anti-rationalism, anti-scientism, anti-positivism, and anti-humanism have lost followers and declined? Not necessarily. Instead, in dialectic philosophy from Hegel to Adorno, when there exist elements "A" and "non-A" that are theoretically opposite to each other, the stronger the element "A" becomes, the stronger the

---

[1]Refer to Fujimoto (2002, 2005, 2010a, b, 2016, 2017) for the concept of "Territory Machine". Refer to Fujimoto (1994, 1997, 1999b, 2000, 2002, 2005, 2010b, 2016, 2017) for "unilateral nature" and "non-transparency" of information transmission.

[2]Refer to Goffman (1963) for "secrecy" and "non-transparency" during communicating face to face. Refer to Fujimoto (1994, 1997, 1999b, 2000, 2002, 2005, 2010b, 2016, 2017) for the dogma of "ideal one-on-one transparent communication".

[3]Refer to Serres (1980), and Fujimoto (1999b, 2002, 2005, 2016, 2017).

antagonizing element "non-A" also becomes, which in turn leads to the possibility of a dramatic reversal or transition to another dimension (Aufheben).[4]

M. Weber argued that the modern rationalization process is a process of being released from enchantment, i.e., "disenchantment."[5] However, based on dialectical logic, the chance of "re-enchantment" also increases simultaneously with the progress of "disenchantment" in the midst of the modern rationalization process.

M. Horkheimer and Th. Adorno discovered that only in the midst of the rational, cultural, and enlightened did "internal natural oppression" progress, which provided an opportunity for the birth and development of fascism as "new barbarism".[6]

Similarly, in the midst of the twenty-first century omnipotent society of scientific technologies, a trend of opposing ideas and cultures may be appearing and developing. In this article, I will discuss how anti-rationalism and anti-humanism were born and are thriving simultaneously by adapting to cutting-edge information technologies.

Since the advent of mobile phones, even with the global popularity of smartphones that provide access to social networking services (SNS) and augmented reality (AR) functions, there has never been a time before today when the distance between technology and the human body was short (both psychologically and physically) in our daily lives and technology was unconditionally trusted by users. Information technologies have become akin to everyday accessories and clothing and have become embedded into the human body and consciousness.

Mobile phones (aka smartphones) are platforms for latest information technologies such as AR, virtual reality (VR), and SNS. They can combine multimedia content comprising letters, voices, still images, and videos in various modes such as transmission, reception, recording, editing, and replaying; they can also freely switch on and off functions of hardware and software content to arbitrarily change these functions.

Apple Inc. released "Newton" (1992–1998) a quarter-century ago based on the concept of the personal digital assistant (PDA), which was a commercial failure. However, Apple's twenty-first century smartphones, represented by the iPhone series, became the ideal "multimedia platform" that realized the dream of PDA.[7]

Interestingly, a dialectical development can be observed, wherein our lives in the twenty-first century are "re-enchanted" as a whole "because of" the popularity of advanced technologies and not "in spite of" them.

---

[4]Refer to Horkheimer and Adorno (1947).

[5]Refer to Weber (1917).

[6]Refer to Horkheimer and Adorno (1947) and Fujimoto (2002, 2005, 2010a, 2016, 2017).

[7]Refer to Fujimoto (1997, 2000), for Mobile Media Terminals as portable device for an individual use in comparison to home appliance.

## 2 "Mobile Media Solipsist" and Growing Anonymous Personalities

This "re-enchantment" drastically changes the relationship between an individual and others, or that between an individual and the society. Through this change, one-on-one, face-to-face, and intersubjective social relationships, such as human versus human, human versus group, and human versus god, will decline. Instead, a super-subjective, transcendental, and solipsistic world view—individual (I) with a sense of omnipotence versus a group of anonymous characters that live in multiple possible worlds ("possible worlds" including this world)—will emerge.[8]

In this world view, beings other than oneself—humans, robots, pseudo-personalities, virtual personalities, animals, animations, gods, devils, fairies, entities, and virtual images—all become characters, personalities, spirits, and guardian spirits (such as Socrates' Daemon) having a diverse and intermediate style of existence. It is an image of self, where each of us holds a smartphone in one hand and walks alone through characters, spirits, and ghosts, while we freely switch between real (offline) and virtual (online) worlds.

Such a theoretical world of mobile media solipsist (solipsist with mobile media) of the "modern 'nagara (doing something while doing something)'-smartphone humans" is extremely similar to the worldview preceding monotheism: for example, the narrative, mythical world of a Greek tragedy's protagonist, such as that of Odysseus or Antigone.[9]

Similar to the world of videogames, lonely heroes = demigods (heroes = half-gods), fight the inevitable fate (moira) while being led or misled by whispers of supporting characters (those standing on the sidelines = para-sites)—such as fairies, spirits, nymphs, daemons and ghosts—that surround the heroes together with songs of khoros (teasing chorus of ancient Greek). This is the worldview of Greek tragedy. Of course, this lonely and obsessive worldview is also comical if one considers it objectively.

The relationships of these fertile groups of characters surrounding the individual entity as a "mobile media solipsist" are quite different from human relationships preceding smartphones. Earlier human relationships gradually spread from the family living together, which was the center of the social circle, to the outer circumference of concentric circles wherein nearby relatives living, friends, acquaintances from work commute, school, and social circles, and strangers are positioned at the perimeters. In other words, earlier formed a "concentric circle structure of intimacy", in which those who were psychologically close (familiar) were also located in close physical proximity.

In contrast, for modern humans = "mobile media solipsists," who live in their own pseudo-Greek tragedy world with a smartphone in one hand, individuals other

[8]Refer to Ohmori (1994), for solipsistic worldview. Refer to Kripke (1980) for the concept of the "possible worlds".

[9]Refer to Fujimoto (2017) for the worldview prior to monotheisms, such as ancient Greek tragedy.

than oneself—families, friends, acquaintances, SNS friends, and groups of virtual characters (including AI and BOTs)—are at a psychologically equal distance of intimacy with homogeneous and equivalent intimacy (the physical distance is zero for all); modern human relationships have a "mirror ball structure of intimacy," in which mottled patterns of shades appear and disappear as the distance drastically changes and yet remains equivalent at each point, based on the interest of the solipsistic subject.[10]

Because this intimacy is different from that experienced in the past, I refer to this concept as the "Invisible Pseudo-Kinship Structure." Rather than signifying human–human relationships, I chose the term "Multiplying Anonymous Personalities" to signify a group of countless characters and avatars both online and offline.[11]

In the process of the "disenchantment" of modern rationalism, Hitler's fascism was already the expression of "re-enchantment". Similarly, we, the "mobile media solipsists" in the twenty-first century, are also facing Greek-tragedy-style "re-enchantment" in the midst of "disenchantment" with an increasing embodiment of advanced technologies represented by information technologies.

Although this differs from the fascists' sense of omnipotence, "mobile media solipsists" also instantly summon both online and offline network, finance, and services (so-called mobilization) in front of oneself and are able to give them lives, delete them all in the next instant, or freely rearrange and edit some portions of them. "Mobile media solipsists" are similar to fascists in the sense that they fall into self-consciousness with a self-righteous sense of omnipotence as if they are a shaman or sorcerer with the power to decide life and death.

Particularly with AR, the avatars, characters, and personalities (persona) of others begin to overlap with reality and simulate the living activity. Owing to SNS, it is impossible to eliminate the sense of having every action and moment seen and monitored by someone (an invisible third party) from the near future to now.

Currently, one is constantly surrounded by lively groups of human/non-human and real/AR characters and personalities that are connected through various SNSs. In a way, they are companions who can become closer than families and friends or at times an irritating observer or parasite. Families, friends, pets, characters, avatars, and personalities become intimate or distant entities with the same qualifications. This is the psychological constellation of the "mobile media solipsists" that we face.

In ancient Greek tragedy, the supporting characters and the chorus (heckling choir) that surrounded the tragedy's hero always played the role of "parasites"—the interferer and bystander—via interception, interference, and distraction. The encircling net containing various third parties with both good and ill intentions is

---

[10]Refer to Fujimoto (2000) for the original type of two classifications: "concentric circle structure of intimacy" and "mirror ball structure of intimacy". It refers to "skewered oden structure" and "three-legged scarecrow structure".

[11]Similarly, refer to Fujimoto (2000).

similar to the modern "mobile media solipsists" being surrounded by AR and SNS networks.

In the fifteenth century BC, it was the world of Greek mythology before tragedies. In that sense, the modern "mobile media solipsists" can be considered similar to Greek mythology. In Greek mythology, gods, humans, animals, and fairies exist only as groups of characters and personalities with the same qualifications. In other words, it was a worldview that was pantheistic as well as animistic (totemistic). It can be said that modern humans are constantly living in such a mythological world. One can have a lonely self-consciousness that constantly lives in such a fairy-tale world with a smartphone in one hand during work, study, and free time as well as when not watching animated movies or being immersed in theme parks.

Horkheimer and Adorno mention the story of Odysseus as a fable for modern humans, where a lonely and righteous hero (or a heroine) fights their fate alone, defeating adversities such as monsters and suffering. During this time, a dialectical thesis—"mythos is enlightening (logical) from the beginning, while logos is magical (mythical) from the beginning"—was born ironically.[12]

## 3 Online Expansion of the Concept of "Negara"

Let us now consider the concept of "Negara" (in Indonesian) in terms of cultural anthropology. "Nagara" (meaning 'doing something while doing something' in Japanese) and "Negara" are very acoustically similar words; however "Nagara" with a Japanese origin and "Negara" with an Indonesian origin began with completely different concepts. Only by applying the "Nagara" concept that I have expanded, do these two words present similar appearances.

"Negara" as a concept refers to a "(theatrical) village, i.e., a theatrical city-state," proposed by cultural anthropologist, C. Geertz. It is a node of a multifaceted small theater group in which each villager (citizen) = amateur actor plays different roles according to a multilayered network, and while remaining one personality, all villagers act as a group of various characters and personalities. Metaphorically speaking, it is similar for each person to be an actor and act in countless different plays as a member of various theater companies. There is no personal identity of modern ego. As an aggregate (node) of such small theater groups, villages, larger cities, and nations become animated, and the people's daily lives are dramatically acted out. This is the concept of "Negara".[13]

Politics, the economy, religions, rituals, and daily lives are all based upon villagers (citizens) = actors, who are theater players, and various other theatrical entities surrounding these actors (such as supporting actors, characters, and stage

[12]Please see Horkheimer and Adorno (1947) and Fujimoto (2002, 2005, 2010a, 2016, 2017).
[13]Refer to Greetz (1981).

equipments). Not only all music, performing arts, preferred foods and goods, props, and artifacts, living organisms, and natural objects but also spirits, fairies, tokens, symbols, and groups of icons, characters, personalities, and avatars are interpreted and used as supporting actors, props, or the stage sets. Villagers (citizens) mutually interpret the significance of the play and exchange improvisational messages (speeches and acts). Traditionally, the whole body of interactions or "Negara," i.e., the accumulation of such layers—e.g., a shadow-puppet theater (Wayang Kulit)—has been performed in Bali. In a certain sense, westernized urban society has aspects similar to that of "Negara".

In the twenty-first century, we are facing not only the offline (real) "Negara" network but also, to a greater extent, the total expansion of nodes for the multi-layered virtual network that is infinitely cast in the online direction. In this regard, the concept of "Negara" constitutes one aspect of our multifaceted "Nagara Mobilism" (simultaneous and parallel mobilization) as it expands online.

By reinforcing Geertz's concept of "Negara," our "Nagara" acquires multilayer properties of the network. Herein, I have critiqued the traditional "transparent" and "one-on-one" communication model in real face-to-face interaction of humans and proposed an "opaque" 'triple junction model' instead. Based on Goffman's "involvement shield" = "opaque/semi-transparent communication" concept and Serres' "parasite (infesting and hearing)" = "noise (interference)" concept, this article theoretically models reality as a metaphor of the 'triple junction model', wherein third parties with either good or bad intentions always interfere and intervene in online and offline competitive scenes.[14]

We were able to dynamically describe such actions of interference and intervention by parasites as "Negara" $\subseteq$ "Nagara".

## 4 Faith in "novelty" and the 'Triple Junction Model' of the Theory of Time

The conflict in an on–off competitive scene is typically considered as a problem with moral and manner called phubbing. It refers to a context of blaming (an inappropriate behavior) that treats a person facing you coldly, such as answering a call or checking SNSs on a smartphone in a face-to-face (offline) setting.

However, these problems should not be minimized as issues regarding morals and manners. The 'triple junction model' considered these problems as theoretical issues instead of ethical issues and theorized them as intentional self-presentation and concealment strategies through $2 \times 2 = 4$ options of exercising powers on both on and off sides.

[14]Refer to Fujimoto (2016, 2017).

However, this 'triple junction model' was a rather "objective model description" that "spatially expressed" social interactions and encounters with a "bird's-eye--view" seen from an "infinitely far perspective."

Next, I would like to describe a "subjective model" that is "internalized" and "temporalized" according to the conscious subjectivity of the actor in any social situation.

In the 'triple junction' state, messages and news arrive continuously, SNS delivers content non-stop, the world of Internet expands infinitely, and a possible world continues to renew itself even when one is in a room alone with mobile phones and computers turned off, without any online/offline contact in social scenes. In other words, because of the reality in which one is constantly connected to others and the outside world, even if one shuts down online or offline contact for a short time, paradoxically, the subjectivity of a person or ego, i.e., we the "mobile media solipsists", cannot delete the abundant existence of others. Even on a deserted island or behind closed doors, modern humans cannot feel "completely isolated," even with smartphones being turned off.

If we differentiate the time called "now," instant by instant, we may be able to feel "completely alone" in one instant. But is that true? Can we conduct a thought experiment?

In terms of the theory of time, it is said since the time of Augustinus that, "they were aware of time, but once questioned and began thinking about time, they could not answer what the time was." In regard to the sense of time, entangled with the cycles of science and religion, circular and linear concepts of time have been discussed since antiquity.

In the modern world, the observation that our sense of time has greatly changed is derived from the fact that it has become "disenchanted" as it was removed from gods and faith. Furthermore, as Benjamin once told a poet, Baudelaire, modern humans have strong interest and desire for nouveauté, in a way replacing gods and faith.[15]

Similar to spatial awareness, in regard to temporal awareness, the "disenchantment" and the opposing "re-enchantment" have simultaneously progressed as a dialectical process in modern times. As a result, we are constantly aware that there are characters other than ourselves—personalities/non-personalities, living/nonliving, and real/virtual objects—around each "mobile media solipsist".

Diverse groups of characters are parallel and equivalent; however, in terms of "novelty," there is strict discrimination and order, where the new is more valuable, while the old is ignored.

[15]Refer to Benjamin (1939).

## 5 Interruptions of "Parasites" and Re-Genesis of "Now"

As "novelty" is valued as the only absolute and transcendental value following gods, "mobile media solipsists" are obsessed with the "now" and experience amnesia and indifference with regard to the past. Simultaneously, they have longing and expectations for the "near future" called "the next moment". A wonderful "future" arrives every moment, immediately after an infinitely short moment as if intending to "interrupt" each "next moment." In the next moment, the "future" becomes the "now," shining with infinitely positive values; then, in the next instance, the "now" instantly becomes the "past," and its value drops to zero or below. It is then forgotten and subsequently disappears.

If we compare this constant process of change to the four Greek elements, i.e., the wind (future) blowing from a distance instantly fuels a burning fire (the present that arrived), becomes water and calms down (passing present), and quickly becomes earth (forgotten past) that disappears from awareness (amnesia). As Benjamin discussed "the Angel of History," while thinking about the future, we must turn away from the future, be exposed to the "gale" from the past, and feel the "progress."

In the flow of time, where Benjamin discussed "the Angel of History," we can only discuss the hopelessly ironic existence of "non-history", i.e., the "Angel of Amnesia (the Angel of Non-History, Non-Past)" (Fig. 1).[16]

In the theory of space, "mobile media solipsists" could control the life and death of the group of characters and personalities that went through diverse "Nagara" development using the right to freely switch on and off the devices we use. However, in the theory of time, self-awareness is even more focused on the point, "hic et nunc" (here and now). In the theory of time, it is misleading to overemphasize the multilayer and multidimensional nature of parallel worlds, i.e., the simultaneous existence of "Nagara," that was emphasized in the theory of space. In the theory of space, many groups of characters could be infinity multiplied in each real/virtual space (possible world). In contrast, in the theory of time, the order and rectifying characteristics of time itself are put into action. Furthermore, mobile media such as smartphones function as "the device of order" and "the device of rectification" for the order of time, causing all focus to fall on "hic et nunc."

This is because in space and time, unity and exclusion of aspects by the self functions in an even stronger manner. There is the example known as the "rabbit–duck illusion" by Jastrow. This artwork can be interpreted as a rabbit and a duck ("Nagara"), but both cannot be simultaneously perceived. According to Wittgenstein, this is considered to be a problem with aspects (aspects and appearances). Humans can "Nagara" acknowledge this figure as two separate

[16]Refer to Benjamin (1940).

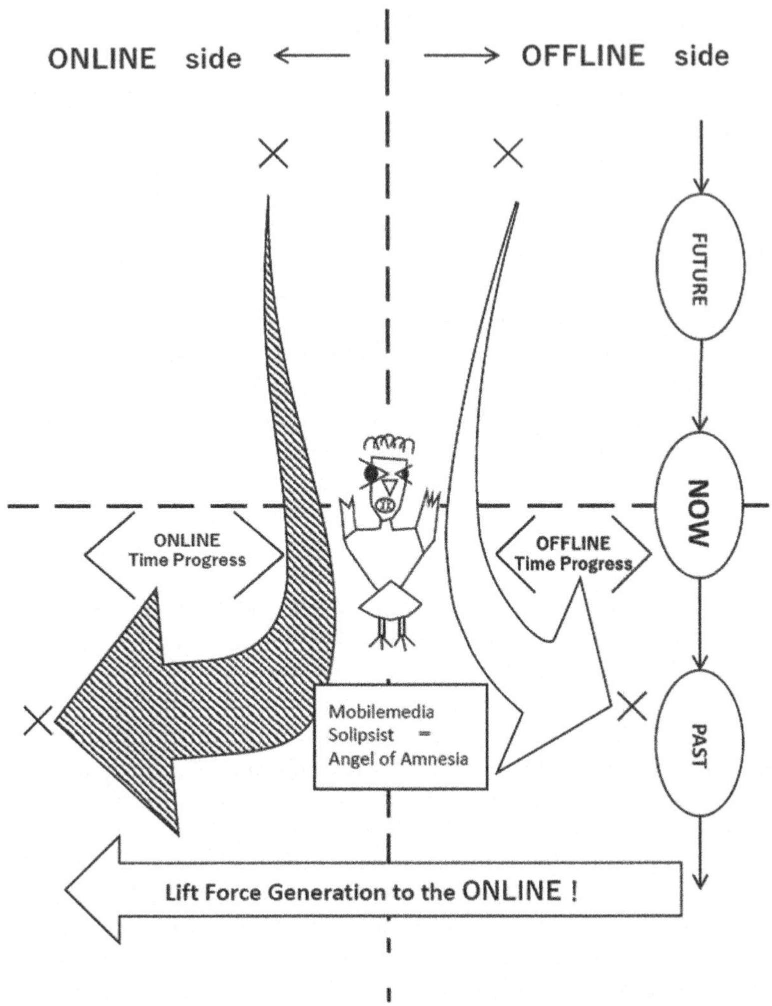


**Fig. 1** "Non-history (non-past) = Angel of Amnesia" re-interpreted by Fujimoto

images of a multi-phase figure in a certain period of time. But within a differentiated instant, it can only be acknowledged as a single-phase image, without "Nagara" acknowledgement.[17]

Perhaps, the "mobile media solipsist" are similarly able to "Nagara" acknowledge an infinite number of "parallel possible worlds" beyond the screen of their mobile devices, but in one instant, they can acknowledge only one of them.

[17]Refer to Wittgenstein (1953) for interpretation of "rabbit-duck illusion" and unity and exclusion of "aspects".

Unity and exclusion of aspects that unconsciously and instantly converge lead to risks of "Nagara smartphone" use on roads and phubbing, i.e., breach of manners (although rights are intentionally exercised by switching between on and off).

Can the limits of human perception, i.e., the "single-phase recognition of aspects" be broken through in the future? This is wishful thinking, but similar to space, the problem of "familiarity" and mastery of sensibility may allow for multifaceted "Nagara" consideration as regards the sense of time. For example, for the driving operation of a bus in the past, two-man operation with a driver and a conductor was the standard, and all tasks other than driving the vehicle were the job of the conductor; two people divided labor.

In other words, tasks such as collecting fees, providing information regarding destinations, providing support for those in need, and communication with the headquarter were the job of the conductor. The driver was not supposed to engage in those tasks and was expected to focus on driving. However today, in most cities around the world including Japan, the operation of buses has become a one-person job. With less opportunities to deal with passengers, drivers of taxis and trucks have been operating alone for a long time. As such, through sensitivity training, humans may eventually be able to perform "Nagara" acknowledgements and actions in a wide range of areas.[18]

Unity and exclusion of aspects at the present time are not limited to the unique media and society of twenty-first century Japan. In the last 30 years of mobile media history, users have utilized multiple devices (including pagers, PDA, and mobile phones), multiple Mobile Media Terminals (MMT), and multiple services and apps. Even if a person is able to "Nagara" use these devices and services with a time lag, it is extremely difficult to "Nagara" use them simultaneously. As modern smartphones such as iPhone became multi-tasking devices, the number of users who have multiple devices decreased. Thus, globally, devices for each user are converging to one specific device. The transition from "single-task and multi-device use" to "multi-task and single-device use" will continue to be the global MMT standard in the future.[19]

I have applied the sense of time of "mobile media solipsists" to the 'triple junction model' proposed herein. As everyone excluding oneself becomes groups of characters and personalities at the same psychological distance, the sense of time called "now" contains constant interruptions to empty space using "it's here!" notifications of new messages, e-mails, news, and BOT information, and the reference point of "zero" is forcibly placed on a number line in the time coordinates ($t$).

However, this "zero = now" concept always has strong intentionality toward the near future called "next"; thus, the number line on the time coordinates ($t$) cannot be said to extend, in axial symmetry, to the past ($-t$) and the future ($+t$) from the

[18]Refer to Fujimoto (2005, 2010a, b, 2016, 2017) for "Nagara" and "Nagara Mobilism".

[19]Refer to Fujimoto (1997, 1999a, b, 2000, 2002, 2005) for the usage behavior of MMT such as pagers, mobile phones, and electronic organizer.

center, “zero”. Metaphorically speaking on the basis of “non-history (non-past) = the Angel of Amnesia,” the time density of the past ($-t$) is low and that of the future ($+t$) is high, presenting an asymmetric structure. Thus, small wings of the angel are violently urged by the strong winds blowing from the future.

The issue with respect to the sense of time of modern humans is that, for “mobile media solipsists” = “non-history (non-past) = the Angel of Amnesia,” who should mediate between online and offline, there are discrepancies in the “months/days” unit on the offline side and in the time unit of “the now opening to the future”, which is the “minutes/seconds” unit on the online side; therefore, it is impossible to adapt to this asymmetry.

For example, the sense of time on the offline side is common with the sense of time for fashionable psychology that gravitates toward new trends. For example, the “current (now)” fashion or the “latest trend” constantly aims for the “next” future and does not look back to the past. Past trends that have passed the season of “now” become somewhat unfashionable after one month, “behind the trend” after three months, and “embarrassing” after one year.

Compared to the offline side of the sense of time that aspires “the now opening to the future” with the “months/days” unit, the online side of the sense of time aspires “the now opening to the future” with a unit shorter than a “second”. For example, the timeline of SNS messages and news apps, which send notifications consecutively and continously, appears to have multiple notifications “simultaneously,” but there is no concept of “simultaneity.” Unity and exclusion of aspects forcibly enters before and after the time series, applying timecode ranking and linearly placing messages without any gap. The instant the next message arrives, the “now” that was being focused on until then is “instantly erased” from awareness, thus disappearing from the awareness.

Comparing the “on” and “off”, each has the same asymmetrical structure of “future–now–past,” but the unit of time is completely different. There is probably a gap on the order of 10,000 to 1,000,000 between offline (progressing on a daily and monthly basis) and online (progressing second by second and minute by minute). Therefore, the online and offline flow of time for “mobile media solipsists” presents an extreme discrepancy between “fast online and slow offline.” Thus, in the subjective sense of time, psychological updraft momentum, which constantly senses psychological inclination that strongly leans to the online side with extremely fast flow, or a type of psychological “lift” toward the online side continues.

The nouveauté worship of Baudelaire and Benjamin discussed earlier is widely shared to this day, but for today’s “mobile media solipsists,” its qualitative change is significant.

In other words, in addition to the nouveauté worship up to the twentieth century, a philosophical discussion of the new twenty-first century sense of time is necessary, where there are now “extreme discrepancies between on and off” and “lift toward the online side,” accelerated by the prosperity of SNS and news apps.

## 6 Five Types of Sense of Time and Transcendental Unbalanced Time

There are five different senses of time for discussion as follows:

1. Primitive time: biological sense of time called "internal clock" or "circadian rhythm";
2. Objective time: Newtonian (physical) time, World Business Time (WBT);
3. Offline subjective time: time sensed offline, for example, when facing someone in person;
4. Online subjective time: time sensed when immersed online such as SNS and Internet; and
5. Transcendental unbalanced (claudication) time: unbalanced consciousness that tries to integrate ①–④ at the metalevel of mobile media solipsists.

Let us first discuss ① primitive time. This is a sense of time humans possess as living organisms, called the "internal clock." It is a diurnal sense of time called the circadian rhythm, which is the cycle of being awake, asleep, and semi-awake (during REM sleep, waking up, or falling asleep). It also includes diurnal fluctuations in mood caused by appetite, sexual desires, desire to sleep, hunger, and the need to defecate.[20]

② Objective time is the time indicated by a clock. This is also known as "Newtonian (physical and astronomical) time." It can also be referred to as the "WBT" as stock markets worldwide and all financial and political activities are strictly regulated by the course of this objective time. Originally, it was established at an observatory in the United Kingdom and was called "Greenwich Mean Time." However, currently, its link to physics and astronomy is not considered. It is an "objective time" that carries through global financial and political activities, and it operates independently from the subjectivity of humans.

If we focus on the "hic et nunc" (here and now), which opens to the future, ③ "Offline subjective time" is "zero = the origin" of the subjective sense of time. For "mobile media solipsists," who are the main subject of actions such as response to the external environment, traditional handling of humans and objects, conversations, and actions, there is no doubt that the sense of time of self, who lives in "hic et nunc" while being affected by ① "primitive time" and ② "objective time", is positioned at the "center of the possible worlds".

Similar to ③ "offline subjective time," if we focus on the "hic et nunc" (here and now), which opens to the future, ④ "online subjective time" is also at "zero = the origin" of the subjective sense of time. Through the screen of "a switching device between on and off = a smartphone," ③ "offline subjective time" and ④ "online subjective time" constitutes the core of our sense of time in a manner similar to coupled mirrors.

[20]Refer to Fujimoto (1993) for discussion of the theory of time in the Lifeworld.

Finally, as these four different times are independently and dependently forced together, they move in an unbalanced and uncoordinated manner, being integrated by the "mobile media solipsists." This leads to the birth of sense of ⑤ "transcendental unbalanced time".

For example, a whirligig beetle, an aquatic insect that freely swims on the surface of water while rotating at an extremely high speed, visually and simultaneously captures enemies and food both above and below the water surface and quickly reacts to chase or flee; therefore, it has evolved to possess a unique nervous system that integrates the visual cortex at a higher order. In other words, insects normally have two compound eyes each on the right and the left, but for the whirligig beetle, the compound eyes have evolved into four eyes (above, below, left, and right), which allows for simultaneous vision above and below the water surface. How do whirligig beetles comprehensively understand visions from four compound eyes while spinning and swimming on the water surface at an extremely high speed? There must be an advanced integration of their visual cortex and nervous system with the sense of time after several billion years of evolution.

Compared to this advanced integration of perception by the whirligig beetle, modern humans' sense of time has a unique meta-consciousness specific to humans called "transcendence"; however, this integration has just begun and is incomplete. As one can see that the operation of smartphones while walking, riding bicycles, or driving a car causes many accidents, not only is there no adaptation to the integration of movements and perceptions of humans but the integration of time and sense of movement is at a more inferior and duller level than that exhibited by whirligig beetles. Yet, we the "mobile media solipsists," must go on living, while attempting to "Nagara" adapt in the flow of time one moment at a time.

The breach of manners that occurs under such circumstances is known as phubbing (ignoring a person in front of oneself by using a phone). A more general problem with the option for exercising this power is the problem of switching on and off, which was formulated as my "triple junction model."[21]

Through smartphones, we can smoothly switch between on and off at any time and exercise the power of making various choices. We can constantly have AR switched on, overlapping countless number of virtual spaces in real space, to be immersed in the possible worlds. We can also delete these worlds instantaneously. We can read and watch various SNS messages, Internet news, and YouTube videos, click "like" and share, and even post our own messages. We are surrounded by countless numbers of timelines, but can delete them all in one instance.

In such instances, the classification of attributes and contexts of each space, e.g., the differentiation between abstract and concrete, and real and virtual, are abstracted, and each of them is recognized as a "possible world" for each possible appearance. In such "possible worlds," the unity and consistency of personality and reality and the independence of an individual are also abstracted, and as a group of anonymous and fragmented elements of letters, sounds, still images, and videos,

[21]Refer to Fujimoto (1994, 1997, 1999a, b, 2000, 2002, 2005, 2016, 2017).

their existence is only recognized in terms of personalities, characters, and icons, based on anonymity, situation, and context.

## 7 "Now" as Gods that Arrive at Each Instant

Let us draw an additional line of theology to the discussions thus far. D. Riesman proposed three types of social personalities: A: tradition-directed; B: inner-directed; and C: other-directed. He argued that modern humans are transitioning to the "other-directed" type that values others' opinions more than the traditional communities, the traditions of national states, and one's own internal guide. If we apply these types of social personalities into our classification of the sense of time (①–⑤), ① primitive time can be classified as B: "inner-directed" sense of time; ② objective time can be classified as A: "tradition-directed" sense of time; ③ offline subjective time and ④ online subjective time can be classified as C: "other-directed" sense of time; and ⑤ "transcendental unbalanced time" by "mobile media solipsists" attempts to integrate them together. More than 60 years after Riesman, an inclination of the sense of time toward C: "other-directed type" is likely increasing.[22]

How, then, can we control this ever-increasing "other-directed" trend and rebuild the integrated sense of time?

The key is in the three types of transitions in Christian faith proposed by a theologian, P. Tillich: D: heteronomy; E: autonomy; and F: theonomy.[23]

In the past, protestants went through the era of D: "heteronomy", when the authority of the church and priests were the source of faith, and arrived at the age of E: "autonomy", when the understanding of the bible and one's inner thoughts were the cornerstone of their faith. Tillich argued that modern humans should move toward the third path—F: "theonomy"—which dialectically exceeds the paths of god and humans while joining the two ("nagara"). He considered that each Advent and grace of God were the opportunities for one to meet others and for humans to meet God and discovered a basis for the new order.

The theological idea of Tillich has restrictions similar to those of Riesman from 60 years ago; however, unlike Riesman who was affirmative and confirmative of the current condition, Tillich criticized the current situation and searched and proposed an opportunity to transcend. Now, modern humans, as "mobile media solipsists," are rocked between "heteronomy" and "autonomy." We are trying to integrate the distortion of the sense of time, but we are struggling with the gaps. Tillich proposed "theonomy" as if he foresaw this uncoordinated and unbalanced sense of time.

---

[22]Refer to Riesman (1950/1964).

[23]Refer to Tillich (1951–1963/2017).

Let us examine the "theonomy" of Tillich using our time model. Each Advent is equivalent to SNS or applications, new messages, news, and YouTube videos—a "rooster", so to speak. The situation where the "near future" is converted to the "now" one after another and arrives is similar to the teaching of dialectic theology in that God descends anew to save us each time (advent).

Of course, for "mobile media solipsists," "the God of Time" that descends every second (more precisely, a plurality of gods) is not the personified god of monotheism. For modern humans, in the midst of the trend of global "re-enchantment," including the followers of monotheism, this god is a god based on primitive, indigenous, and folk belief preceding the time of monotheism or a god of new animism (including totemism of spirits, animals, characters, and personalities) that manifests post monotheism.

Gods living in the possible worlds beyond the screens of the smartphones we use are rich groups of characters from ancient, folksy, and polytheistic festivals (for example, Easter, Halloween, Valentine's day, summer solstice, and winter solstice); mythology, fairy tale, and fantasy (for example, the "Lord of the Rings" and 'Harry Potter' series); animated films (for example, films by the director Hayao Miyazaki); electronic games (for example, "Dragon Quest" and "Pokémon"); theme parks (for example, Disneyland); and art work (for example, the works of Miwa Yanagi).

Appearances of these gods (icons) are routinely emphasized by VR, AR, games, and amusement parks, disseminated by SNS and are abundant around us. In our "re-enchanted" world, such broad iconolatry and animism are seamlessly connected with traditional faith in monotheism. Particularly in polytheistic Hinduism, Tibetan esoteric Buddhism, and Asian faiths such as Japanese Shinto, the faiths are integrated and are mutually complementary with iconolatry and animism (totemism) that continue to be disseminated through smartphone screens.

For modern humans, objective operation of the clock and direct conversation with friends and families, who exist in front of us, do not constitute the sense of time for the "now and present." The objective (physical) time of the clock is a "stocked" sense, wherein time is accumulated as a quantity. Subjective (psychological) time brought by real conversations is a "flowing" sense that deeply immerses in time (which is a quality in this case) and forgets the passing of time. Both are types of real senses of time, but for us, it is not a symbol of the sense of time that indicates the "now and present".

In contrast, what is the symbol of the "now and present" for modern humans? It is the new arrival of SNS, news apps, and YouTube videos (and anticipation, longing, and faith in new arrivals). Humanity and territory such as the identity of the sender or contents of the messages are completely unimportant to us. As long as the arrival is "new," it is okay, even though the information is uninteresting and trivial and was sent by a stranger.

Only Nouveauté is spark of life. The fact that we are anticipating new SNS messages and following them with our eyes, i.e., being conscious of the new arrival, is the only thing that affects the qualification of the "index of time called 'now'."

In this regard, for "mobile media solipsists," interruptions by new information consecutively arriving "now" by an unfamiliar third party (broad sense of parasites such as those who intervene, hear, eavesdrop, and disturb with noise) are "the index of time called now," and the sense of time of "mobile media solipsists" is the symbol of expectation, which was "anticipated and externalized," and the god that is regenerated each time to descend (advent).

Essential requirements for the descending "gods" (aka advent) are that they were not "summoned" by us; instead, they forcibly and externally interrupt from the empty space of the possible worlds, which is in "nowhere," i.e., beyond our consciousness.

"New arrived SNS messages" as the external expression of time can be anonymous, non-personal, and invisible. However, because of the faith in "the novelty that progresses second by second and minute by minute", and of the faith in "the holiness of the moment when the future in possible worlds changes to the present," and of the faith in "the fragility of now being born from nothing, becoming the past, and returning to nothing", we discover the anonymous godlets of telling the time striking every second, i.e. tiny gods plural small pop gods (characters and personalities).

In the early 1990s in Japan, a phenomenon of "bell-pal (aka electronic pager-friend)," in which a stranger was chosen through a random number to exchange messages, became explosively popular among female high school students. At that time, the "bell-pal" was considered as "a mysterious interaction with anonymous friends who came from unknown locations." I analyzed this phenomenon as "spiritual customs and beliefs where young women of similar ages meet electronically," which was an electronic reconstruction of Japanese folk traditions such as "divination by planchette," "fortune telling," "fortune slip," and "young sisterhood house (musume-yado in Japanese)." It was a typical case of "re-enchantment" under "disenchantment," and its example was the "bell-pal as a god of notification."[24]

The "spiritual interaction" of the mid-1990s spread worldwide across all age groups about 20 years later. Though it expanded and changed from short texts to SNS with massive multimedia information and videos with AR effects, its essence has remained constant. In other words, they qualitatively and quantitatively became gods similar to fortune telling, messages from god, oracle, charms, guardian spirit (Socrates' daemon), obstruction, interference, bystanders (chorus in Greek tragedy), and fellow game players as a global phenomenon.

Aristotle categorically called the subjects of such "spiritual interaction" Psychês, i.e., soul/spirit/butterfly, which was translated into Latin as anima, i.e., animated objects/animals/spirits. These are all subjects of animism (spirit worship/totemism) that cover various intermediate forms including fairies, spirits, animals, totems, fictional lives, animation, characters, and personalities.

A modern Japanese artist, Miwa Yanagi, implies the worldview of modern humans without directly depicting "mobile media solipsists." "The Elevator Girl" series (1997–1998) expressed non-humanity, anonymity, and multiple human

[24]Refer to Fujimoto (2000, 2017).

characteristics through the images of modern female occupation called elevator girl. Subsequently, the "My Grandmothers" series (2000–2009) metamorphosed the time–space by having young women performing a costume play of their own image 50 years later. Through positively characterizing (self-deification) their old selves, the series attempted to surface the virtual and real and "present and future" senses of time. The "Fairytale" series (2004–2006) visualized a group of possible worlds, in which one can be simultaneously a protagonist of a fairy tale and other characters (antagonist, meddler, or a third party with good intentions); in other words, it presented a worldview based on dialectical logic, wherein a little girl and an old woman or a princess and a witch can constantly change their positions as the protagonist and the supporting characters.

Her artwork can be considered as an attempt to symbolize the sense of time of "mobile media solipsists".[25]

## 8 Conclusion: Five Implications of "Nagara"

If we summarize the above article, there are five implications of "Nagara Mobilism" herein.[26]

(1) <simultaneous/parallel> Nagara: multiple things and actions simultaneously exist in the same direction or independently, randomly or in parallel (while performing the action)
"move(do) while ~ing/with something ~ing".
(2) <simultaneous/opposite> Nagara: multiple things and actions simultaneously exist in opposite directions in parallel (despite ~)
"move (do) despite ~ing".
(3) <dialectical> Nagara: Multiple phenomena that are theoretically opposite (prograde and retrograde) progress simultaneously.
(4) <multilayer networking> Nagara: "Nagara" as multiple layers that connect nodes of countless network layers, where multiple networks of human relationships (offline) or "Negara" (including the concept of Indonesian work by Geertz) is expanded to the modern online setting.
(5) <different time/unbalanced (claudication)> Nagara: "Nagara" as a transcendental sense of time that stares at temporal phenomena existing both online and offline, which are the progress of time from the future to the present.

As such, we can summarize the five implications of "Nagara" that are pluralistic, yet echo as one.

[25]Refer to Yanagi (2004).

[26]Refer to Fujimoto (1997, 1999a, b, 2000, 2002, 2005, 2010a, b, 2016, 2017) for the concepts of "Nagara" and "Mobiles".

Consequently speaking, Nagara implications and their realizations spread widely over the whole worlds (both real and imaginary), we are becoming the Mobile Media Solipsists and living in the Re-Enchanted 'Possible Worlds' in the twenty-first century more than before.

## References

Benjamin W (1939) Baudelaire ou les rues de Paris. In: Das Passagen-Werk: Die Straßen von Paris: Einer der Grundlagentexte materialistischer Kulturtheorie-Blick in die Jetztzeit des Spätkapitalismus. Tokyo:e-artnow

Benjamin W (1940) Theses on the philosophy of history (trans by Stuart Jeffries). https://www.versobooks.com/blogs/2791-the-storm-blowing-from-paradise-walter-benjamin-and-klee-s-angelus-novus

Fujimoto K (1993) A wind blows, without why: notes on 'Primordial Time' of Swatches' Fashion (Kaze wa Naze Fuku, Naze nashini Fuku—Swatches no 'Gensei Jikan-Ron' Oboe-Gaki in Japanese). In: The Bulletin of Mukogawa Women's University, Everyday-Life Ethestics (Mukogawa-Jyosi-daigaku Seikatu-Bigaku Kenkyusyo Kiyou) vol 3

Fujimoto K (1994) Singing submariners or the ocean fulfilled with feminine listeners (Utau Submariners aruiha Kikimimi de ippai no Umi in Japanese). In: Kadono Y et al (eds) Expressive power of Osaka: from giant signs to the local dialect, searching for the city's attractions (Osaka no Hyougenryoku—Kyodai Kanban kara Osaka-ben made Purezen-Toshi no Miryoku wo Saguru). Parco, Tokyo

Fujimoto K (1997) Girls' pager revolution: introduction to media folklore (Pocket Bell Shoujo Kakumei—Media Folklore Josetsu(in Japanese). Etore, Osaka

Fujimoto K (1999a) A cultural sociology of 'mobiles': 300 years-history of home, automobile, and the body ('Mobiles' no Bunkashakaigaku—Ka-Do-Tai no 300 Nenshi in Japanese). In: Fashion environment (Fashion kankyou), vol 8-3

Fujimoto K (1999b) Anonymous, noisy, and parasitic: icono- logic of X and Y among pager friends (Tokumei, Zatsuon, Kisei—Beru-tomo wo meguru X to Y no Zuzou Ronrigaku (in Japanese). In: Unhealthy enjoyment, depressed health (Fukenkou no Etsuraku—Kenkou no Yuutsu). Gendai Fuzoku Kenkyukai, Kyoto

Fujimoto K (2000) Syntony, distony, virtual sisterhood, and multiplying anonymous personalities: invisible Pseudo-Kinship structures through mobile media terminal's literacy. Senri Ethnol Stud 52:117–141

Fujimoto K (2002) Shrill feminine voices, thick masculine voices: mobile space and literary criticism surrounding 'Yipes' and 'Overbearing Voices' (Ousei/Kigoe, Dakusei/Damigoe—Kya to Dami wo meguru Keitai kukan/bungakuron (in Japanese). In: Saitou M (ed.) Beyond literature and super literature (Datsu-bungaku to chou-bungaku). Iwanami Shoten, Tokyo

Fujimoto K (2005) The third period paradigm: the anti-ubiquitous 'Territory Machine' from 'Girls' Pager Revolution' to 'Mobile Aesthetics'. In: Ito M, Okabe D, Matsuda M (eds) Personal, portable, pedestrian: mobile phones in Japanese life. MIT Press, Massachusetts

Fujimoto K (2010a) Nagara-Mobilism in the clutches of cutie mobs. In: Yoshida M et al (eds) Welt in der Hand. Spector Books, Leipzig

Fujimoto K (2010b) Smart mobs, pager girls and nagara mobilism (Smart Mobs, Pocket Bell Shoujo, Nagara Mobilism). In: Japan Sociological Society (ed) Encyclopedia of sociology (Shakaigaku Jiten in Japanese). Maruzen, Tokyo

Fujimoto K (2016) The 'Triple Junction Model' of mobile media: two dogmas of the 'Myth of Communication'. In: Tomita H (ed) The post-mobile society: from the smart/mobile to second offline. Routledge, London

Fujimoto K (2017). From "Nagara" to "Negara"—Dégagement or engagement in the theatrical contextualism? (My Oral Presentation of Intenational Symposium, July 2nd). In: Are you second offline?—The diversity of post-mobile society. Kansai University, Osaka
Geertz C (1981) Negara: the theatre state in nineteenth-century Bali. Princeton University Press, New Jersey
Goffman E (1963) Behavior in public places: notes on the social organization of gatherings. The Free Press, New York
Horkheimer M, Adorno Th (1947) Dialektik der Aufklaerung. De Gruyter, Berlin
Kripke S (1980) Naming and necessity. Wiley-Blackwell, New Jersey
Ohmori S (1994) Time and being (Jikan to Sonzai in Japanese). Seidosya, Tokyo
Riesman D (1950/1964) The lonely crowd: a study of the changing American character. Yale University Press, New Haven
Serres M (1980) La Parasite. Bernard Grasset, Paris
Tillich P (1951–63/2017) Systematische Theologie I•II. De Gruyter, Berlin
Weber M (1917) Wissenschaft als Beruf. Reclam, Leipzig
Wittgenstein L (1953) Philosophische Untersuchungen. Suhrkamp, Berlin
Yanagi M (2004) Miwa Yanagi. Hatje Cantz Pub, Stuttgart

**Kenichi Fujimoto** is Professor, Dept. of INFORMATICS and MEDIOLOGY, Fac. of Human Environment Sciences, Mukogawa Women's University (Nishinomiya, JAPAN). He is also a member of Mukogawa Institute of Esthetiucs in Everyday-Life. He is studying SOCIOLOGY, PHILOSOPHY and ESTHETICS of media cultures, at Osaka univ. and on the job (art, design, editorial, advertising) activities. Focused on MOBILE MEDIA, from interdisciplinary points of view, mobile i.e. TERRITORY MACHINE, NAGARA MOBILISM, SHIKO-HIN (REFRESHING FAVORITES). His defied MOBILE MEDIA includes not only information tools, but also art works (mobile), portable foods, cars and housings. Articles available in English: Kenichi Fujimoto, 'Syntony, Distony, Virtual Sisterhood, and Multiplying Anonymous Personalities : Invisible Pseudo-Kinship Structures through Mobile Media Terminal's Literacy', Senri Ethnological Studies: SES (52)2000. Kenichi Fujimoto, 'The Third–Stage Paradigm: Territory Machines from the Girls' Pager Revolution to Mobile Aesthetics, in Personal, Portable, Pedestrian: Mobile Phones in Japanese Life (MIT Press, 2005)..

# The Importance of Place in the Second Offline Life: Geographical Differences in Social Media Usage and Online Gaming Behavior

**Misa Matsuda**

**Abstract** In this chapter, I argue that "place" plays an important role in this globalized world, as do our existing (or offline) social relationships. The spread of smartphones is contributing to an increasingly globalized world. However, geographical differences in young Japanese people's social media and online gaming behavior reflect differences in their personal networks. I analyzed a survey that was conducted in November 2015 among 20-year-olds living in two municipalities, Suginami Ward, Tokyo, and Matsuyama City, Ehime Prefecture in Japan to underscore how diverse young people's second offline lives really are. For example, LINE is the dominant social media platform among young people in both areas, but young people in Suginami tend to use a greater mix of communication tools. And young people in Matsuyama are more likely to play games in general than those in Suginami. I exposed geographical differences in the way people relate to social media and online gaming. I also showed how these geographical differences relate to differences in personal networks, living environments, and daily routines—in other words, to factors that are heavily dependent on place.

## 1 Introduction

We live in what Tomita (2016) has dubbed a second offline world—in which online information permeates our everyday activities. If you observe a train at rush hour, you will find passengers using their smartphones to message friends, interact on social media, read up on the latest news or gossip, and play games. When arranging meetups with friends, we use social media to decide on the time and place. We also use social media to check reviews of the restaurant where the meetup will take place. No matter the time or place, we can instantly access the information we seek and act upon it. This second offline existence is a mixed blessing. When we visit somewhere for the first time, we can reach our destination without getting lost on

---

M. Matsuda (✉)
Faculty of Letters, Chuo University, Tokyo, Japan
e-mail: mmatsuda@tamacc.chuo-u.ac.jp

 
H. Tomita (ed.), *The Second Offline*, Advances in Information and Communication Research 3, https://doi.org/10.1007/978-981-16-2425-4_10

the way by looking up the destination online. On the other hand, even during a vacation, we can never quite turn off—an urgent message may pop up at any moment, tearing us away from our relaxation. In this way, our personal time and space become inseparable from our online time and space.

That said, online time and space do not affect everyone in the same way. Each person has different ways of interacting with online space, disconnecting from it, or attempting to do so. The same online content, though it can be used uniformly, will in practice be used differently depending on the user in question. Simply put, people's offline lives dictate their online lives. Given that our online lives generate our second offline lives, we could say that our second offline lives reflect our first-offline lives.

Geographical differences in young Japanese people's social media and online gaming behavior reflect differences in their personal networks. The spread of smartphones is contributing to an increasingly globalized world. However, I argue that, nonetheless, place plays an important role in this world, as do our existing (or offline) social relationships. In this article, I analyze differences in people's second offline lives by counterpoising them with their first-offline lives. In doing so, I aim to underscore how diverse people's second offline lives really are.

## 2 Review of the Literature

The impact of urbanization on personal networks has garnered interest in urban sociology. Fischer (1982) discussed this matter and proposed a subcultural theory of urbanism. According to this theory, people living in larger cities interact more with people on a daily basis, and thus have more opportunities to form diverse networks. Because they have a greater range of subcultural network options, these urbanites have greater homophily in their networks and they "were definitely involved with more 'just friends'—the large category of associates called 'friends' who share no other social context with" (258) them. Matsumoto (1992, 2005) and Akaeda (2011) discussed whether Fischer's theory is applicable to Japan.

With the Internet becoming ever more ubiquitous, sociologists are increasingly interested in how people's online behavior affects the social networks they form. Does the Internet increase our options for forming personal networks in a similar way as urbanization? Rainie and Wellman (2012) coined the expression "networked individualism" to describe how people use information and communications technology (ICT) to increase their connectedness to strong ties (close friends) while maintaining a large network of weak ties (more superficial friendships). In a Japanese study, Iwata (2014) compared two nationwide surveys conducted by the Mobile Communication Research Group in 2001 and 2011. Iwata's aim was to determine how mobile phone use had affected friendships over the 10-year period between the surveys when mobile use had proliferated. He reported that people aged between 12 and 69 had fewer friendships in 2011 than they did in 2001,[1] but that people who spent more time online, using either a mobile device or PC, had more remote friends.

The spread of the Internet has encouraged communities of shared interests whose members span the globe. This is evident in the way young people use their smartphones. Young people use smartphones to connect with their friends at any time and from any place, but they also use them as devices for connecting to social media. In other words, they use smartphones to interact with a broad range of users, play online games, watch stream movies, or catch up on topics that are trending on Twitter or on user-generated websites.

A question then arises: Does such online behavior affect young people's personal networks uniformly, or does it depend on the level of urbanization in their living environment? Are young people in different living environments equally likely to seek online content to suit their preferences and develop personal networks around shared interests? To explore this question, it is necessary to analyze how geographic differences affect social media and online gaming behavior. What does the literature have to say on social media and online gaming?

Let us first focus on social media. Since 2000, we have an increasingly diverse array of options for contacting friends and interacting anonymously with strangers online. Some of these options involve one-to-one communication (e.g., email, chat, messenger) while others involve multiple participants and are open to public view (e.g., message forums, social media). The method people use depends on who they want to communicate with and what the situation is. Ishiguro (2018) compared the results of a 1993 and 2014 survey, both of which were conducted among married people aged 20–65. He argued that the spread of ICTs had led to more close-proximity friendships among young women during the 20-year period. In discussing why women were limiting themselves to close-proximity friendships, Ishiguro suggested that this is because women place more value in friends as supportive resources than men do. Kobayashi (2018) also analyzed the above surveys and included a 2015 follow-up survey in this analysis. He found that social media is not effective for increasing the size of networks of friends with strong ties. However, it can be effective for increasing the size of networks with weak ties if these networks are small and if the person concerned lives in a highly urban environment.

As I discuss later, social media took off in Japan during the mid-2000s. Since then, the number of young people using PCs to send emails is declining, as is the number of those who use smartphones to send emails or text messages. According to the literature, the tools that individuals frequently use to communicate online vary depending on where they live. If the living environment correlates with online behavior, then presumably it also correlates with personal networks.

[1]However, Iwata suggested that the 2011 Great East Japan Earthquake might have contributed to the lower number of friendships in 2011.

What about online gaming? Mobile-based social network games became popular around 2010. By "social-network games," I mean smartphone-based games that use a free-to-play model and involve competing against or interacting with other players. Such social-network games have proven popular among demographics with no previous interest in gaming, such as middle-aged to old men and women and young women. Tsuji (2016) examined geographic differences based on the survey conducted in 2005 and reported that young people living in municipalities in or near large urban centers are more differentiation-oriented, while those in more provincial municipalities are more other-directed. Tsuji also found that young people in more urban environments tended to seek hobbies that suited their own particular interests, while those in less urban environments were more likely to follow the dominant interests of their peers.

Given that the Internet has made it easier for people to interact around a common interest, regardless of where they live, is one's address becoming irrelevant to the interests that one pursues? If, on the other hand, Tsuji is correct, and geography does shape cultural preferences, does a shift in popular game design from single- to multiplayer reflect a corresponding shift in the gamer population?

I analyzed a survey that my colleague and I conducted in November 2015 among 20-year-olds living in two municipalities in Japan. The first is Suginami Ward, Tokyo, and the second is Matsuyama City, Ehime Prefecture.[2] We conducted this survey to obtain data on contemporary youth culture and how it has changed. Accordingly, we designed the survey in such a way as to allow comparison with previous periods (1990, 2005, and 2009). In this way, we were able to track changes over time (between the 2005 and 2009 surveys) in both municipalities.[3] Suginami Ward is a highly residential district in Tokyo's Yamanote area. Matsuyama City is a hub city in the Shikoku region, which is situated in the western part of the Japanese archipelago. Both municipalities have a similar population; as of the 2015 national census, 563,997 people were living in Suginami and 514,865 in Matsuyama.

The data I analyzed pertains only to 20-year-olds. However, given that young people tend to use new media actively, the sample is suitable for the purpose of examining the impact of such media. Another advantage is that I could compare change over time in two municipalities with different levels of urbanization (one is situated in a metropolis and the other is a regional hub city).

---

[2]The sample size was 2000: 1000 in Suginami and 1000 in Matsuyama. Of the former, 259 (25.9%) people returned the questionnaire and, of the latter, 214 (21.4%) people did. Please see Tsuji et al. (2017) for more about the survey. There were no differences in gender or marital status between the Suginami and Matsuyama samples. But there was a difference in educational level: 80.7% of the Suginami sample had completed (or were undergoing) undergraduate or graduate-level education; in the Matsuyama sample, this was 57.5% ($p < 0.001$).

[3]The 2005 and 2009 surveys were conducted by Matsuyama Daigaku Shakaichosa Shitsu. Both surveys used the same locations (Suginami and Matsuyama), sample (20-year-olds), and sample size (1000 in each location). See Matsuyama-daigaku Shakaichosa-shitsu (2006, 2010) for more on these surveys.

# 3 The Dominance of the Smartphone and the Importance of Place

## *3.1 The Shift from the PC to the Smartphone, and from Email to Social Media*

Before analyzing geographic differences in young people's smartphone behavior, let us first see the kinds of ICT devices that Japanese people have commonly possessed and used over the past decade.

To illustrate Japan's online trends, I will present data from a 2017 white paper, Information and Communication in Japan, released by the Ministry of Internal Affairs and Communications, which shows the household penetration rates of different ICT devices (i.e., the percentage of households owning each device). Since 2003, more than 90% of households have a mobile phone or smartphone, denoting that these ICT devices have become virtually ubiquitous in Japan. The smartphone's household penetration rate began at 9.7% in 2010 and soared to 29.3% in 2011 and 49.5% in 2012 before reaching 71.8% in 2016. With regard to PCs, more than 80% of households had this ICT device in 2005, and the rate rose to 87.2% in 2009. Since then, the rate has gently declined, dipping to 73.0% in 2016. As for tablets, after entering the table at 7.7% in 2010, the rate for this ICT rose sharply. As of 2016, approximately one-third of households own an ICT device. Since 2010, two new ICT devices—the smartphone and tablet—have rapidly spread among Japanese households. Meanwhile, the PC penetration rate has declined, although it still features in more than 70% of households (Fig. 1).

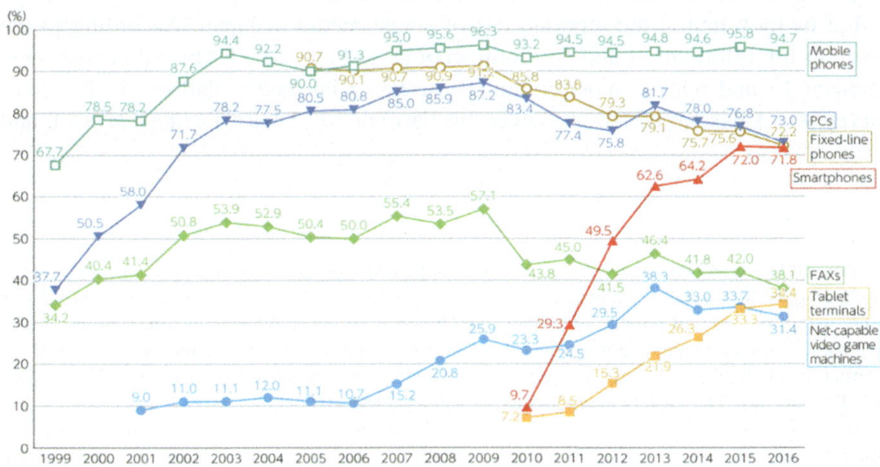


**Fig. 1** Household penetration rates of ICT devices in Japan (Ministry of Internal Affairs and Communications 2017)

Young people are particularly likely to own a smartphone. According to the same white paper, in 2016, 56.8% of people owned smartphones. Of these, 81.4% were aged 13–19, 94.2% were aged 20–29, and 90.4% were aged 30–39. The prevalence of smartphones suggests that more people are using smartphones rather than PCs to go online. On average, people in their teens spent 32.4 min a day online using a PC, and 75.7 min a day using a mobile in 2012. The gap between the two devices has widened with each successive year and, as of 2016, teens were spending only 15.2 min a day online using a PC and as much as 108.2 min a day using a mobile. As for people in their twenties, who are much more likely to use a PC for work, in 2016, they were online using a PC for only 31.4 min a day and as much as 124.8 min a day using a mobile. As this data shows, the smartphone has surpassed the PC as the device that young people commonly use to go online.

Simply put, fewer young people in Japan are using PCs. The 2015 Program for International Student Assessment (PISA) surveyed 15-year-old students in the 46 Organisation for Economic Co-operation and Development (OECD) countries about, among other things, their use of ICT devices (OECD 2016). In his analysis of the survey, Sakurai (2017) noted that Japanese students were at least 20 points below the OECD average in terms of how frequently they use desktop, laptop, and tablet computers, printers, and USB memory sticks. Sakurai noted, in particular, the change in reported PC use between 2009 and 2015. In Japan and 32 other OECD countries, reported desktop use significantly declined over this period (between 6.3 and 30.8 points). Meanwhile, most of these countries saw a rise in laptop use (between 4.3 and 55.6 points). Japan was the only exception; both desktop use and laptop use declined significantly (desktop use falling 13.1 points and laptop use falling 5.3 points).[4]

As young people increasingly favor smartphones over PCs as their device for accessing the Internet, they are also shifting from email to social media as their go-to tool for communicating with friends and family.

Let us look first at the reported use of social media in Japan. According to the Institute for Information and Communications Policy (2017), among people aged between 13 and 69, the most commonly used social media platform in the 2016 survey was LINE, at 67.0%, followed by Facebook (32.3%), Twitter (27.5%), and

[4]Compared to students in other OECD countries, Japanese students were significantly less likely to use ICTs outside of school, whether for leisure or for schoolwork. Japanese students spent 90 min a day using the Internet outside of school, which is the second-lowest daily time among OECD countries. The OECD average was 146 min. The percentage of Japanese people who accessed the Internet for the first time before they turned seven years of age was 9.4%, which ranks 27th among OECD countries. The OECD average was 17.4% (Sakurai 2017).

In examining why Japan was the only OECD country to see a decline in both desktop and laptop use among 15-year-olds, it becomes apparent that the spread of smartphones cannot be the only factor. Other likely factors include the fact that Japanese students started accessing the Internet relatively late and the fact that they spend relatively few hours using a PC outside of school for leisure or schoolwork.

Instagram (20.5%).[5] Among teens, the most commonly used social media platform was LINE (79.3%), followed by Twitter (61.4%), Instagram (30.7%), and Facebook (18.6%). Those in their twenties use LINE (96.3%) followed by Twitter (59.9%), Facebook (54.8%), and Instagram (45.2%). Thus, people use a variety of social media platforms, and LINE most of all. Young people spent much more time using social media than they did using email. Teens spent an average of 58.9 min on social media and only 20.2 min using email on the average weekday. Among those in their twenties, these times were 60.8 and 25.7 min.[6]

From the above data, we can form an idea of the ICT trends among young Japanese people; they are more likely to use a smartphone than a PC and are more likely to spend time using social media (particularly LINE) than emailing. Do these trends reflect any geographic differences?

## *3.2 Geographic Differences in Social Media Behavior and the Factors Behind Them*

**Suginami—A Mix of Platforms; Matsuyama—LINE Alone**

In 2005 and 2009, more than 80% of young people in both Suginami Ward and Matsuyama City used mobile phones. In 2015, the rates in both municipalities were near 100%; the rate in Suginami was 97.3% while that in Matsuyama was 97.7%. No geographic difference was evident during any of the three years.[7] In 2005 and 2009, however, young people in Suginami were more likely than their counterparts in Matsuyama to report using the Internet in the past month. This gap disappeared in 2015, however, with a rate of 98.1% in Suginami and 97.7% in Matsuyama City. Thus, as of 2015, geographic differences in mobile/smartphone or Internet use have dissipated.

On the other hand, the 2015 survey does indicate geographic differences in email and social media behavior. In Suginami, 48.0% of young people reported using a PC (desktop, laptop, or tablet) for email in the past month, compared to 33.3% of young people in Matsuyama; 46.9% of young people in Suginami, and 59.2% in Matsuyama reported never using a PC, and 5.1% in Suginami and 7.5% in Matsuyama reported that they do not have a desktop, laptop, or tablet computer ($p < 0.01$). Another geographic difference is that young people in Suginami were

[5]Google Plus is actually in fourth place at 26.3%. However, I decided not to include it in my analysis because it is easily confused with the search engine Google; in this data, the rate of use of Google Plus was high among people in their 50s and 60s.

[6]Respondents were asked how much time they spent on social media platforms such as Twitter, LINE, and Facebook (viewing content or messaging). Viewing video-sharing sites or playing online games were categorized separately.

[7]Hereinafter, average values are based on a t-test while all other values are based on a chi-squared test.

more likely to send text messages or send other mobile carrier mails (43.4% compared to 32.9% in Matsuyama; $p < 0.05$). Likewise, young people in Suginami were more likely to send emails (for example, Gmail) with a smartphone (34.4% compared to 15.0% in Matsuyama; $p < 0.001$). According to the 2011 survey by the Mobile Communication Research Group, 96.1% of men and 100% of women in their twenties reported using a mobile device for email (Matsuda 2014). If we relate these results to the 2015 survey above, we can clearly understand that young people have drifted away from using mobile-based emails over the past few years.

If young people are abandoning mobile-based emails, what are they using instead? As I have mentioned already, many are using LINE. We found no geographic difference in the use of LINE; in Suginami and Matsuyama, 95.4% and 96.7% reported using the platform, respectively. However, those in Matsuyama spent significantly more time using the platform (143.63 min compared to 108.78 in Suginami; $p < 0.05$). It may be related that young people in Matsuyama were significantly more likely to use each LINE function, the exception being phone calls —young people in Suginami Ward were more likely to use this function (Table 1).

As for other social media platforms, there was no geographic difference in Twitter use (68.9% in Suginami, 61.2% in Matsuyama), but young people in Suginami were more likely to use Facebook (41.3% in Suginami, 22.5% in Matsuyama; $p < 0.001$) and Instagram (36.6% in Suginami, 20.1% in Matsuyama; $p < 0.001$).

In summary, LINE is the dominant social media platform among young people in Suginami and Matsuyama, but young people in Suginami tend to use a greater mix of communication tools. Specifically, they send emails using a PC or mobile phone more frequently than those in Matsuyama. They are also more likely to use social media platforms other than LINE, including Facebook and Instagram. Young people in Matsuyama, on the other hand, tend to use LINE more exclusively. They also use each LINE function more extensively and spend more time on LINE.

#### Relating Differences in Social Media Activity to the Size of Personal Networks

How do these geographic differences relate to the particularities of each social media platform? What do young people use social media for? Let us consider the social media platforms that young people frequently use: LINE, Twitter, Facebook, and Instagram.

We will start with the dominant platform, LINE. Young people commonly use LINE for daily communication with their friends. LINE has a "read receipts" feature—the sender can see whether the recipient has read their message. Twitter is used in more diverse ways, including chatting with friends and acquaintances. Young people frequently use the platform to tweet with their friends. However, many also have several alternative accounts, which they use to interact anonymously around common interests. With Facebook, however, users do use real name accounts. Facebook's popularity among young people has declined. Young people use the platform for posting updates or messaging with their friends/acquaintances. They are more likely to use a Facebook update, rather than a tweet on Twitter, to

**Table 1** Usage rates of each LINE function by region

| | Suginami (%) | Matsuyama (%) | |
|---|---|---|---|
| Phone calls | 83.4 | 75.8 | $p < 0.05$ |
| Timeline | 26.3 | 40.1 | $p < 0.01$ |
| Gaming | 15.4 | 33.3 | $p < 0.001$ |
| News | 17.0 | 23.2 | |
| Coupons | 8.9 | 12.1 | |

announce major life events (Economic Research Office, Ministry of Internal Affairs and Communications 2017: 116). They also use Facebook Messenger to communicate with people outside of their peer group or to stay in touch with their overseas friends. As for Instagram, this photo-sharing platform is proving popular among young women, as suggested by the fact that "Insta-bae" (meaning Instagenic or Instagram-worthy) won the 2017 Japan buzzword award.

We noted earlier that young people in Matsuyama tend to use LINE more exclusively, while those in Suginami use LINE as well as various other platforms. If we relate this difference to the social media trends described in the above paragraph, we can surmise that young people in Suginami have broader interpersonal relations.

A review of smartphone contact lists bears this supposition out; young people in Suginami have an average of 103.59 friends in their contact lists, while their counterparts in Matsuyama only have 77.55 ($p < 0.001$). No such geographic difference was apparent in the 2005 survey—young people in Suginami had an average of 160.3 friends listed in their contacts, while those in Matsuyama had 149.6. However, a difference emerged in 2009—the averages were 171.1 in Suginami and 126.4 in Matsuyama ($p < 0.001$).

LINE friend lists provide further evidence. Young people in Suginami had an average of 177.61 friends, while those in Matsuyama had 120.91 ($p < 0.001$). If we look at LINE groups, which one can create for group communication at any time, the results are what we would expect: in Suginami, young people interacted "regularly," with an average of 5.28 LINE groups compared to 3.34 LINE groups in Matsuyama ($p < 0.001$), and they interacted "occasionally" with an average of 24.47 groups compared to 13.19 in Matsuyama ($p < 0.001$). These results indicate that young people in Suginami have larger LINE groups—or more extensive personal networks.

This geographic difference correlates with the difference in numbers of friends between the two municipalities. According to the data in Table 2, while the number of close friendships does not differ between the municipalities, young people in Suginami have more medium-level friends and acquaintances than their counterparts in Matsuyama, and this trend persists over time.

**Table 2** Number of friends by region (in 2005, 2009, and 2015)

| | 2005 ($n = 515$) | | | 2009 ($n = 558$) | | | 2015 ($n = 473$) | | |
|---|---|---|---|---|---|---|---|---|---|
| | Suginami ($n = 266$) | Matsuyama ($n = 249$) | | Suginami ($n = 308$) | Matsuyama ($n = 250$) | | Suginami ($n = 259$) | Matsuyama ($n = 214$) | |
| Extremely close friendships | 3.92 | 3.50 | n.s. | 3.98 | 3.54 | n.s. | 3.65 | 3.59 | n.s. |
| Medium-level friendships | 18.47 | 14.36 | $p < 0.01$ | 19.87 | 17.54 | n.s. | 18.23 | 13.51 | $p < 0.01$ |
| Acquaintances | 64.52 | 44.80 | $p < 0.001$ | 70.60 | 49.59 | $p < 0.01$ | 71.30 | 42.53 | $p < 0.001$ |

**The Localized Smartphone**

Fischer's (1982) subcultural theory states that greater urbanization leads to more extensive personal networks. This theory has at least been proven valid in the case of Suginami and Matsuyama; young people in Suginami—the more urbanized of the two—had more extensive personal networks, and they had larger collections of contacts on their smartphone contact and LINE friend lists. Moreover, young people in Suginami had more LINE groups with whom they interacted regularly or occasionally, and they used a broader selection of social media platforms.

The survey asked the respondents whether they engaged in clubs or communities for shared interests outside of school or work. Those in Suginami were significantly more likely to answer " yes" than those in Matsuyama (46.9% vs. 36.3%; $p < 0.05$). In both municipalities, "school" was the most frequent response to the question of where the young people established their extremely close and medium-level friendships. However, young people in Suginami were more likely than those in Matsuyama to cite "lessons and clubs or communities of shared interests outside of school or work" (14.1% vs. 6.7%; $p < 0.05$).[8]

Thus, the fact that young people in highly urbanized environments have more friendships correlates with the fact that they have more LINE groups and use a broader range of social media platforms. Although there was no geographic difference in use of Twitter—a platform with a relatively large user base—there was a geographic difference in other platforms, including Facebook and Instagram. This difference may be related to how new services proliferate in more urbanized environments earlier than elsewhere. In any case, more research is needed to explore how the same kinds of social media are used in different ways depending on the environment.

## 4 Geographic Differences in Online Gaming

### *4.1 Online Gaming in Japan During the 2000s*

Online PC gaming took off in the late 1990s when more people had started using the Internet. In Japan, however, online PC games proved less popular. Multiplayer online role-playing games (MORPGs) and massively multiplayer online role-playing game (MMORPGs) famously failed to capture the Japanese market. Koyama (2016) wrote a history of Japan's gaming industry, starting from the release of *Space Invaders* in 1978 up to the 2010s, when smartphone gaming

[8]Otani (2007) analyzed a 1993 survey conducted among university students in a municipality connected to a large urban center—Izumi City, Osaka Prefecture—and in a more provincial municipality—Matsuyama City. The students in Izumi reported a larger subjective number of friends. They also reported having more friends outside university and having more options for making friends.

became popular. He described how the Japanese PC gaming market expanded rapidly in 2003 and peaked in 2011, but how PC gaming remained within approximately 2–30% of the Japanese console game market, which was equivalent to about 100 billion yen (0.91 billion dollars). Koyama gives two reasons why MORPGs and MMORPGs failed in Japan despite proving popular elsewhere: the first was that the console game market was too successful; the second was that Japanese game developers lacked the design and technical know-how to create game content suitable for the gaming market outside the console market (2016: 228).

Mobile-based gaming in Japan began in the early 2000s. By this time, it was standard for mobile phones to come with an Internet connection (this trend began with NTT Docomo's release of i-mode in 1999). It was in the mid-2000s that mobile gaming really took off. A major factor behind the explosion in mobile gaming was the popularity of social-network games that existed on the social networking sites of the time. Gaming-oriented social networks such as Mobage and Gree commanded many subscribers. Meanwhile, the social media platform Mixi had achieved a hit with its farming game *Sunshine Ranch*.

Koyama (2016: 321) defined early-era social-network games as games that focus on fun and involve competing, cooperating with, or interacting with other players. He noted that many of these games featured a simple premise, consisting of cooperative or competitive gameplay. According to Koyama, one reason for this simple design was that mobiles had more technical restrictions than PCs. Another reason was that many mobile users were people who do not traditionally play games, such as young women and middle-aged to old people of both genders.

Like many other online games, social network games follow the free-to-play model. While the base game is free, players who wish to play the game when and how they want (without spending many hours grinding, for instance) may have to pay fees. In other words, players must pay fees to access certain in-game items or content, which will allow them to progress in the game or gain advantages over other players. By monetizing such content, game developers can generate substantial revenues. While players understand that they can play the game for free, many are tempted to pay fees because they want to gain prestige among their companions. Such pay-to-win mechanics attracted controversy around 2010, with reports of children spending a fortune on games unbeknownst to their parents.

Just as the gaming industry began to respond to this criticism, the smartphone explosion began. As Fig. 1 shows, the smartphone's household penetration rate stood at 9.7% in 2010, but the rate soared and, by 2013, it was as high as 62.6%. This trend led to the dominance of native mobile game apps, which users can download directly from the App Store or Google Play. In 2010, sales revenue from game apps surpassed 100 billion yen, and 2012, it surpassed 444.8 billion yen, overtaking console sales. Sales revenue continued to rise in subsequent years (Gz brain 2017).

One game app that achieved a hit in 2012 was *Puzzle & Dragons*. Koyama (2016: 336–337) highlighted two aspects of this game that differentiated it from previous social-network games. The first was that the game stood alone without the social networking aspect. In other words, the game offered fulfilling single-player content that players could enjoy during their spare time. The second aspect was that the player could play for no charge to a considerable degree.[9] A number of other games adopted this precedent. Yonaga (2016: 1110) dubbed these types of games "social-network games that don't use social graphs." More confusingly, some call them *sosha-ge* (a contraction of "social games")—which is the same moniker used for social-network games.

So, who are playing these mobile and smartphone games? Do they differ from traditional gamers?[10]

I will now outline gaming trends by referring to three surveys that the Computer Entertainment Suppliers' Association (CESA) conducted in January 2006, January 2011, and January 2016.[11] These three surveys are close in time to the surveys we conducted in Suginami and Matsuyama (November 2005, November 2010, and November 2015). In 2006, 28.0% of "current game players" (respondents) who answered, "I habitually play games now" to any of the questions about games habits reported that the games they played most frequently were console games 18.8% answered "handheld gaming consoles," and 13.8% answered "PC games" (excluding online games). In 2011, 35.1% of current game players answered "games playable on portable game machines," 18.4% answered "games playable on household game machines," and 16.5% answered "mobile phone games." In 2016, 57.1% of current game players answered "smartphone/tablet games," 14.9% answered "PC games," and 11.9% answered "handheld games." Thus, gaming consoles were the most popular gaming device around 2005, but mobile phones surpassed them around 2009. Around 2015, game apps playable on smartphones and tablets reached the top spot.

In the January 2016 survey, CESA sampled general consumers from ages 3 to 79. In this survey, 38.0% of the respondents answered that they regularly play games. Many of these respondents were young males; 80.2% of male respondents aged 15–19 and 70.3% of those aged 20–24 gave such a response. By contrast, only 64.4% of female respondents aged 15–19 and 47.3% of those aged 20–24 gave such a response, when compared with males. Focusing on respondents in the 20–24 age range, the range that applies to the respondents in Suginami Ward/Matsuyama City surveys (20-year-olds), 57.7% of males and 43.4% of females in this group cited smartphones/tablets as the gaming hardware they used on an ongoing basis. Next, 39.0% of the males and 17.5% of the females cited video game consoles, and 29.0% of the males and 7.9% of the females cited PCs.

[9]These two aspects were also cited by the creator of *Puzzle & Dragons*, namely, Suzuya (2014).

[10]The data I have analyzed is from November 2015. *PokÃ©mon GO* launched in the summer of 2016. Therefore, I have not included the influence of this game.

[11]See CESA (2006, 2011, 2016). CESA has surveyed gaming trends since 2000, but the method is not consistent for all the surveys, so care is needed when comparing the data.

## 4.2 Geographic Differences in Gaming

**The Popularity of Social-Network Games Among Women**
With regard to my surveys, what are the gaming trends among 20-year-olds?

Traditionally, gaming is more of a male pastime than a female one. Yet, women were significantly more likely than men to play LINE-based games (M 19.1% vs. F 29.9%; $p < 0.01$), and men did not play games on social media any more than women did (M 20.5% vs. F 19.4%).

On the other hand, when asked what they did online, men were significantly more likely than women to report playing online games (including social-network games) (M 42.7% vs. F 29.5%; $p < 0.01$). Furthermore, when asked about their current hobbies, men were significantly more likely to answer gaming (M 47.7% vs. F 34.7%; $p < 0.005$).

What we have learned so far is that, while men remain the predominant users of videogames, PC games, and mobile games as they were in the past, after LINE and social media-based games emerged in the late 2000s, many women started playing games too. They access most of these games from smartphones.

**The Growing Popularity of Games in Matsuyama**
As we saw in 3-2, young people in Matsuyama are more likely than those in Suginami to use LINE to play games. Table 3 further presents this geographic difference by gender. The figures for "plays games often"* indicate the total rates of those who answered either "agree" or "agree somewhat." For all other items, the figures indicate those who selected the item concerned

In Matsuyama, men were more likely to report gaming as a hobby and to report playing games often. Both men and women in Matsuyama played LINE and social media-based games more extensively than their counterparts in Suginami. Young people in Matsuyama play games more than those in Suginami, but the women in Matsuyama are particularly likely to do so: 41.6% of the women reported playing games on LINE, and 28.2% reported playing social media games. This finding underscores the extent to which social network games have penetrated the municipality.

In the 2005 survey, we asked the respondents whether they played video games. The responses to this question did not indicate any geographical difference. Among the men, 47.1% of those in Suginami and 60.2% of those in Matsuyama answered "yes." Among the women, the rates of affirmative responses were 10.0% (Suginami) and 14.8% (Matsuyama). In the 2015 survey, we asked respondents about their current hobbies and included "gaming" as an answer option. In 2009, we asked similar questions and found that, among the men in that year, there was no significant difference between the municipalities in likelihood of selecting the gaming option (56.8% in Suginami, 64.8% in Matsuyama). Among the women, however, those in Matsuyama were significantly more likely to select this response (25.3% in Suginami, 34.8% in Matsuyama; $p < 0.05$). We cannot make a direct comparison since the question format differed between the three surveys. That said,

**Table 3** Ratio of game players by gender and region

| | | Suginami (%) | Matsuya (%) | |
|---|---|---|---|---|
| Current hobby: Gaming | M | 39.8 | 56.7 | $p < 0.05$ |
| | F | 32.5 | 37.4 | n.s. |
| Play games often* | M | 63.4 | 77.8 | $p < 0.05$ |
| | F | 53.6 | 60.5 | n.s. |
| Play games on LINE | M | 10.7 | 28.2 | $p < 0.01$ |
| | F | 20.6 | 41.6 | $p < 0.001$ |
| Play online or social-network games | M | 39.4 | 46.5 | n.s. |
| | F | 28.1 | 31.1 | n.s. |
| Play games on SNS | M | 10.8 | 31.8 | $p < 0.001$ |
| | F | 12.3 | 28.2 | $p < 0.001$ |

the results do suggest that gaming is becoming an increasingly popular activity among women, and that women in Matsuyama are more likely to play games than those in Suginami.

**What Underlies the Geographic Difference in Gamers?**
Traditionally, gamers were predominantly young men. However, the rise of the smartphone has broadened the gaming market. The results of our surveys show that women are playing games on LINE more than men are. They also indicate that young people of both genders in Matsuyama are more likely to play games in general than those in Suginami.

Where one lives has no bearing on the gaming device itself, nor on how easy it is to access the game content. If that is so, then this raises the question of why Matsuyama's young people—of both genders—have a greater propensity to play games than those in the other municipality. To address this question, we need to consider it from various points of view, such as the kind of daily routines they have, how gaming relates to their other leisure activities, and the role of social relationships.

With regard to daily routines, the creator of *Puzzle & Dragons*, Suzuya (2014) claimed that many people play social network games during their morning commute (7:00–8:00) and at noon. Play activity then picks up again after the school- or work-day finishes (17:00) and peaks between 23:00 and midnight. Suzuya also mentioned that developers of social-network games time the in-game events around people's daily routines. By synchronizing in-game time to real-world time, social-network games fit themselves around users' daily routines more closely than other games do. This overlap between in-game time and real-world time is a core component of social-network games.

Next, we look at how gaming relates to the other activities that young people enjoy. When we look at the changes across the three-time points, it becomes apparent that the upward trend in the number of women in Matsuyama playing games correlates with a downward trend in television viewing. In data between 2005 and 2015, women generally spent more time watching television than men did, and people in Matsuyama spent more time watching television than those in Suginami did. When we compare the geographic differences for each gender, we find no such difference among the men. Among the women, a geographical difference existed in 2005 and 2009, but not in the 2015 survey. Watching television used to be the main way people spent their spare time, but it may have been surpassed by gaming.

Finally, let us now consider how young people's social relationships may affect their gaming behavior. If gaming is a hobby, then the way people pursue this hobby presumably reflects the influence of other people to a large extent. In any given environment, people's motives for playing online games will vary. Some may be avid gamers who regard online gaming as a way to connect with fellow gamers. Others may have simply followed the crowd—they see their acquaintances playing online games, so they join in the trend. In a 2017 survey, Gz brain (2017) asked people aged between 10 and 59 which information sources or tools they use when searching for a new mobile-based game. The top response was "I seek the opinions of my family, friends, or acquaintances" (35.2%), followed by "I get information from television advertisements" (29.6%) and "app stores like the App Store or Google Play" (26.9%). As this data shows, the opinions of others powerfully shape people's decisions on which mobile game to play, and single-player app games are surely no exception to this. Although online gaming is equally accessible irrespective of where you are, we nonetheless find geographical differences in online gaming behavior. This paradox tellingly demonstrates how locally rooted flesh-and-blood networks remain as important as ever despite the March of globalization.

## 5 Conclusion: The Importance of Place in the Smartphone Age

As long as we have a smartphone close at hand, we are one touch away from the online world—hence, we live a second offline existence. That said, smartphones are physical things, and we carry them around in real-world environments. In connecting to the online world through our smartphones, we never fully detach ourselves from the physical place in which we are operating the device. Moreover, our online behavior will always be shaped in some way by our personal networks, which in turn reflect our particular social situations. In this article, I exposed geographical differences in the way people relate to social media and online gaming. I also showed how these geographical differences relate to differences in personal networks, living environments, and daily routines—in other words, to factors that are heavily dependent on place.

This article neither belittles nor dismisses our attempt to form networks that span physical locations, or the way we use online content to transcend physical boundaries. In fact, by understanding how our first-offline lives shape our second offline lives, we are better able to map out viable possibilities for the latter.

As Rainie and Wellman (2012) emphasized with the term "networked individualism", ICTs increase our mobility, which allows us to expand our sphere of activities, transcend social and physical barriers, and exercise greater freedom in who we socially interact with. In other words, ICTs play a powerful role in our social interactions. However, I have shown that ICTs do not affect us all uniformly irrespective of time or place. This finding—as unsurprising as it may be—challenges technological determinism. It also underscores the need for more empirical and theoretical inquiry into the role of place—particularly the differences and user diversity it describes—in the context of an increasingly widespread second offline world.

This paper is a revised version of Matsuda (forthcoming) and I would like to thank Editage for English language editing and financial support of the Telecommunications Advancement Foundation in 2017.

## References

Akaeda N (2011) Reexamination of urban effects on primary ties in Japan: community lost or saved or transformed? Japan Sociol Rev 62:189–206 (in Japanese)

CESA (2006) 2006 CESA games white paper (in Japanese)

CESA (2011) 2011 CESA games white paper (in Japanese)

CESA (2016) 2016 CESA games white paper (in Japanese)

Economic Research Office, Ministry of Internal Affairs and Communications (2017) The report on the survey of economical aspects of smartphone (in Japanese). http://www.soumu.go.jp/johotsusintokei/linkdata/h29_01_houkoku.pdf. Accessed on 18 Sept 2018

Fischer CS (1982) To dwell among friends: personal networks in town and city. The University of Chicago Press

Gz brain (2017) Famitsu mobile game white paper2018. Gz brain (in Japanese)

Institute for Information and Communication Policy, Ministry of Internal Affairs and Communications (2017) Report on the survey of the usage of the ICT on 2017 (in Japanese). http://www.soumu.go.jp/main_content/000492877.pdf. Accessed on 18 Sept 2018

Ishiguro I (2018) The change of network size. In: Ishiguro I (ed) Kawariyuku nihonjin no network. Keisoshobo, pp 45–72 (in Japanese)

Iwata K (2014) Dose keitai change friendship? In: Matsuda M, Dobashi S, Tsuji I (eds) Keitai in the 2000s: Maturation of Japanese mobile society. University of Tokyo Press, pp 171–200 (in Japanese)

Kobayashi T (2018) The diversification of ICT usage and network size (in Japanese). In: Ishiguro I (ed) Kawariyuku nihonjin no network. Keisoshobo, pp 187–206

Koyama Y (2016) The history of Japanese digital game industry. Jinbunsyoin (in Japanese)

Matsuda M (2014) Keitai in 2000s. In: Matsuda M, Dobashi S, Tsuji I (eds) Keitai in the 2000s: maturation of Japanese mobile society. University of Tokyo Press, pp 1–19

Matsuda M (forthcoming) Media usage and personal relationship. In: Tsuji I, Matsuda M, Asano T (eds) Glocalizekasuru wakamono sekai. Iwanami Shoten (in Japanese)

Matsumoto Y (1992) What does urbanism produce?: The innovation of urban theory. In: Morioka K, Matsumoto Y (eds) Toshishakaigaku no frontier 2: Seikatsu kankei bunka. Nihon Hyoronsha, pp 33–68 (in Japanese)
Matsumoto Y (2005) Urbanism and friendship: structuration of social networks in a metropolis. Japan Sociol Rev 56:147–164 (in Japanese)
Matsuyama-daigaku shakaichosa-shitsu (2006) Life and culture of youth (in Japanese)
Matsuyama-daigaku shakaichosa-shitsu (2010) Life and culture of youth (in Japanese)
Ministry of Internal Affairs and Communications (2017) WHITE PAPER 2017: Information and communications in Japan. http://www.soumu.go.jp/johotsusintokei/whitepaper/eng/WP2017/2017-index.html. Accessed on 18 Sept 2018
OECD (2016) PISA test. http://www.oecd.org/pisa/test/. Accessed on 18 Sept 2018
Otani S (2007) The sociology of "urbanism". Nineruva Shobo (in Japanese)
Rainie L, Wellman B (2012) Networked: the new social operating system. The MIT Press
Sakurai N (2017) ICT usage in school and well-being of students(in Japanese). In: National Institute for Educational Policy Research (ed) OECD Seito no Gakushu toutatsudo hosa PISA 2015 nen chosa kokusaikekka houkokusho seito no well-being. http://www.nier.go.jp/kokusai/pisa/pdf/pisa2015_20170419_report.pdf. Accessed on 18 Sept 2018
Suzuya N (2014) Why are you crazy about Pazudora?. Futabasha (in Japanese)
Tomita H (ed) (2016) The post-mobile society: from the smart/mobile to second offline. Routledge
Tsuji I (2016) The culture of local orientation among youth. In: Kawasaki K, Asano T (eds) "Wakamono" no yukai. Keiso Shobo, pp 147–176 (in Japanese)
Tsuji, I., Okura H., & Nomura, Y.(2017). How does Youth Culture Change in 25 Years (in Japanese). *Kiyo Shakaigaku/Shakaijohogaku*, *27*,107–137. Faculty of Letters, Chuo University
Yonaga R (2016) The birth, present and future of social game. Jyoho Shori 57:1106–1110 IPSJ (in Japanese)

**Misa Matsuda** is a professor at Chuo University in Tokyo, Japan. Her research focuses on media and society, particularly the impact of new technologies on everyday life. Her publications include co-edited collections about mobile communication: Personal, Portable, Pedestrian. (MIT Press, 2005). She is also interested in rumor and has published Uwasa toha nanika in Japanese (Chuko Shinsho, 2014). Her recent article "How to use twitter to make fan-friends through 'Ensei(fan tourism)'." (The Annual bulletin of the Institute of Social Sciences, Chuo University.23, 2019 in Japanese) focuses on media usage and interpersonal relationship on fan tourism.

# Media Literacy and Emerging Media in Education

**Eriko Uematsu**

**Abstract** After looking briefly at some concepts of media literacy in education, this paper sets out the results of research carried out between September 2016 and March 2017 into the use of emerging media in education in countries including Japan, Singapore, New Zealand, the UK, and Finland. The paper describes examples including use of AR (augmented reality), VR (virtual reality), fintech (financial technology), and apps in the classroom. Trends witnessed include internet use, integration of emerging media into lesson content, use of IT and data to direct individual learning via personalization, and BYOD (bring your own device). The paper concludes that emerging media is contributing to the rapid evolution of educational resources, systems, and teaching methods around the world, and that our ability to collect data means that it ought now to be possible to study, over time, the relationship between the use of emerging media in schools, and the formation of pupils' future careers. At the same time, use of emerging media in education is vital in order to foster children's media literacy in a relevant way that reflects how they will have to interact with and employ emerging media as part of their daily lives going forward.

## 1 Introduction

The aim of media literacy education is to raise children who understand the nature of media as well as how to use and interact with it. With the rise of digital media, digital media literacy is becoming more and more important. The proliferation of digital devices such as smart phones and tablets has brought huge changes to the environment in which children grow up. It is not uncommon for children to communicate using social media. This is highly convenient, enabling communication anywhere, anytime, and yet at the same time has led to examples of new kinds of bullying, as well as the posting of inappropriate content on Twitter, etc. It

E. Uematsu (✉)
Department of International Communication, Musashino Gakuin University, Saitama, Japan
e-mail: eriko.uematsu@u.musa.ac.jp



H. Tomita (ed.), *The Second Offline*, Advances in Information and Communication Research 3, https://doi.org/10.1007/978-981-16-2425-4_11

is thus vital that children be given a thorough grasp of this and other kinds of emerging and digital media, so that they can use them to their advantage, whilst understanding the potential risks.

Society has changed dramatically as a result of the advanced information and communication technologies enabled by information networks. The frameworks of this changing society are what support our education systems, with society and education involved in a relationship of mutual influence.

This paper will look at some concepts of media literacy, past and present, and then at the situation of media literacy education in Japan, and how, despite not being an official subject under the Japanese curriculum, emerging media is playing an ever-expanding role in education.

We will then go on to describe the results of research carried out between September 2016 and March 2017 into the current state of education in light of the progress of technology, focusing on emerging media and media literacy. Examples of teaching materials and methods from Singapore, New Zealand, the UK, and Scandinavia are used in an attempt to understand what forms media literacy takes, and whether use of the latest emerging media can be shown to have a synergistic effect on understanding.

The countries included in this study share a common characteristic, that is, regardless of any differences in the scale of each respective country or its educational system, they all offer advanced examples of the proactive application of ICT in education. Furthermore, these countries were included because their educational systems have responded to recent changes, including those in the current technological landscape, and to the growing expectation that students will need to learn a revised skillset throughout their education.

## 2 Concepts of Media Literacy

Originally, literacy referred to the ability to read and write. In recent years, however, the word "literacy" has been combined with various other concepts, including that of "media." In the 1960s, UNESCO proposed the idea of "functional literacy," defining the ability to read as important to be able to interact with society as an educated citizen. In 1997, Suzuki suggested as an example of functional literacy the need for citizens to be able to access and critically analyze and evaluate media in the context of society, and to devise various ways of communicating (Suzuki 1997).

Much has been written about children and media literacy. The Convention on the Rights of the Child, adopted by the United Nations in 1989, says that "The child shall have the right to freedom of expression; this right shall include freedom to seek, receive and impart information and ideas of all kinds, regardless of frontiers, either orally, in writing or in print, in the form of art, or through any other media of the child's choice" (OHCHR 1989). The Children's Charter on Electronic Media, drawn up at a global summit held in London, states that programs for children should be educational and interactive, and that children should be involved in their production (Von Feilitzen 1998).

The explosive spread of the internet from the 1990s onwards changed our view of media, and led to a dramatic overhaul in the concept of literacy in the twenty-first century. Children find themselves growing up in a vastly different media environment, complete with new types of media such as online games and e-books. This is when a definition of media literacy that includes the ability to use a variety of devices, networks, software, etc. to communicate began to gain traction, and media literacy began to evolve alongside media itself (Uematsu 2012).

Around the year 2000, a concept of media literacy emerged that divided media competencies into three levels: "ability to use" media devices and software, "ability to understand", which involves understanding and critically interpreting information, and "ability to express", where media are used to express the individual's thoughts and feelings (Mizukoshi 2002).

The first example of media literacy being incorporated into an educational curriculum came from Ontario in Canada in 1987, and since then different countries have incorporated it in various forms.

## 3 Media and Information Literacy (MIL) Curriculum for Teachers

The phrase "media and information literacy (MIL)" is now used internationally. MIL combines media literacy and information literacy, and was proposed by UNESCO. In an interview with the author, the manager of the United Nations MIL project, Jordi Trent, said that one element of MIL involves growing intercultural understanding interactively through the use of various media.

UNESCO has released an MIL curriculum for teachers (Wilson et al. 2011). As well as media, the curriculum refers to literacy of information, news, computers, the internet, digital, cinema, television, freedom of information and expression, libraries, advertising, and games (Fig. 1). It can be said that this diversity is reflective of the diversity of communication methods now available, as exemplified by the internet. The MIL curriculum speaks of the need to develop education and implement lessons featuring these new concepts.

The concept of MIL is founded on the global standard competency-based view of academic ability, and the PISA understanding of reading comprehension (OECD 2010). Under PISA, comprehension was formerly based on printed texts, but now includes digital texts accessed via computers and the internet. This change reflects the type of reading comprehension needed to handle a wide range of new phenomena, and represents key competencies required to solve a variety of real-world issues.

**Fig.1** Media and information literacy curriculum for teachers. *Source* Wilson et al. (2011)

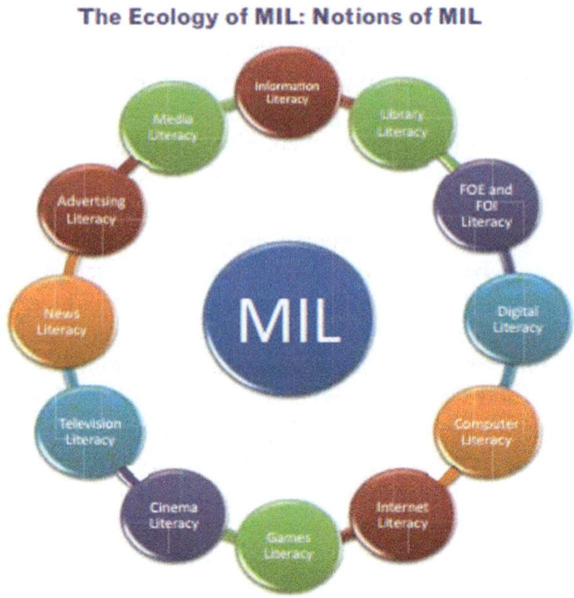


Since 2011, media have evolved even further, giving rise to a need for literacy to encompass such things as augmented reality (AR), virtual reality (VR), robotics, and artificial intelligence (AI).

## 4 Japan

With the rapid proliferation of mobile devices, more than 90% of senior high school students in Japan now own a mobile phone or a smartphone, and approximately 50% of junior high school students also own a mobile device (Benesse 2013). It is common to see junior high school students downloading applications onto their smartphones and participating in social gaming or online shopping. One in three junior high school students uses SNS (social networking services such as Facebook, Twitter, and other social media), and data show that at least 20% of all junior high school students have more online than offline friends. Interactions that were previously performed via short message service (SMS) on mobile phones have now been superseded by SNS. As a result of the frequent use of SNS, the way in which friends socialize is also changing (Uematsu 2014).

Developments in information and communication technology (ICT) have not only introduced new ways to communicate with friends but also led to new educational activities. For example, students may actively use SNS to exchange opinions with other students in adjoining classrooms or in another community before reflecting on the activity.[1] In addition, some lessons incorporate peer assessments[2] in which learners evaluate one another's work through sharing over the Internet. The work created during the activities included in these kinds of lessons can be saved in an e-portfolio.[3] Furthermore, in a so-called "flipped classroom" model, teachers publish videos for students to watch at home online before the class. This leaves the actual class time for answering questions. Lessons that have traditionally been held offline have changed a great deal through the use of the Internet.

### *4.1 Changes in the Use of Digital Media in Educational Settings in Japan*

Even before the widespread use of personal computers, paper textbooks and teaching materials were enhanced by radio and television educational programs and other multimedia educational materials, such as overhead projectors. Computer classrooms were established in schools as the Internet continued to grow in popularity. This is what is referred to as Phase one of the use of ICT in education since the emergence of the Internet.

Phase two refers to the ubiquitous phase, during which connection to the Internet became possible anytime and anywhere. Children started to own their own mobile phones, and some primary and junior high schools began to distribute electronic devices to all students. Learners were now able to view educational materials on their own devices at any time that suited them. The removal of constraints on time and place marked the start of a mobile learning society in which assigned tasks could be studied anytime and anywhere. Progressive educators who were able to foresee these changes began to recognize a variety of possibilities for the use of mobile devices in educational settings. This was the start of an innovative merger between education and technology known as Edtech.

Phase three represents a more evolved version of Phase two. In this phase, learning is impacted by a deepening of the mutual understanding among learners in response to their newfound ability to share their expressive activities via the Internet. Extracurricular activities, such as excursions to museums and historic sites, which traditionally occurred in offline spaces, are now enhanced by activities using mobile devices connected to the Internet. For example, learners can exchange

[1]Reflection on instruction is also used in teacher training. One such example involves teachers in Northern Europe watching videos and exchanging opinions about one another's lessons.

[2]Peer assessment refers to mutual evaluation. Until recently, learning outcomes were primarily produced on paper; therefore, teacher evaluations and self-evaluations were the main modes of evaluation. However, the ability to share work digitally now allows learners to evaluate one another's learning outcomes.

[3]An e-Portfolio is a record of learning that is saved and organized in the form of files (photographs, documents) or a blog; it can assist with the verification of learning and ability.

opinions about the "space", share their virtual experiences, and participate in learning activities together. This type of learning represents a departure from conventional notebook- and pencil-centred lessons. Other examples of this phase include textbooks that incorporate augmented reality (AR) technology, hands-on learning using 3D technology, and image recognition using QR codes to display certain images on the student's own device. Furthermore, flipped classrooms, open education, and opinion sharing through SNS represent new learning activities that transcend the classroom.

## *4.2 Use of AR in Japanese Education*

AR is being incorporated into lesson practice in Japan. The use of AR is creating a new sense of place by adding virtual content, which is created on computers using virtual reality (VR) technology, to real spaces, thereby creating a "virtual-real space". At the same time that the AR of Hatsune Miku was a hot topic in Japan in 2007, small steps were also being taken to apply AR to education through hands-on activities.

An example of the use of AR is a location-based service in which location is confirmed using GPS or Wi-Fi. This type of AR would, for example, allow students visiting a historic site on a school trip to use their smartphones to trace the locations displayed on ancient maps. Learners would be able to efficiently check for information related to historical content at museums or resource centres as well as exchange opinions with other learners who have visited the same site. Learners could also connect with experts in the subject. An example of this kind of application is provided by ATR (http://atr-c.jp/burari/).

Image recognition is another type of AR in which QR codes and images are used to display specific content. When these codes appear in books, they can be used to display 3D computer graphics, enabling experiential learning. These kinds of AR applications, which allow learners to gain hands-on experience, access information with QR codes, and have experiences that "upgrade" their ideas, are creating new learning spaces not previously encountered in conventional learning settings.

In Japan, some secondary schools are already using textbooks containing AR features (Tokyo Shoseki 2017). If students install an application that links their paper textbook to these AR features, they can view related content simply by holding the corresponding page up to their iPad or iPhone and scanning the code. The type of content that pops up on screen can include items such as videos of science experiments, geometrical shapes (e.g. regular polyhedrons), and animations of quadratic functions. Connecting textbook illustrations and photographs with CG animation and videos allows students to view three-dimensional rotating images, which helps them understand the concepts being taught. Students can also view stars in the solar system in 3D or create a model, which they can hold in their own hands, using a 3D printer.

### *4.3 The Concept of Media Literacy in Japanese Education*

All of the above examples require children to acquire varying degrees of media literacy. Nevertheless, media literacy education as such is by no means universally implemented in Japan. In Japan, education that centres on the use of devices such as computers occurs under the subject headings of information technology, general studies, or technology. Education involving visual media, on the other hand, takes place in diverse forms and across a number of subjects, including audio-visual education, information technology, general studies, and Japanese language. We have seen above examples of emerging media incorporated into different subject lessons. However, since media literacy is not implemented systematically, but rather largely at the discretion of the individual teacher, the reality is that schools vary greatly. This variance is linked to the problems facing media literacy education in Japan.

The main problem is that despite the fact that conventional reading comprehension alone does not equip students with the skills needed to embrace the twenty-first century, the Japanese education system does not stipulate under which subject media literacy should be taught. Furthermore, despite the advanced examples given above, these are by no means universal, and the fact that many schools either ban mobile phones on school premises or prohibit their use in class demonstrates a resistance by some schools to confronting emerging media.

There is a sense in which media literacy does not fit into the traditional teacher-centric teaching method. It requires collaborative learning methods, and yet the means by which to assess collaborative learning in Japanese schools are not yet formally established. While some schools do implement rubrics for assessment, elsewhere the criteria are deemed too ambiguous, whilst some do not believe that media literacy needs to be assessed at all.

Further, whereas media literacy education calls for critical thinking, the specific Japanese word used to translate the concept of "critical" has negative connotations, increasing reluctance to teach it. The fact that, of course, "criticism" here has the meaning of analysis, rather than disapproval, appears to get lost in translation.

## 5 Singapore

### *5.1 Use of VR and AR at ITE*

The Institute of Technical Education (ITE), Singapore, is a public institution of secondary education established in 1992. It functions as a kind of vocational training college, teaching applied sciences, business and service, design and media, electronics and IT, engineering, hospitality, etc.

Use of virtual reality (VR) and augmented reality (AR) in lessons is common at ITE. Several classrooms have VR spaces that allow learners to experience a variety of activities without leaving the classroom. One lesson observed was for would-be wedding planners. Students were able not just to imagine where they would situate chairs and flowers for a beach wedding, but to actually visualize the set-up using VR. VR was also used to experience work on a building site, thus avoiding exposing students to the multiple dangers of a real building site.

In the lessons observed that made use of AR, the technology was used to simulate the effect of drag on aeroplane components. Teachers explained that AR now forms a vital part of their lessons, which they can no longer imagine teaching without. Aeroplane components are precision instruments, and one small mistake in their adjustment can lead to fatal consequences. Although students often have access to actual aeroplane fuselages in their lessons, they can also experiment risk-free, using their tablets alongside AR and VR-compatible components.

# 6 New Zealand

## *6.1 Fintech in Primary Education*

The New Zealand example shows how fintech (financial technology) is being used in primary schools to teach about finance. In public primary schools in New Zealand, lessons on finance form part of the formal curriculum. The fintech tool used in this example is called Banqer (https://www.banqer.co/), and consists of a virtual space, created specifically for schools, where learners can experience online banking in a number of creative ways.

Banqer uses a virtual currency called Banqer dollars. "Money" passes electronically between teachers and pupils and between pupils. For example, pupils might have a basic weekly income of 500 dollars, with the opportunity to earn an additional 200 for picking up litter in the classroom, helping out around the school, or coming top in a spelling test, with the amount and qualifying criteria being set by the teacher. Teachers may also stipulate fines for lateness etc.

Further capabilities enable students to experience loans, interest, rent, and tax in a virtual environment. The teacher sets a rate of interest to be paid on learners' virtual savings accounts each week, and pupils can apply to their teacher for a loan which they can choose to accept or reject. Pupils can decide to buy a virtual property which they can then rent out, paying 40% of the rent they receive towards capital repayments on their virtual mortgage.

Jolene Buston, year 6 and 7 teacher at Churton Park School, New Zealand, related how pupils are motivated to acquire a wide range of financial skills and competencies. She explained that some pupils have tried to set up an actual bank account, and are clearly taking an interest in asset management. She described Banqer as helping to build financial literacy and knowledge that will benefit their future careers.

### 6.2 Careers Education

Technology is also used for age-appropriate careers education. Students create CVs and apply for jobs from a list provided by the teacher. From the second year of primary school, pupils learn about job-hunting through virtual experiences. Studies have shown that this leads to increased motivation. By participating in active learning, pupils are acquiring life skills and increasing their financial understanding in a way that will stand them in good stead for the rest of their lives.

## 7 The UK

In 2014, the English curriculum replaced ICT with a new subject: Computing. Computing consists of three elements: computer science, information technology, and digital literacy. As well as evolving education in line with the changing times, there was also a desire to nurture world-leading talent, and the curriculum created to do this also sets out to make use of the latest technology, including emerging media.

Organizations such as Digital Schoolhouse provide primary school teachers with much-needed support, connecting them with local secondary schools where they can take their younger pupils to participate in computing workshops. They also provide teaching materials, lesson plans, and a network of like-minded teachers for mutual support.

At a visit to Townley Grammar School in England, computing lessons for both 11–12 and 16–18-year olds were observed. Pupils had access to a computer each, and lessons were pupil-driven, with individuals using the Internet to solve problems set by the teacher.

## 8 Finland

In Finland, media education was incorporated into Finnish language lessons in the primary curriculum in the early 1970s. One notable method of teaching used in Finland is to have children from the lower year groups upwards come up with a story using a method similar to mind mapping, then create their own picture book to be published online.

### 8.1 Tablets and Apps

Programming has been a compulsory subject in Finnish primary schools since 2016. A pre-curriculum was introduced in 2014, which saw the start of project-based-cross-curricular learning. Schools also make use of a school website and administration system accessible from smart phones (Wilma 2017). In all the schools visited, there was significant cross-over between subjects.

At Olarin Koulu Ja Lukio secondary school, a variety of subject lessons were observed. As all high school final exams are sat on a computer screen, it is important that students use computers in class from the first year of school. Even in lessons such as philosophy and ethics, iPads are used to exchange opinions, with programming featuring in lessons across a range of subjects. In a religious education class, for example, the teacher brought an element of programming into the lesson by getting students to create software for the exchange of opinions. This saved time and repetition in class by allowing students to respond to questions, and the teacher to view their answers, simultaneously, and was particularly helpful for sharing the results of group work within the class.

### *8.2 Teacher Training via MOOC*

At Olarin secondary school, teacher training in programming takes place via MOOC (Massive Open Online Course). Professor Lauri Malmi of Aalto University's computer science faculty explained that the MOOC was set up by Aalto and Helsinki Universities. Many of the courses provided consist of 10 sessions, and teachers can watch them any time they like, though many choose to view one session a week. Some watch at school after-hours, while others study at home before discussing what they have learnt with their colleagues in a flipped classroom style of learning.

## 9 Sweden

In Sweden, media education has been compulsory since 1980, and is now taught as part of Swedish language lessons in primary and secondary education. Lessons look at things like media content creation, using media, and the responsibilities that come with media activity, and focus on the acquisition of skills such as thinking critically about information gathered and considering the ethical and aesthetic value of content. The Swedish Educational Broadcasting Company produces teaching materials for media education. Some local authorities fund audio-visual centres where film and video education is carried out. Non-profit organizations frequently hold seminars for teachers, and media education is intended to be relevant to real life.

In both Finland and Sweden, educational apps have long been used in lessons from the lower years of primary school upwards, and many schools operate a BYOD (bring your own device) policy.

**Fig. 2** Pupils at Jindalee State School on the outskirts of Brisbane in Queensland, Australia, bring their own devices to school to access the Internet and make use of digital teaching materials (August 2014)

## 10 Australia

In Queensland, Australia, children are taught to make use of technology from the lower years of primary school. Even in nursery school, in the year before entering primary, some classes make use of tablet devices. Some schools operate a BYOD policy (Fig. 2). Using the Internet becomes normal practice, and the curriculum requires children to use email from the second year of school. Classes are not necessarily restricted to a single subject, but can feature a combination of subjects. Unlike media literacy education that focuses purely on traditional media, these classes emphasize the acquisition of literacy that is closer to home and relevant to our times.

## 11 Conclusion

The written word is no longer the only means of acquiring information, and this is being reflected in the changing definition of literacy and the way it is reflected in education and learning around the world. Merely being able to operate a computer and to use word processing and spreadsheet software, or to find information on the Internet, is not literacy. The new form of literacy involves knowing how to obtain information, how to use that information creatively, and how to apply it to one's own life, and involves familiarizing children with a wide range of digital and emerging media that play an increasing role in daily life.

All of the schools visited during this survey used the Internet on a daily basis. In England, the aim was not just to make use of the latest technology, but to improve the curriculum by actively integrating an understanding of IT into lesson content. In

Finland, pupils and teachers made active use of emerging media to direct their own learning, with every class in every subject making use of tablets, teacher training being carried out via MOOC, and pupils making use of educational apps to learn creatively. In a lot of cases, the teaching method employed was that of bring your own device (BYOD), where pupils bring in their own device from home on which to access the Internet. Examples of the BYOD method are seen around the world.

Meanwhile, in many countries, the technical ability to upload personal data onto the cloud and to personalize learning to suit the individual allows for flexible styles of learning that can be changed to suit the learner and the needs of the time. We witnessed examples of classes using virtual currency, VR, and AR to show the relevance of lesson content to future careers and to allow students to experience the outside world without leaving the classroom. In some schools that make use of terminals in class, every lesson features active learning, and collaborative learning is used on a daily basis.

It would appear that this use of emerging media along with the latest teaching methods in schools is what has, in some cases, given children of secondary-school age the ability to trade shares, and even to start up their own venture companies. Our ability to collect data means that it ought now be possible to study, over time, the relationship between use of virtual currencies, VR, and AR in class, and the formation of pupils' future careers. In fact, such studies have already begun in some countries. Around the world, emerging media is one of the factors contributing to the rapid evolution of educational resources, systems, and teaching methods as we progress towards a super-smart IOT society. At the same time, use of emerging media in education is vital in order to foster children's media literacy in a relevant way that reflects how they will have to interact with and employ emerging media as part of their daily lives going forward.

## References


Benesse (2013) Mobile phone usage survey—number one. Retrieved 25 Aug 2017. from http://berd.benesse.jp/berd/data/dataclip/clip0001/index.html (in Japanese)

Mizukoshi S (2002) Digital media society. Iwanami, Japan (in Japanese)

OECD (2010). OECD Programme for international student assessment. Retrieved 26 Aug 2017, from https://www.nier.go.jp/kokusai/pisa/index.html (in Japanese)

Office of the High Commissioner for Human Rights (1989) Convention on the rights of the child. Retrieved 26 Aug 2017, from https://www.ohchr.org/en/professionalinterest/pages/crc.aspx

Suzuki M (ed) (1997) For people studying media literacy. Sekaishisōsha, Japan (in Japanese)

Tokyo Shoseki (2017) Introduction to AR in textbooks. Retrieved 26 Aug 2017, from https://ten.tokyo-shoseki.co.jp/text/hs1/math/book001/level5/index.htm (in Japanese)

Uematsu E (2012) Concepts of media literacy. In: Okada T, Matsuda M (eds) Mobile society theory. Yuhikaku, Japan, pp 135–136 (in Japanese)

Uematsu E (ed) (2014) Survey of smart device use among young people. Broadband Association (in Japanese)

Von Feilitzen C (1998) The second world summit on television for children. News Child Violence Screen 2(1):10–11. Retrieved 26 Aug 2017, from https://www.nordicom.gu.se/sites/default/files/specialthemes-pdf/NL_1_1998.pdf

Wilma (2017) Website of Wilma school management program. Retrieved 26 Aug 2017, from https://wilma.edu.hel.fi

Wilson C, Grizzle A, Tuazon R, Akyempong K, Cheung C-K (2011) Media and information literacy curriculum for teachers. UNESCO

**Eriko Uematsu** is an Associate Professor at Musashinogakuin University. Her research efforts and implementation of media literacy in education stem from her experience teaching at the junior- and senior-high school levels. Dr Uematsu obtained a PhD degree in Education from Niigata University and lectures there on a part-time basis. She is a research fellow at the Graduate School of Modern Society and a visiting research fellow at the International University of Japan (GLOCOM). Dr Uematsu's goal is to construct a new form of education that is in sync with today's continually evolving information-oriented society and makes best use of new technologies. Publications: ICT Education in Media Literacy Education, Eriko Uematsu, The Journal of Information Processing Society of Japan, pp. 322–326, 2015.

# The Bodily Mode of the *Selfie*

**Kyoung-hwa Yonnie Kim**

**Abstract** This article focuses on the corporeality of mobile photography from a historical exploration of vernacular photography, and discusses the bodily mode of the *selfie*. *The Hidden Mother* (2013), a book collection of old daguerreotype portraits, is the historical reference for excavating the forgotten relationship between the photographer's body and the camera. The specific mode of the *selfie* is juxtaposed as a contemporary example to show how the bodily mode of photographic practices has changed and how the physical distance between the photographer and the photographed is dissolved and converged into a single unit of creative practice. It suggests that the corporeality of the practice could be a relevant aspect for understanding the changeovers brought about by mobile technology from the subject's viewpoint. The possibility of the outbreak of a second offline situation in everyday life will also be mentioned.

## 1 Introduction

McLuhan's (1964) notion of "media as the extensions of man" suggests that the emergence of electronic technologies would not only affect the nature of our social information but also have created a new condition for perceiving and understanding the world around us. This idea implies that the changes brought about by media technologies would be comprehensive and more inclusive rather than being possibly calculated just in the dimension of social interactions; it rather notes that they are necessarily to be probed also as ways of the transition of human conditions and the corporeal relationship with the outer world. The second offline concept (Tomita 2016) basically refers to the effect of advances in mobile technologies on the reshaping of modes of social information and the generation of a hybrid reality that crosses the physical and virtual worlds. This article is an attempt to advance the concept from the perspective of user's body and the corporeal relationship mediated

K. Y. Kim (✉)
Department of International Communication, Kanda University of International Studies, Chiba, Japan



H. Tomita (ed.), *The Second Offline*, Advances in Information and Communication Research 3, https://doi.org/10.1007/978-981-16-2425-4_12

by digital technologies, as the examination of its bodily aspect could contribute to a better understanding of the second offline from the subject's viewpoint.

The focus will be on the *selfie* as a unique cultural mode of mobile photography; herein, I will describe the changeover of the bodily mode of the practice of photo-taking in relation to the rise of mobile photography, and explore the physical aspect of those visual practices. Mobile photography, as one of the most conspicuous phenomena brought about by the advent of smartphones, has so far received quite lot of attention both socially and academically. Many discussions have focused on the social role of mobile visuality, facilitating and communicating with visual images, as well as managing virtual identities in social networks (e.g., Van House et al. 2005, 2011; Van Djick 2007, 2013). Debates regarding the *selfie* phenomenon have also tended to focus on its social implication as the self-documentations of everyday lives and self-observational practices in social networks (e.g., Mota 2016; Jurgenson 2019). However, here, I would rather concentrate on the bodily mode of these narcissistic practices, and discuss the corporeality of mobile digital photography in line with the materiality of technologies. By doing so, I will address an unspoken aspect of the changes associated with the second offline situation: the human's body under a new technological juncture.

## 2 A Hidden Aspect: Body-Technology Relations of Photography

### *2.1 The Rise of Mobile Vernacular Photography*

Regarding the authentic account of photography's history, Batchen (2003) noted that the ordinary use of the camera to portray everyday life, common family rituals, and neighborhood activities had been constantly neglected. While professional or journalistic photographs had been praised for their artistic presentations and social messages—typically displayed and recalled at museums and galleries—vernacular photographs (although such examples outnumber those involving so-called historical photography) have long been isolated from these areas and have, therefore, not received historical acclaim.

Since the snapshot camera was introduced at the end of the nineteenth century, vernacular photography has continually expanded the boundaries of photographic practices to document, archive, and memorialize daily social activities, (e.g., as ceremonies, family events, tourism). As Sontag (1977) noted photography became a symbolic ritual for ascertaining and upholding crumbling interpersonal relations and social bonds. In the 1970s, the snapshot camera had already become popular for hobbies and merchandising among the American public; prices had decreased, thus facilitating middle-class affordability and possession of the device as a household item. The film industry was also growing rapidly at that time, and town shops were often equipped to develop negative film into printed photos. As mass consumer society continuously encouraged members of the middle class for their artistic tastes and aesthetic hobbies, the practical spread of vernacular photography could be read as the rise of "middle-brow art" (Bourdier 1965) in which ordinary people pursued their aesthetic desires through artistic hobbies and mass consumption. Despite Batchen's scholarly concern about the biased historical narrative, vernacular photography always had a value of its own.

Since the rise of the smartphone, the emergence of the mobile camera in association with wireless networks has again created the opportunity for fundamental changes in photographic practices in everyday life. The smartphone has enabled people to take digital snapshots anywhere and on every occasion; consequently, taking photos has become the most common practice globally. Equipped with the ubiquitous accessibility to the Internet, the smartphone also enables people to transmit digital images into networked virtual spaces, dramatically facilitating sharing and circulating activities as well as public communications regarding photos. The entire process, from shooting to editing, printing (i.e., developing in a traditional form), storing, sharing, and discussing, is simplified and integrated into a single portable device. Only requirements are a smartphone and wireless accessibility.

Incalculable visual snapshots of all sorts of objects, such as celebrities, ordinary people, nature, food, flowers, and households, are uploaded by global participants for availability across vast network locations. The plethora of digital images on virtual networks has transformed the social mode of photography from a fixed position of being gazed at to a dynamic visual artefact that can be shared and repeatedly discussed. The overwhelming amount of vernacular photography in social networks has also changed our involvement with the outer world not only in terms of digital visuality, but also in terms of real-world creativity. As Lee (2010) described and argued, people are actively synchronizing digital images with real-world experiences, creating a hybridization of physical and digital visuality.

Traditional arguments about vernacular photography have focused on the amateurism of the subject in terms of plain aesthetic tastes and cherished cultural meanings. However, given the new circumstances, a different approach may be required to examine vernacular photography. Gómez Cruz and Lehmuskallio (2016) were correct in suggesting "practice-based approaches" for studying digital photography and adding the framework of materiality as a critical aspect for understanding a contemporary photographic practice. As I mentioned elsewhere (Kim 2020), the habituation and routinization of photography has seldom earned critical examination, despite its ramifications. The seamless availability of technology has made the practice of digital photography an unexciting routine, thus making casual desires or habitual obligations direct motivations for moving forward with photography. Now, it is quite common for people to carry hundreds or thousands of photographic images in their mobile devices—a result of the smartphone's feature that enables the addition of photos in quick succession.

Though repetitive and habitual moments are portals to the motivation for photographic creation, the associated banality and mundaneness may be keywords for understanding actual motivations for creative practice. Common and casual moments, such as everyday dinners, casual gatherings, atmospheric and uplifting parties, or encounters with worn-out visual clichés, call for the social ritual of turning on the camera application of one's smartphone. How can we approach this practical context of vernacular photography that has increasingly extended its social and cultural boundaries alongside mobile technologies (specifically, the smartphone) and the ubiquitous existence of networks? As an interface closely associated with the material feature of mobile media, the corporeality is regarded in this chapter as a pivot for grasping this aspect. Beginning in the next section, I will draw upon a historical example of the daguerreotype (an old camera prototype) as a guideline for delineating the corporeality in line with visual practices. I will also relay crucial points for understanding the bodily mode of mobile photography, which will not only contribute to the social circumstances associated with the practice but also frame the physical arrangement.

## *2.2* The Hidden Mother *and Daguerreotypes*

*The Hidden Mother* is a book collection of old photographs published by Italian photographer Nagler (2013). The book was central to her installation titled *The Hidden Mother,* wherein hundreds of old and anonymous daguerreotype portraits were presented. The portraits were extraordinary because they repeatedly showed bizarre images of children sitting in the laps of veiled figures (Photo 1). Although the main objects of the photographs are children—situated in the center of each picture—the shrouded figures behind them are more likely to attract attention because of the grotesque atmosphere. Although Nagler revealed that the lurking figures were the mothers of photographed children, curiosity still remains. Why did these mothers hold their children in such strange ways? What made these mothers hide themselves behind dark veils, thus effacing themselves from the pictures?

Since their first introduction in New York in 1840, by the 1850s, more than 100 daguerreotype studios had appeared there; further, several hundred were reportedly in Paris. City workers were ready to open their wallets to visit these studios, which purportedly charged one week's pay per production. Although not cheap, it was an acceptable price for the luxury of preserving family memories. Making a daguerreotype portrait of a loved one remained a popular practice among urban residents until the early twentieth century. The film camera made its debut in professional productions (e.g., cinemas), and Kodak introduced the first snapshot camera in 1883. However, it took several decades for the snapshot camera to become a popular consumer item. Daguerreotype studios instead enjoyed prosperity during this transition. As a matter of fact, the daguerreotype photographs presented in *The Hidden Mother* date back to the late nineteenth and early twentieth centuries.

Batchen, who wrote an expository commentary for this collection (Nagler 2013, p. 4), rationalized the strange postures as corresponding to a technological issue regarding the daguerreotype, an early antecedent to the film camera. Although the daguerreotype was renowned for creating realistic, sharp, and clear images, it was

**Photo 1** Daguerreotype portraits in a book collection titled *The Hidden Mother*

deficient in that it required a comparatively long exposure time (a few minutes for the earliest model and several seconds for the most recent). Thus, the subject had to remain still for minutes while the device was plating a stable image on a photosensitive board; otherwise, the resulting photograph would be blurred or not clearly identifiable.

Yet, the longer exposure time then was by no means a critical weakness. In the late nineteenth century, the daguerreotype studio was a new business that competed with painters who produced celebrities' portraits by hand. Hand-painted portraits normally required days or weeks for painters to complete; even then, poor likenesses were sometimes the result. By comparison, the daguerreotype could create clear and exact images of objects in just a few minutes. Although many contemporaries might have seen it as a flaw, the exposure time for the daguerreotype was short compared to painters' handwork—a key advantage for daguerreotype studios, which attracted visitors in towns where they were situated.

Nevertheless, the exposure time might have become a particular problem when taking photos of children, who were less likely to remain in uncomfortable positions. Mothers tried to solve this problem by sitting behind their toddlers, whom they held and supported during the necessary exposure time. Hence, children were able to participate in the creation of memorable pictures; with the help of their mothers, they remained still in front of the daguerreotype during the promised exposure time.

There is no clear ground for explaining why the pictured mothers chose not to reveal their figures in the portraits resulting in a bizarre sort of posture. However, from the fact that similar photographic images existed in large quantities, it is presumable that the setting was generally accepted for children's daguerreotype portraits. Batchen (ibid) suggested that high infant mortality rates might be the background for this abstruseness. As posthumous child portraits were common at that time, mothers might have tried to hide themselves behind cloth as a signal that the pictured children were still alive.

In any case, it seemed clear that the daguerreotype's specification influenced the object's physical condition and extraordinary posture as a result; The strange arrangement was made wherein veiled mothers would support their children behind a scene. The bizarre daguerreotype images in *The Hidden Mother* enlighten us to the fact that photography was not only just a visual presentation but also the result of bodily practice and a corporeal relationship with a tool. Creating daguerreotype images of children could not be completed only by the photographer. Instead, the tripartite cooperation between the daguerreotype technician, child (subject), and the child's mother (who supported the child's body from behind the veil) made the production of a single photograph possible.

## 2.3 Body-Technology Relations

Extraordinary photographs in *The Hidden Mother* invite us to look behind the scene; A relationship between the apparatus (the daguerreotype) and human bodies (of the daguerreotype technician, children, and mothers) that tactically cooperated to create photographic images. It suggests that the relationship between the photographer's body and that of the photographed might be unstable, against the robust images of photography produced in the era of film cameras. Thus, this particular historical case opens a way for us to understand the nature of relations between the camera and human bodies, which had remained invisible and taken the self-evident position throughout photography's history, from a different view point: Body-technology relations.

Diverse frames have hitherto been applied to understand bodily practices as social and cultural artefacts. For example, Mauss (1968) explained techniques of the body as institutional outputs built from social education and cultural habits. For Goffman (1963), communication was a better model for demonstrating the delivery of social messages and symbols with nonverbal performances (e.g., gestures, bodily moves, and facial expressions). Yet, our bodies in the era of mobile technology are not always translated within those socio-communication frames. Bodily activities nowadays tend to be directly connected to the use of technological gadgets, as we carry personal computers, mobile media devices, and other mechanical items throughout the day. We need to properly use these devices to communicate, socialize, remain productive, and even survive. In the contemporary era, our bodily modes tend to lay stress on how to involve technological devices.

In this context, Richardson and Wilken (2012) apparently suggests "body technology relations" as a pertinent framework for describing bodily performance in the digital world. They defined the concept as our corporeal schema, which is "under continuous modification by artifacts, tools, techniques, and more complex technological ensembles, which are always already embedded in a palimpsest of cultural milieus and collective habits" (p. 182). Their approach partly coincides with the concept of "affordances" (Gibson 1979) in that it describes the interface between individuals and their external environment. However, while emphasizing the subject's intention and practical control over the apparatus, this concept more directly applies to the concept of media practices in cultural studies.

# 3 The Corporeality of Mobile Photography

## *3.1 The Practical Changeover of Photography*

Nowadays, people take photos with smartphones rather than with cameras. Certainly, this is a change in the engaging mode of the photographer's body—from pressing the shutter of the camera to touching the screen of a versatile mobile device. Yet, it still seems a trivial changeover compared with the dramatic transition from the daguerreotype to the handheld film camera in the early twentieth century. The advent of the snapshot camera, which introduced the use of film instead of silver plates, emancipated photography from a designated location (i.e., daguerreotype studio), and the treatment of a technician (daguerreotypist). It not only streamlined the process of creating and duplicating a photo but also changed the social and physical mode of the photographic practice. A purchasing event accompanied by a visit to a daguerreotype studio was transformed into an independent and creative practice by lay people. The labor involved in going to a studio and paying a daguerreotypist to take a picture was eliminated and the way was opened for the autonomous practice involving a handheld camera of one's own.

When Barthes (1980) related photography to the metaphor of a *camera lucida* counterposed to the traditional and historical reference of a *camera obscura* (meaning "dark chamber"), he attempted to interpret and relocate photography as similar to the "eye." Different from the *camera obscura*—a closed and darkroom-like apparatus considered a forerunner of the camera—the *camera lucida* was a light optical device that helped painters reproduce visual objects. While the metaphor of the *camera obscura* implicates the optical procedure for duplicating the visual and producing photographic images, the *camera lucida* describes the subject's experience of capturing the vision and creating a photograph. In this regard, a transition from daguerreotype to the snapshot camera literally brought about the practical changeover of practice of creating photography from the spatial mode of a "room" (i.e., the daguerreotype studio) to the visual mode (i.e., the eye), combining the sense of capturing and gazing into the single unit of an apparatus (snapshot camera) and a practice of using it.

In terms of the transformation of the bodily mode, the rise of camera-embedded mobile phones was less impressive rectification than the transition from daguerreotype, as both the snapshot camera and the smartphone were portable, independent, and individual items for personal use. Thus, the migration from the snapshot camera to camera-embedded mobile media was comparatively smooth, as the two devices did not generate significant differences in terms of the body practice. As Manovich (2002) defined digitization as a revolutionary shift in replacing continuous analog information into numerically represented data, the transformation from analog to digital photography was a significant technological progress. However, separate from a radical alteration at the technological level, user experiences of creating photographs have rather maintained similarities.

Although vision is undoubtably a core sense in photography, the history of photography, in turn, suggests that its corporeality cannot be fully explained with the metaphors of vision and visuality. Bizarre images in *The Hidden Mother* help to generate an understanding regarding the relationship, wherein a visual apparatus, a photographer's body, and the bodies of those photographed would engage together and exquisitely collaborate to replicate images and to produce a photo. Thus, the practice of photography would not be just about the adaptation to individual devices for appropriate use, but also about the relocation of bodies and material conditions under certain physical and social circumstances. Beginning with the next section, I will move onto the *selfie* to exemplify a new corporeality of vernacular photography in the era of mobile media.

## 3.2 *The Bodily Mode of* Selfie*: Gazing at Oneself*

Despite the tendency to connect the expansion of mobile photography with the uplifting use of smartphones across the globe (Palmer 2012), in countries such as Japan and South Korea (leading adopters of mobile technology), mobile photography has already become a usual practice in the second-generation mobile phone era. Since the smartphone gained global popularity nearly a decade later, a narcissistic photo taken by oneself has made frequent appearances in virtual networks, resulting in the newly coined word "*selfie.*" In South Korea, the colloquial word *selka* (a combination of "self" and "camera," referring to the practice of self-photography using a mobile phone) was widely used among younger generations at the beginning of the 2000s, suggesting that it had become a common media practice before the introduction of the iPhone or SNS-based technologies, such as Twitter and Facebook.

The history of self-portrait photography is relatively long, having been reported since the daguerreotype era. The narcissistic portrait started to be perceived as an independent photographic genre in the early film camera era (Rawlings 2013). Thus, the rise of the *selfie* was considered as the remediation (Bolter and Grusin

1999) of existing practices. Previous literature tended to highlight its newness in relation to social networks with the plethora of mobile photographs and visual identification. For example, Mota (2016) predicted that the *selfie* would be the most popular type of self-representation in social networks, such as Instagram, whereby many women would practice and engage with microcelebrity and self-branding in the global media landscape. For Jurgenson (2019), the *selfie* is paradigmatic and the most notorious type of social photography, devoted to the ongoing process of identity construction that had become conspicuous with the emergence of mobile photography.

In these discussions regarding the *selfie* so far, the importance of visuality has dominated. However, because the self-portrait is far from new in the history of photography, the role of the smartphone deserves more acknowledgement as a powerful catalyst responsible for the overwhelming presence of the *selfie* in social networks. Different from precedent genres of the self-portrait representing a photographer's narcissism, the nature of the *selfie* significantly concerns the material features of the smartphone as a mundane portable device. Serving as a one-stop center for visual creation not only for capturing and editing photographs but also for circulating them via virtual networks and discussions, the smartphone ushered in a myriad of photographic creations. The possibility of sharing images with viewers with the expectation of receiving immediate reactions is an obvious influence in this dynamic context, diversifying and enriching the actual motivations behind mobile digital photography, including the *selfie*.

The peculiarity of the *selfie* lies in the bodily mode of using a camera for oneself and the unique photographic composition resulting from the body's position. In the *selfie,* the physical arrangement between the photographer and the photographed, as previously mentioned in the case of *The Hidden Mother,* matters in a different way. The bilateral structure between the subject of an object dissolves and converges into a single unit. The subject stretches her/his arm as far as possible to secure a focusable distance. Yet, because of the limited length of the arm, the object is usually close to the lens, causing the subject's face to be captured up close with other objects in the background. Experienced practitioners of the Internet offer extensive advice on how to take better *selfies*, usually addressing how to pose one's body. For instance, many recommend positioning the mobile camera 45° at an upward angle from the face to obtain a cool and slimming perspective. Many *selfie* takers follow this advice, thereby explaining similar visual presentations in most *selfie* portraits.

Thus, the *selfie*'s extraordinary expression comes from the specific bodily arrangement of the subject taking the picture of herself/himself and relying on her/his body. The composition resulting from this body position (despite being far from the assessment of aesthetically balanced photography in a conventional term) is generally being accepted and recognized as emblematic for the *selfie* genre regardless cultures and regions. Just as we perceive daguerreotype photographs of *The Hidden Mother* as an odd phenomenon in the history of photography, a future generation may gossip about the burlesque posture characteristic of the *selfie* as a dominating genre of the former smartphone era.

Although taking a *selfie* tends to be imagined as a lonely practice, many performers would refuse this proposition since many *selfie* photographs contain multiple objects (Photo 2). In fact, the social meaning of the *selfie* lies in the subject's involvement with the collectivity, both physically and virtually. The *selfie* is not just about *gazing at oneself*; it is also about *justifying the self-gaze* as a social means of seeing and archiving. For either case, the bodily dimension may be the most essential aspect of the practice.

The growing use of the *selfie stick*—a popular aid for taking the *selfie*—depict how the bodily dimension of the practice has actually intervened and reframed the social norm in public places. Although the *selfie stick* is widely utilized by tourists and weekenders, their favorite visiting sites—such as public landmarks and theme parks—started to ban its use by law for security and safety reasons. Although not so

**Photo 2** A *selfie* shot of several people, illustrating a typical composition of the genre wherein the photographer's face is situated up close (in the corner)

outspoken, some people sometimes consider the practice of taking the *selfie* as unpleasant and uncomfortable. This, in turn, implies that the corporeality of the *selfie* is crucial for the social contexts of physical places. Though such opposition to the *selfie* may be derived from concerns about privacy invasion or hostility toward the ubiquity of the practice, it is be notable that opposition is also the result of a sense of alienation,i.e., a person who physically exists in a given location is more involved in a virtual space and thus socially camouflaged (Tomita 2006). Both human bodies and physical spaces are mutually connected in this way and together consist of the material reality of a place. By focusing on the bodily dimension of the *selfie*, we begin to understand how mobile technology and its seamless usage can transform the social meaning of place.

## 4 Conclusion: Further Implications

In this article, I have discussed two contrasting examples of vernacular photography —from the history of the early camera (daguerreotype) and from the latest trend (the *selfie*). Though both examples present interesting insight into the historical trajectory of vernacular photography, my intention is to demonstrate how technological and material features of devices intervene with the rearrangement of the body during its use, and, in turn, how the human body works as a dynamic assignee to seek and find affordable conditions for technology that are relevant to photography.

Mobile photography, in particular, is worthwhile to note in this context because digital photos may be the most prominent media for building connections between online and offline communities in everyday lives. Locations where crowd-pleasing events take place—festival sites, live concert venues, or even targets attacked by terrorists—spontaneously receive many reactions from mobile photographers and are replicated with numerous photos uploaded onto social networks. As Shanks and Svabo (2014) notes, mobile photography is about a spatial engagement by which the excitement offline soon turns into a clamor on social networks. On the other hand, a proliferation of practices of mobile photography often leaves the physical place is devoid of social interactions and communication. At those geographical places and events that are famous as backgrounds for taking pictures (i.e., Instagrammable attractions and so on), you can only see crowds preoccupied with their smartphones (taking pictures and sending them online via wireless networks). While people are passionately communicating with virtual participants whom they have never met, as a consequence, the meaning of the physical place is emptied and replaced according to the logic of virtual networks. In this situation, on behalf of the living reality of online information, parts of the offline world are lost, which could be described as the outbreak of a second offline context.

The social impacts of seamlessly accessible mobile technologies are consistently growing, thereby causing the intersection across offline places and online spaces in many facets of everyday life. While the boundary between online and offline communities is becoming increasingly ambiguous, the corporeality might be a crucial aspect for understanding this emerging phenomenon, as the human body is serving as a substantive platform for enacting, retreating, and controlling these crossovers. The body could be a novel subject for understanding a fundamental but invisible layer of people's adoption of technology, which requires a more careful assessment either in terms of body-technology relations or as an element comprising the social context of technologies in actual use.

**Acknowledgements** I thank Linda Nagler for her generosity in permitting the reprinting of daguerreotype portraits from *The Hidden Mother* (2013).

## References


Batchen G (2003) Each wild idea: writing, photography, history. The MIT Press, Cambridge, MA

Barthes R (1980) Camera lucida: reflections on photography (trans: Howard R). Hill and Wang, New York

Bolter JD, Grusin R (1999) Remediation: understanding new media. The MIT Press, Cambridge, MA

Bourdier P (1965 = 1990) Un art moyen: essai sur les usages sociaux de la photographie, Les editions de minuit. Japanese Edition: Shasinron: Sono syakaiteki kouyou (trans: Yamagata H, Yamagata N). Hosei University Press, Tokyo

Gibson JJ (1979) The ecological approach to visual perception. Houghton Mifflin Harcourt, Boston

Goffman E (1963) Behavior in public places: notes on the social organization of gatherings. The Free Press, New York

Gómez Cruz E, Lehmuskallio A (eds) (2016) Digital photography and everyday life: empirical studies on material visual practices. Routledge, London and New York

Jurgenson N (2019) The social photo. Verso, London

Kim KY (2020) Tactile photography. INTERIM: Vis intermed 25(1):101–120

Lee D (2010) Digital cameras, personal photography and the reconfiguration of spatial experience. Inf Soc 26:266–275

McLuhan M (1964) Understanding media: the extensions of man. McGraw-Hill Education, New York

Manovich L (2002) The language of new media. The MIT Press, Cambridge and London

Mauss M (1968–1973) Sociologie et anthropologie. Presses Universitaires de France. Japanese edition: Syakaigaku to Jinruigaku II (trans: Arichi T, Yamaguchi T). Koubundo, Tokyo

Mota S (2016) "Today I dressed like this": selling clothes and playing for celebrity. In: Gómez CE, Lehmuskallio A (eds) Digital photography and everyday life: Empirical studies on material visual practices. Routledge, London and New York, pp 35–51

Nagler L (2013) The hidden mother. Mack, London

Palmer D (2012) iPhone photography: Mediating visions of social space. In: Hjorth L, Burgess J, Richardson I (eds) Studying mobile media: cultural technologies, mobile communication, and the iPhone. Routledge, London and New York, pp 85–97

Rawlings K (2013) Selfies and the history of self portrait photography. Oxford University Press Blog, 11.21.2013. Retrieved January 23, 2020, from: http://blog.oup.com/2013/11/selfies-history-self-portrait-photography/

Richardson I, Wilken R (2012) Parerga of the third screen: mobile media, place, and presence. In: Wilken R, Goggin G (eds) Mobile technology and place. Routledge, London and New York, pp 181–197

Shanks M, Svabo C (2014) Mobile-media photography: New modes of engagement. In: Larsen J, Sandbye M (eds) Digital snaps: the new face of photography. I.B. Tauris, London and New York, pp 227–246

Sontag S (1977–979) On photography. Japanese edition: Shasinron (trans: Kondo K). Syobunsya, Tokyo

Tomita H (2006) "Fukugou-genjitsu-shakai": Augmented reality-to-social camouflage. ("Mixed reality society": augmented reality and social camouflage). Jpn Soc Inf Commun Res J 24 (1):1–8

Tomita H (ed) (2016) The post-mobile society: From the smart/mobile to second offline. Routledge, Oxon and New York

Van Djick J (2007) Mediated memories in the digital age. Stanford University Press, Stanford, CA

Van Djick J (2013) The culture of connectivity: a critical history of social media. Oxford University Press, Oxford

Van House N, Davis M, Ames M, Finn M, Viswanathan V (2005) The uses of personal networked digital imaging: an empirical study of cameraphone photos and sharing. In: CHI 2005, Portland, Oregon, USA, ACM SIGCHI, 2–7 Apr 2005

Van House N (2011) Personal photography, digital technologies, and the uses of the visual. Vis Stud 25(1):125–134

**Kyoung-hwa Yonnie Kim** is a media anthropologist and a part-time lecturer at the Kanda University of International Studies in Chiba, Japan. Her research focuses on the cultural and transformational aspects of digital technology and social networks, particularly in terms of the materiality of the medium and creative media practices. She has published English articles such as "The landscape of keitai shôsetsu: Mobile phones as a literary medium among Japanese youth," and "Tactile photography". Her recent book Everything has begun with Internet: Six stories you need to know for digital literacy (2020, Darun publishing, in Korean) discusses on the everydayness of networked technologies in the Internet age. Kim received her Ph.D. from Graduate School of Interdisciplinary Information Studies of the University of Tokyo.

# Social Media and Mobile Society

# Spatial Practices of the Second Offline

**Jason Farman**

**Abstract** How we represent a space deeply affects how we live in that space. Representations of a location (how we visualize it in our media) directly impact the ways that we think about that space, and thus ultimately practice everyday life in that space. In the second offline, how we layer our space through technology shapes the ways that we live in those spaces and even image what is possible in those locations. One important way that this is done is through the ways we can represent data in (and about) our spaces. Data, in the mobile media age, has become site-specific. This site-specificity affords users a new window into the meaning of complex data and ideas. This chapter draws on a range of examples in augmented reality (AR) and mapping visualizations to demonstrate how location-aware mobile media work as signifying tools for how we think about the world and how we orient our bodies in these spaces. Rather than functioning as two distinct spheres, the "virtual" of the digital interface and the "material" of the physical space are mutually constructive, functioning in a co-constitutive relationship that produces each other.

## 1 Introduction

During a recent trip to Seattle, Washington, I was attempting to use my mobile device to locate a good coffee shop near my hotel. I loaded a map on my phone, hit the button that would request my location, and noticed the blue dot that located me at an intersection. I looked at the nearby street corner signs, which did not match the place that the map located me. I knew that my mobile map was representing my location incorrectly. I also knew the name of the nearest intersection. But, I had no idea where I was! Though I had barely taken a few steps outside of the hotel, I was already lost. With no one nearby to help clarify the discrepancy, I tried a few techniques to get the map to show my correct location, so I could find out which restaurants were within walking distance. I did a search for my hotel and discovered

J. Farman (✉)
Department of American Studies, University of Maryland, College park, USA



H. Tomita (ed.), *The Second Offline*, Advances in Information and Communication Research 3, https://doi.org/10.1007/978-981-16-2425-4_13

that the map was placing me about a half-mile from my current location. What struck me most about this situation was the feeling of displacement I had until the map lined up with my physical location. I had an odd anxiety about being lost but couldn't quite figure out why. It dawned on me that as I typically move through a new place, I use my mobile device to inform me of the context of my location. The "virtual" world of the mobile interface deeply affects the way I move through my everyday life. Like many mobile media users, I savor the context-aware information my mobile device provides me and, when the representation of my environment on my device does not match up with the material space around me, I feel that one of my lenses to the world has been broken.

Increasingly, we are living in what has been termed as the "second offline," where our movements through physical space are informed by digital technologies (Hidenori 2016). Thus, rather than seeing the virtual and the real as distinct spheres, users are coming to find a meaningful experience in the way that the virtual and real are layered and permeable. In fact, by tracing the history of the term "virtuality," we immediately see that the intimate relationship between the virtual and the "actual" has always been historically assumed. For Grosz (2001), this dissolve takes place at the level of the perceptual, noting that the most striking transformation heralded in by digital technologies is the "change in our perceptions of materiality, space, and information, which is bound directly or indirectly to affect how we understand architecture, habitation, and the built environment" (p. 76).

In this recent shift, I want to continue an argument that has been advocated by me and other cultural geographers: how we represent a space deeply affects how we live in that space. Representations of a location (how we visualize it in our media) directly impact the ways that we think about that space, and thus ultimately practice everyday life in that space. As I have argued in *Mobile Interface Theory*, the ways that we represent space deeply affect the various ways that we embody that space (Farman 2012). Our concepts of culture, identity, and agency all spring from our understanding of bodies' relationships to the spaces they exist in and move through. Such understandings are conceived out of the various ways space is represented and visualized.

## 2 The Virtual Versus the Real

In order to build this argument and extend the scholarly work that has been done over the last decade to untangle the binary opposition between the real and the virtual in mobile media studies, I want to draw on the long history of the term virtual. Historically, our embodied relationship to the virtual was always linked to the phenomenologies of multiplicity. That is to say, an experience of the virtual is always an experience of the virtual in conjunction with another concept such as the "actual." The term "virtual" comes from the Latin *virtus*, which is typically translated as "virtue" or being "effective in respect of inherent natural qualities or powers" (Oxford English Dictionary). This was the common use of the word "virtual" in English until the late 1400s, when it began to stand in for ideas of force and power. The virtual as a force or power is always conjoined with ideas of actualization or realization. As John Rajchman (1998) writes, "The virtual lies in those forces or potentials whose origins and outcomes cannot be specified independently of the open and necessarily incomplete series of their actualizations. Such is their multiplicity (or complexity) that it can never be reduced to a set of discrete elements or to the different parts of a closed or organic whole" (p. 116). Thus, the virtual is not the opposite of the real; instead it is a component of experiencing the real. The virtual serves as a way to understand the real and as a form of actualization that serves to layer and multiply an experience of that which is already realized. In terms of our embodied engagement with mobile media, which simultaneously takes place in our everyday spaces (which have been "realized") and in the ways this space is augmented by virtuality infused from our interfaces, the terms cannot be used in isolation from one another. The realized or actualized is always implicated by the virtual (broadly defined) and such an implication is produced through embodied practices.

What takes place across the "virtual" space of mobile computing is almost always founded on social interaction in the material sphere (i.e., to learn how to practice embodiment in virtual space we must initially experience embodied practice in material space). However, since the two realms are so intertwined, the embodied practice of space on mobile networks strongly reinforces our sense of embodiment in the material sphere. In other words, our sense of embodied self can be developed and thrive from interactions that take place across geographically distant places. When it comes to intimate interpersonal connections, face-to-face is now implicated and informed by the virtual.

This approach contrasted the early descriptions of mobile media practices, in which the incorporation of mobile technology into everyday spaces prompted a distinction between the actual space of the physical and the virtual space of a mobile screen. While the mobile media space of pervasive computing often prompted a comparison between the "real" and the "virtual," such dichotomies do little to inform the embodied experience of this kind of space, especially in an age when the perceptive interaction with the digital environment offers a significant embodied experience. We might even ask, what distinguishes the "real" space when a virtual interaction offers a very "real" experience. Instead, by understanding the space of the digital and the space of the material to have constant interplay and permeability between one another, distinguishing the space of the virtual from the space of the real does not inform a nuanced understanding of pervasive computing space, mobile media space, or space broadly conceived.

Computing culture and history took the term virtual and recast it in a very different light than the historical understanding. In 1959, it began to be used in computing terms as that which is "[n]ot physically existing as such but made by software to appear to do so from the point of view of the program or the user" (Oxford English Dictionary). This use of the virtual as that which is not physical but emulates the physical (such as "virtual memory" or "virtual machine") gestures back to the 1600s when people used it to refer to metaphysical ideas related to

Christianity, especially in distinguishing between the physical practices of faith—such as taking communion or getting baptized—and the metaphysical/"virtual" components of faith—such as the inward belief and connection to God. Connecting the virtual to the spiritual illuminates the historic idea that virtuality is non-physical and largely about potential or a process of becoming. However, this definition of the virtual had never been opposed to that which is real. For people of faith, sometimes that which is "virtual" and metaphysical is even more real than the physical world in which they live.

This definition is only one approach to the virtual. Accompanying this approach to the virtual is the idea of the virtual as simulation. The extended history of using the virtual to stand in for ideas of simulation is traced by de Souza e Silva and Sutko (2009) and is what they term the "technological virtual." They write, "Because the Internet was mostly accessed through fixed interfaces (e.g., personal computers) that were physically attached to a home or office space, physical spaces were perceived as independent from digital spaces. Accordingly, digital worlds, such as chat rooms and multiuser environments, were considered 'virtual' because they allowed people to meet in nonphysical, simulated spaces" (p. 25). The emergence of the relationship between virtuality and simulation is linked to a shift in computing from a "culture of calculations to a culture of simulations." De Souza e Silva and Sutko note, "In the culture of simulations, everything is taken at interface value" (p. 26). The simulation as a screen representation that stood in for physical spaces has since caused a significant amount of cultural anxiety due to the potentials present in these forms of representation (from fears of children committing acts of violence after playing a violent videogame to people being so distracted by their devices that they no longer pay adequate attention to the physical space around them). De Souza e Silva and Sutko rightly trace this anxiety back to Plato's anxiety over art as a representational form that would draw us away from the "real" world. This fear has extended into contemporary discussions of digital interfaces as spaces that threaten to become more important—and will thus eventually subsume—"actual" space. As Umberto Eco has argued, once there is a 1:1 relationship between the representation and the thing it represents (such as a map that is the exact size of the space it represents), the former will destroy the latter. They are unable to coexist (De Souza e Silva and Sutko 2009, p. 29).

These theories of virtuality and simulation fail us in important ways: they do not take into account what I call a "sensory-inscribed" experience of virtuality, which is when our bodies encounter the world both through the senses and through the ways we "read" or analyze the world. Simulation—as opposed to the second offline—is a concept that tends to ignore the materiality of the second offline. The virtual, and its companion experience as second offline in the mobile media age, has been experienced throughout history as not a privileging or erasing of one space over another. The virtual is instead an experience of multiplicity. It is an experience of layering, and the constant interplay that bonds the virtual and the actual together is the pleasure of virtuality. As Rajchman writes, citing Proust: "The virtual is 'real without being actual, ideal without being abstract'" (p. 116). This constant interplay—without a full dissolution of one space into another—is the key to the success of virtuality. He continues: "The actual is then what manifests and effectuates the virtual, but the actual never completely shows or activates all that the virtual implies. Something always remains."

Playwright Tony Kushner, author of Angels in America, relates this kind of experience of multiplicity to the reasons that representational forms (from plays to maps) are effective and powerful. He says,

At the end of Hamlet, you think, "What was Shakespeare thinking? You have somebody die at the end of a swordfight?" Well, if you've ever done stage fencing you know, at the end of the fencing when he falls dead he's just been running around the stage with Laertes waving his sword, so he's going to lie on the stage and he's going to be [breathing heavy]. It's always—every Hamlet—there's the body, bellows breathing. And yet, in a good production of Hamlet, when Horatio says, "Goodnight sweet prince; and flights of angels..." it kills you. Of course, Shakespeare knew exactly what he was doing. He wanted you to see that body breathing and to have this double experience. That's how you understand, if you can develop that in yourself: if you can learn to read the world, if you learn to understand that fundamentalism and literalism are inimical to human progress (and, I think in a certain sense, to human happiness and to decency and justice and liberty and all sorts of good things). If you are a literal reader of texts, you're never going to understand anything. If you don't have the ability to interpret, you're missing the whole point of being alive, the whole point of being alive with a brain. And you'll be—that's what Shakespeare says—you'll be the fool of time, the fool of history, the fool of the world instead of being someone who can understand (Kushner 2011).

The doubleness that Kushner argues for is essentially the multiplicity that is the experience of virtuality. It is experienced as a multiplicity that "can never be reduced to a set of discrete elements or to the different parts of a closed or organic whole. (This is what Bergson called 'qualitative' rather than 'quantitative' multiplicity)" (Rajchman 1998, p. 116). Thus, as we experience the virtual through our mobile interfaces, it is vital to note that virtual space always implies a counterpart, such as Gilles Deleuze's coupling of the virtual with the actual. For Deleuze, these are not oppositional terms; instead, they serve as counterparts indelibly linked to one another. In this view, the virtual would never fully dissolve into the actual because it is already an integral part of the ways we have always experienced the actual. From our interfaces to our imaginations, the virtual and the "realized" have historically been tandem and complementary elements of our experiences of everyday life.

Yet, the virtual and the real continue to be discussed as opposites. One reason we are so drawn to discussing space in such bifurcated terms is largely due to a significant shift in our experience of space with the advent of mobile computing, especially with internet-capable devices. The move from personal computing to pervasive computing, a shift characterized by the move from immobility to mobility, has allowed for online space to interact with material space in unprecedented ways. Smartphones allow us to go online from any place with an internet connection, a fact that is quite amazing after connecting online for years while attached to non-mobile places. By having a device (one we carry with us wherever we go) that is able to interface with the world in a way that transforms our everyday experience of space into an experience of multiplicity, the production of virtual space is with us on seemingly unprecedented levels. This experience of virtuality, it must be noted, extends Deleuze's (and later the work of N. Katherine Hayles) idea that the virtual is a "process of becoming" (Deleuze 1994). Instead, the virtual better represents "being-as-becoming." Mobile technologies' impact on the production of space demonstrates how the virtual is always understood as a state of being that is intertwined with a state of becoming. This being-as-becoming is a present-tense experience of embodied space informed by past and future potentials. Essential to this experience of virtual space is the way that the practice of materiality is informed by various modes of representation. Examples from mobile and locative media and the second offline will demonstrate how the production of embodied space is enacted.

## 3 Spatial Layering in the Second Offline

In the second offline, how we layer our space through technology shapes the ways that we live in those spaces each day. One important way that this is done is through the ways we can represent data in our spaces. Data, in the mobile media age, has become site-specific. This site-specificity affords users a new window into the meaning of complex data and ideas. The transformation of complex information into manageable visual layouts is the ultimate goal of practitioners of "information visualization." Information visualization is important to the ways that locative media utilize the convergence of material and virtual spaces. One key technology that allows for this organization and display of spatial data is augmented reality (AR). This technology, in essence, superimposes data onto an object (or person) through a mobile device. These forms of visualization, according to artist Corby (2008), are able to "capitalize on humans' natural ability to spot patterns and relationships in visual fields (cognition). This enables an intuitive identification of structures, which would not be available if presented in purely numeric form" (p. 462).

AR on mobile devices is also being utilized in the arts and the preservation of histories. In 2010, the Museum of London released an iPhone application called Streetmuseum, in which users go to a variety of places around the city that correspond to one of the many historical photographs and paintings in the museum's collection. Users are able to utilize the phone to overlay the historical photographs onto the material landscape. Based on location and the direction you are facing, you are able to juxtapose images from the past with current surroundings. Additionally, users can access information about the image and the historical context. For example, a user can go to the gates of Buckingham Palace and bring up a photo taken in 1914 of the arrest of Emmeline Pankhurst (Fig. 1). Holding the phone up toward the gates will position the photograph on top of the live image of the space captured through the phone's camera. Tapping on the image offers a caption for the photograph, this one saying, "Emmeline Pankhurst arrested outside Buckingham Palace. Carried past reporters to be taken to Holloway prison, Emmeline shouted 'Arrested at the gates of the Palace. Tell the King'. The arresting officer died two weeks later of heart failure." Pankhurst, one of the leaders of the British suffragette movement, who was arrested on several occasions during protests for the right of women to vote, is here juxtaposed with our present-day context. Similarly, if a user of the Streetmuseum application stands at 23 Queen Victoria Street, the application will bring up an image of the Salvation Army International Headquarters tumbling to the ground soon after the night raid on May 10, 1941, "the most severe attack London had sustained throughout the Blitz," as described by the caption in the application (Fig. 2).

AR applications like Streetmusuem demonstrate the ways that mobile technologies are able to imbue space with meaning, thus transforming a space by giving it a sense of place. Additionally, beyond the ability to implace people, mobile technologies are able to offer users new ways of visualizing information. The transformation of space into place is linked to what Edward Casey calls "implacement." Related to Heidegger's Dasein (roughly understood as "being-in-the-world"), implacement locates our situated nature and our sense of proprioception with others and with objects in a space. Implacement serves as the counterpoint to displacement, which "represents the loss of particular places in which their lives were formerly at home." This loss of place is "tantamount to losing one's existence" for many (Casey 2009, p. 36–37). Embodied implacement gives us the sense of direction in a particular place—direction not only in movement but also in purpose. Implacement gives us a sense of embodied integrity in a particular locale and also answers the questions "Which way am I going?" and "What am I doing here?" Implacement offers context for embodied being-in-the-world: "What is my history with this place?" For emerging generations, such questions no longer prioritize between material space and digital space since these spaces simultaneously inform our experience of implacement. Our lived conception of space, especially the online realm, is very much a situated experience always contextually informed.

Landscapes, it can be said, have become information interfaces much like the graphical user interface of a computer screen. The landscape around us can serve as a type of interface where data of all types can reside, from the quotidian rankings of various restaurants to the mobile mapping of crisis zones after a major natural disaster. Our places have always served as a type of information interface long before the advent of digital technologies. Information is communicated about a space in a variety of ways, most of which are not digital. From street signs to graffiti and from statues to billboards, cities have used the urban landscape as a site of information. Our embodied interaction with a locale offers insights into the meaning of the place and our situatedness there. However, a locale's context is limitedly known and much may remain unknown to us during our interactions with that place. For example, people can often spend most of their lives in a particular place without knowing certain significant facts about that location. Even the events that

**Fig. 1** A screen capture from the iPhone application Streetmuseum, overlaying an image of the arrest of Emmeline Pankhurst at Buckingham Palace in 1914 onto a present-day backdrop. © 2010, The Museum of London

are known are understood in a limited way. Context, it must also be understood, is ongoing and never settled.

Many site-specific and location-aware technologies are addressing both the desire for further context and the engagement with ongoing contexts so that we may transform locations into locales. Therefore, while AR interfaces may not do anything revolutionary in regards to historicizing a place (people could, for example, simply take the 1914 photograph of Emmeline Pankhurst and hold it up to the gates

**Fig. 2** The Streetmuseum application showing imagery of the Salvation Army International Headquarters crashing to the ground after a night raid during the Blitz. © 2010, The Museum of London

of Buckingham Palace instead of using a smartphone to do it for them), the major shift here is the implication of the user in the act of defining the site. By utilizing technologies that draw on a person's location through GPS, a user is understood as being situated in relationship to technology and thus experiences the world as a collaboration between digital and material interfaces. While this notion harks back to many discussions held over the last 20 years about "what's new about new media," my brief reply, especially in connection to mobile interfaces, is that our embodied relationship to these interfaces uniquely structures our experience (and thus conception) of the world around us. Therefore, while holding a photograph of Pankhurst up to Buckingham Palace is one experience of that place, using the exact same photograph in the exact same place but on a digital interface like an iPhone will be an altogether different embodied experience. The same is true of reading a print newspaper and the exact same content but on a mobile device. The embodied experience of content is non-transferable across media. Instead, by investigating the media specificity of our engagement with cultural objects, we can see that interfaces shape our embodied engagement with space and the ways we practice space as a lived place. This extends Manovich's (2001) distinction between media and "new" media: "All existing media are translated into numerical data accessible for the computer. The result: graphics, moving images, sounds, shapes, spaces, and texts become computable, that is, simply sets of computer data. In short, media become new media" (p. 25). Thus, the transformation of our cultural objects into binary data, such as a photograph of a significant event in front of Buckingham Palace, also transforms our embodied engagement with these objects. Here, the "sensory-inscribed" mode of embodiment developed in the previous chapter again becomes significant. Our experience of place through mobile technologies is at once a phenomenological engagement with this particular medium and a mode of reading the significance of that mode of engagement. Our bodies sense the world as a collaboration between material and digital spaces while simultaneously interacting with the cultural inscriptions written into the experience, such as the privacy implications of disclosing your location to businesses and other users.

## 4 Mobile Maps and the Second Offline

One area of mobile culture where the second offline and embodiment can be studied is in the many ways that maps get utilized in a range of projects. Maps are signifying tools for how we think about the world and how we orient our bodies in these spaces. They are also representations of the ways that we want to practice the world. Following Lefebvre's (1991) argument that space should not be considered as an empty container that we fill with our bodies (and instead should be understood as produced co-constitutively with bodies), the embodied practices of space are how it takes shape and is given meaning (p. 89–90). Space is produced and practiced; it is not a given (i.e., it does not exist a priori). Space always must be understood as existing within the cultural constraints that impact the ways that we practice space and even think about it. Representations not only frame our thinking about a space but also serve as modes of spatial production that make the space fit with our understanding of the world. There is thus a dialogical relationship between representational objects like maps and our embodied engagement with spaces. It is therefore not surprising that many mobile media projects use maps as their primary interface. What is surprising is the use of maps in such body-centric media like locative media despite the fact that maps have traditionally offered representations of space as "objective." That is, maps (if they are "correct") are understood as standing in as an objective, often scientifically produced, index of reality (to borrow a phrase from Charles Sanders Peirce). Peirce's (1998) semiotic approach argued that "representations have power to cause real facts," (p. 322) and maps (especially those comprised of GPS or areal photography) are indexes of reality, "in contrast to the icon's relatively straightforward resemblance and the symbol's conventionality or arbitrariness" (Doane 2007, p. 2).

While historical maps did offer a sense of representing space objectively (i.e., trying to capture, through scientific approaches, the accuracy of the landscape), contemporary maps have increased their perceived objectivity due to the data gathering methods and modes of photographic representation. Since many of our maps are represented through satellite visualization, a mode of capture which perceived to be detached from human agency since the imagery is taken not from a human's point of view but from a machine's, it can be (and has been) assumed that maps are an index of reality (Farman 2010). Yet, theorists and cultural geographers have sought to trouble this alignment by extending or augmenting Baudrillard's (1994) famous aphorism, "The territory no longer precedes the map, nor does it survive it" (p. 1). As Kitchin et al. (2011) have noted, many cultural geographers have followed Baudrillard by arguing that "a territory does not precede a map, but that space becomes territory through bounding practices that include mapping." They continue, "And since places are planned and built on the basis of maps, so space is itself a representation of the map; maps and territories are co-constructed.... In other words... space is constituted through mapping practices, amongst many others, so that maps are not a reflection of the world, but a re-creation of it; mapping activates territory" (p. 6).

When engaging a locative media project that uses maps as the primary interface, we interact with the map in a way that reflects it as an "interfaceless interface," a term that Bolter and Grusin (1999) use to describe the immediacy of a medium that delivers content without drawing attention to itself as a medium (p. 23). Indeed, maps tend to obscure their own authorship to deliver their content, thus seeming to erase the interface (and its politics) entirely. As a result, the networks of circulation that allow maps to arrive are often obscured. Such obscuring of a map's networks of circulation results in spaces and media that address some bodies and not others. Objects like maps reveal their essence by what they allow people to do with them; when we look at a map in the Streetmuseum app, we know what it signifies and the various conventions of how to orient the map with our bodies and our bodies with the map. This commonsense approach to the perceived affordances of a map obscures the fact that, as Ahmed (2006) puts it, "an object tends toward some bodies more than others." She continues, "So it is not simply that some bodies and tools happen to generate specific actions. Objects, as well as spaces, are made for some kinds of bodies more than others" (p. 51). Thus, when we ask the questions, "Who does this map address and who does it exclude?" or "Who is this locative media project intended for?" we begin to uncover the fact that, as representations of our locations, maps present the space from particular perspectives and omit others. Maps thus tend to reiterate the practices and ideas about a space that reinforce the existing power dynamics of the space.

## 5 Locative Arts and Cartographic Practices

The invisibility of these power dynamics in the maps that we use for mobile media projects demonstrate that maps can be extraordinarily effectual tools for those in positions of power to maintain the status quo practices of the space by presenting them as commonsense. As Craib (2000) has convincingly argued, "[N]o other image has enjoyed such prestige of neutrality and objectivity [as the map has].... The most oppressive and dangerous of all cultural artifacts may be the ones so naturalized and presumably commonsensical as to avoid critique. Like any other production, a map is contingent on its sponsor and its producer and on their cultural, social, and political world desires" (p. 8). Many locative media artists and producers have utilized this relationship between objectivity and commonsense as the launching pad for their own work. These artists have sought to critique the objectivity of maps by utilizing them in ways that critique the very nature of mapmaking and cartography and instead insert the human body's subjective perspective as the primary way of seeing the world. These works range from Paula Levine's creation of maps that overlay distant places onto nearby ones (such as her layering of San Francisco and Baghdad during the first Gulf War) to Christian Nold's creation of "emotion maps" of various cities by having volunteers wander the space while he monitored their stress levels with a mobile galvanic skin response machine (i.e., a mobile lie-detector that measured heart rate, perspiration, and breathing among others). These projects seek to make the embodied perspective of individuals the primary way of encountering the map. Orienting yourself through these maps and navigating the space with them ultimately allows us as participants to question the very process of orientation and cartography.

Perhaps most notable is the work of Esther Polak, whose Amsterdam REALtime is widely regarded as one of the first forays into locative mapping, blending the "virtual" of the screen with the data created by bodies utilizing GPS mobile technologies to trace out their movements across the city. In this project, she equipped around 60 participants with GPS receivers and tracked their movements throughout the city. Instead of having an existing map as a base layer, she began with a black background that slowly transformed into the lived map of Amsterdam as people left behind traces of their pathways around the city over a period of 6 weeks. Her subsequent locative projects explored the relationship between visualization and embodied practices of space. As Hansen (2014) notes, Polak's recent projects, Souvenir and NomadicMILK, "address the difference between the person being tracked and the person trying to make sense of the tracks.... both projects show how the tracked participants negotiate and navigate structures of politics, economy, and the concrete landscape through their movements" (p. 134). Rather than mapping space (as a pre-existing container), these projects map movement and, subsequently, create maps of the body's engagement with space.

The visualizations created in these projects often look very little like what we expect a map to look like. Creating maps of people's movements related to food and milk production in the Netherlands and Nigeria (the subjects and spaces of Souvenir and NomadicMILK), Polak's traces of tractor movements through a field or pathways of a nomadic dairy farmer in Nigeria produce images that do not serve as mimetic representations of the spaces. Instead, the traces created by the movements of these people create visualizations of the "trajectories [that] are experienced by the people making them. Using the GPS receiver as a storytelling tool, she accesses individual stories about everyday practices and how individuals experience their relationship to the larger structures that are part of their movements." As Hansen (2014) goes on to argue, "I understand Polak's projects as site-specific narratives that both 'write' and 'read' a location with the heterogeneous 'voices' of those who embody the place" (p. 130).

For emerging locative media projects, there is immense power in the ability to take something so familiar (and commonsense) as the map and get people to engage it in a new and unexpected way. Much of the power of locative media is found in the ways that these projects engage participants as embodied actors producing the space around them. When these participants are able to completely reimagine their relationship to the ways that their spaces are visualized, the impact is profound: people are able to have critical distance on their own practices of space that have been taken for granted due to the invisibility of the map's networks of circulation. As such, locative designers, artists, and participants can take the map and creatively misuse it to design unexpected ways of visualizing (and thus practicing) the spaces they move through.

The project demonstrates collaborative cartography that is deeply connected to users' bodies and their movements through everyday space. Here, mobile devices show the lived space of the city through the bodies navigating through space. Such a map can serve to represent the lived and embodied nature of that space. Another key example of this mode of mobile cartography is Christian Nold's Biomapping project. Biomapping offers a perfect example of the representation of space working in collaboration with mobile technologies and information visualization. The project, which began in 2004 and has thus far taken place in four cities including San Francisco, Paris, Greenwich, and Stockport, equips participants with a mobile device similar to the technology used on a polygraph machine that tracks their galvanic skin response (GSR), logs their GPS coordinates, and allows them to annotate their locations as they navigate the city on foot. As they walk, their stress is visualized on a map, with each person represented by a different color wall that traces their movement and shows the spikes when they experience heightened physical encounters (Fig. 3). In his article on the uses of information visualization in the arts, Tom Corby nicely summarizes the procedures behind Biomapping:

As part of the University of Westminster exhibition, self-selecting student volunteers were introduced to the project in a workshop situation. Each was fitted with a device and sent out on an hour-long walk of the university and its immediate environs, which includes a hospital and a densely built-up urban environment. While this was happening each student's changing location and level of arousal were sampled every 4 s by the device and the data downloaded to a memory chip. This information was then fed into Google Earth and visualized as three-dimensional forms to produce, what Nold calls, an "emotion map" of the area (Corby 2008, p. 465).

As they moved (and even after the fact upon reviewing their map) participants were able to tag certain locations they note as high stress or high stimulation areas. In San Francisco, for example, a participant tagged an area with, "Noticed an ambulance and decided to follow," which is then followed by the tag, "Could see the guy on the stretcher." As Perkins (2007) writes about the project, "There is a relationship between GSR response and emotional arousal: anger, being startled, fear and sexual feelings can all produce similar responses. Using this system it is possible to construct individual tracks and display the ridges and troughs of

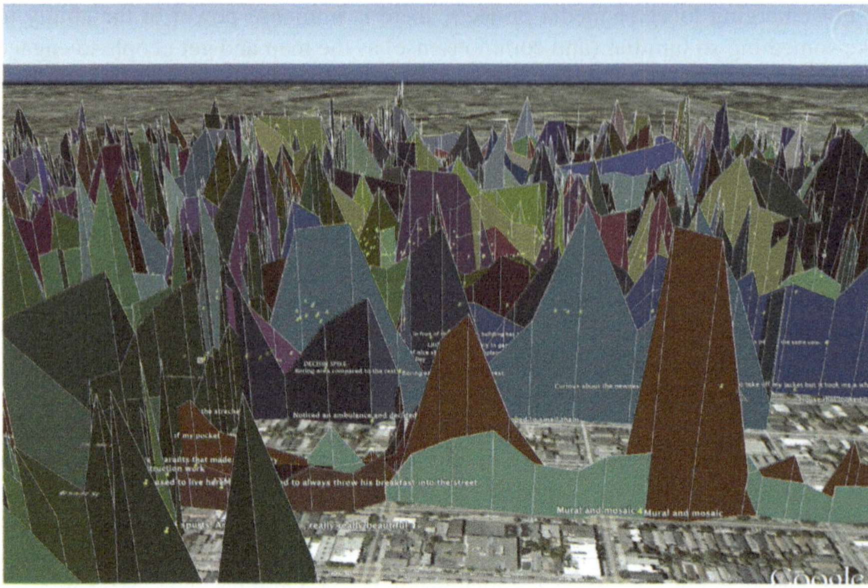

**Fig. 3** Christian Nold's San Francisco Biomapping project, showing the visualization of people's emotions as they walk through the city. Used by permission

emotion on a map. Results can be merged into composite maps reflecting wider social responses" (p. 128). Corby develops the consequences of user-generated mapping and annotations in Biomapping:

These conversations allowed a number of interesting outputs to accrue. For example, consensual interpretive processes allow participants a deeper purchase on ownership of their data. By taking analysis and information-gathering out of the hands of experts, persons normally considered as "subjects" of study are enabled to construct understanding of results in any way they see fit. Thus, the work provides an alternative to institutionally directed visualization practices that is rooted in what Nold has described as social or "bottom-up" data gathering. (p. 465).

The map in Nold's project represents a lived locale, the practice of space that transforms it into lived place. These representations go far in dismantling the separation of the sensory body in space and the cultural inscriptions of that space. The map and the body are unified in a sensory-inscribed experience of the urban space. The fact that Biomapping utilizes mobile technologies as its primary interface are significant in transforming the site of the map into a sensory-inscribed mode of implacement. The collaboration between the mobile device and GPS satellites positions the human body within space, yet it is the experience of that space coupled with a reading of the location that imparts meaning to the space. To elaborate, the act of walking through San Francisco offers one mode of sensory-inscribed engagement; to walk through the city with a mobile device provides further levels of implacement and signification. That is, while using a mobile device to trace my exact movements through a city and chart my emotional state, I experience my body in the city as being inscribed by the technologies that locate me. With these technologies, users are able to precisely know their location in space and time through GPS satellites. Simultaneously, users have to contend with the fact that they are being surveilled constantly, not only by the satellites but also by the people monitoring their emotional state through the GSR device and by passersby who inscribe the user's interactions with the mobile devices with certain significance (usually trying to "read" what you're doing and why you're there).

Another project that demonstrates the notion of the virtual and the second offline is Paula Levine's San Francisco ↔ Baghdad, which is part of her series Shadows from Another Place (see Fig. 4). This project overlays a map of the city of Baghdad onto a map of San Francisco and, at each place where a bombing occurred in Baghdad, Levine maps corresponding points onto coordinates in San Francisco. Once these corresponding nodes have been created, Levine places a geocache container at each location. Her goal, one that resonates throughout her work as a whole, is to make the foreign something that is familiar. She writes, "Collapsing 'foreign' and 'domestic', these maps bridge local and global, and allow walkers/viewers to experience spatial and narrative contiguity between separate and distant locations" (Levine 2009). Levine's San Francisco ↔ Baghdad project, while offering a new mindfulness of the city, simultaneously subverts the militaristic foundations of GPS. By using a tool created by the United States military to critique the military, Levine's work allows participants to reimagine the uses of mobile and locative technologies and the ways we understand our representations of place. By mapping the city of Baghdad onto San Francisco using a mobile device, people engage the tension between embodied space and the tools used to signify place. Engaging this project also forces users to participate in an embodied way with the historical conflict between maps and empire. Here, subverting the map by using the very technologies designed by the power structures that typically draw the map, the grounded nature of the map as a static signifier comes into question. As Edney (1990) has argued in Mapping an Empire, "Imperialism and mapmaking intersect in the most basic manner. Both are fundamentally concerned with territory and knowledge" (p. 1). He continues by noting that the "maps came to define the empire itself, to give it territorial integrity and its basic existence. The empire exists because it can be mapped, the meaning of empire is inscribed into each map" (p. 2). In Levine's project, the map critiques the imperial agendas of the war in Iraq instead of reinforcing the power structures behind the map.

As seen in the projects discussed in this chapter such as San Francisco ↔ Baghdad, Biomapping, and Amsterdam REALtime, there are obvious correlations between representations of space and power structures. Maps are not simply representations of ontological reality; instead, they signify space in a very particular way that is designed to be read to fit with the current cultural hegemony. With mobile technologies, the ways that space is represented is a practice of lived space. The movement through space and the collaboration between material environment and representations of that environment inform an embodied meaning of space.

**Fig. 4** The map of Paula Levine's San Francisco ↔ Baghdad project, showing the overlay of Baghdad onto San Francisco. The dots are the locations of bombing sites in Baghdad. At these sites, Levine placed a geocache container with a list of military personnel who had been killed in the war. © 2010, Paula Levine, http://shadowsfromanotherplace.net. Used by permission

## 6 Conclusion

Our representations of place using mobile media demonstrate the ways that mobile interfaces are transforming the information landscape around us in the context of the second offline. Our interactions with the landscape as an information interface is still developing; however, some technologies are pointing the way to what future instantiations of mobile technologies could look like. The projects described here exemplify the transformations that can take place through interactions of the second offline with mapping technologies. Whether it be connecting a historical image (as seen in Streetmuseum) and moment to our current experience of that location or the community mapping of a city (such as the emotion maps of San Francisco), the ways we experience these spaces has everything to do with the representations we interact with of those spaces. Developing information landscapes—especially spaces we can collaborate in and contribute to—demonstrates that context is never grounded, but is instead lived, ongoing, and enacted. The role of these context-rich environments in transforming landscapes into information interfaces also demonstrates the role these visualizations play in our experience of community space as second offline and virtual, a deep layering of data and embodied experience.

**Acknowledgements** Portions of this chapter have been reprinted from *Mobile Interface Theory: Embodied Space and Locative Media* (Routledge Press 2021) by permission of the Taylor and Francis Group.

## References

Ahmed S (2006) Queer phenomenology: orientations, objects, others. Duke University Press, Durham, NC
Baudrillard J (1994) Simulacra and simulation. In: Glaser SF. The University of Michigan Press, Ann Arbor
Bolter JD, Grusin R (1999) Remediation: understanding new media. The MIT Press, Cambridge, MA
Casey ES (2009) Getting back into place: toward a renewed understanding of the place-world. Indiana University Press, Bloomington
Corby T (2008) Landscapes of feeling, arenas of action: information visualization as art practice. Leonardo 41(5):460–467
Craib RB (2000) Cartography and power in the conquest and creation of New Spain. Latin Am Res Rev 35(1):7–36
de Souza e Silva A, Sutko D (2009) Merging digital and urban playspaces: an introduction to the field. In: de Souza e Silva A, Sutko D (eds) Digital cityscapes: merging digital and urban playspaces, pp 1–17. Peter Lang, New York
Deleuze G (1994) Difference and repetition. Columbia University Press, New York
Doane MA (2007) Indexicality: trace and sign: introduction. Differ J Feminist Cultural Studies 18 (1):1–6
Edney M (1990) Mapping an empire: the geographical construction of British India, 1765–1843. University of Chicago Press, Chicago
Farman J (2010) Mapping the digital empire: Google earth and the process of postmodern cartography. New Media Soc 12(6):869–888
Farman J (2012) Mobile interface theory: embodied space and locative media. Routledge Press, New York
Grosz E (2001) Architecture from the outside: essays on virtual and real space. The MIT Press, Cambridge, MA
Hansen LK (2014) Paths of movement: negotiating spatial narratives through GPS tracking. In: Farman J (ed) The mobile story: narrative practices with locative technologies. Routledge Press, New York
Hidenori T (2016) What is second offline. In: Hidenori T (ed) The post-mobile society: from the smart/mobile to second offline. Routledge Press, New York
Kitchin R, Dodge M, Perkins C (2011) Introductory essay: conceptualising mapping. In: Kitchin R, Dodge M, Perkins C (eds) The map reader. Wiley-Blackwell Press, Oxford
Kushner T (2011) A conversation with tony Kushner. University of Maryland, College Park, Dean's Lecture Series
Lefebvre H (1991) The production of space (Donald Nicholson Smith Trans). Blackwell Publishing, Oxford
Levine P (2009) Shadows from another place. In: Proceedings of the media in transition 4 conference. MIT, Cambridge, MA
Manovich L (2001) The language of new media. The MIT Press, Cambridge, MA

Oxford English Dictionary Online. Virtual, adj. (and n.), Feb 2021. https://www.oed.com/view/Entry/223829
Peirce CS (1998) New elements. In: The essential Peirce: selected philosophical writings, vol 2. Indiana University Press, Bloomington
Perkins C (2007) Community Mapping. Cartographic J 44(2):127–137
Rajchman J (1998) Constructions. The MIT Press, Cambridge, MA

**Jason Farman** is a Professor at the University of Maryland, College Park where he is the Director of the Design Cultures & Creativity Program and a faculty member with the Human-Computer Interaction Lab. He is a Faculty Associate with Harvard University's Berkman Klein Center for Internet & Society. He is author of the book Delayed Response: The Art of Waiting from the Ancient to the Instant World. This book was awarded an Alfred P. Sloan Foundation Grant for the Public Understanding of Science and Technology. He is also the author of Mobile Interface Theory, winner of the 2012 Book of the Year Award from the Association of Internet Researchers. He is the editor of the books The Mobile Story (2014) and Foundations of Mobile Media Studies (2016). His work has been featured in The Atlantic, GQ, Aeon, Vox, the Wall Street Journal, the New York Times, NPR, 99% Invisible, Atlas Obscura, ELLE Magazine, Brain Pickings, and others.

# Carrying Relationships: Cities, Social Networks, and Mobile Media

**Kunikazu Amagasa**

**Abstract** In this chapter, I want to address a conceptual extension of this doubling of time and place, namely, the "doubling of social relationships." This social-relationship doubling is a contemporary phenomenon not seen previously in mobile media and is characteristic of the use of mobile communications media such as cellphones or smart phones are. "Behind" the smartphone's display screen are people, who are involved in the phone's communications via a variety of social networking services (SNS), messaging tools, etc. In today's communications environment, such social relationships go beyond what is visible on a phone display: They create intricate circumstances which, in turn, impact mutual, face-to-face interactions. Thus, the relative social status of the people involved is the most fundamental information needed to consider the differences in the "doubled relationships" the art manifested through the (smart) phone medium. This paper seeks to investigate the role that social status plays in these relationships.

## 1 Introduction

> And the resulting networks swirl around, fluid-like, changing the fixing of place and bringing unexpected new places 'into' play. (Urry 2007:275)

I wonder where you, the reader, are reading this now? As "brain stimulation" just before you roll over to go to sleep? In a university research lab, as you think about the contents of your next paper? Relaxing in your favorite coffee shop, the aroma of coffee filling your senses? Surely, you represent a variety of people in various situations. As the deadline approaches for this book, I am writing, while sitting in a local cafe, one of many similar shops for mobile workers in Tokyo, as I partake of my "morning set" of coffee and ham and cheese on toast. The glass curtain wall",

K. Amagasa (✉)
Faculty of Humanities and Social Sciences, Showa Women's University, Tokyo, Japan
e-mail: amagasa@swu.ac.jp

 
H. Tomita (ed.), *The Second Offline*, Advances in Information and Communication Research 3, https://doi.org/10.1007/978-981-16-2425-4_14

allows for ample sunlight, making this cafe a refuge for me when I "get stuck" in my writing. Here, one sees many businesspeople: The one closest to me has his personal computer plugged into the outlet at his table with materials scattered across the tabletop, and he appears to be creating some kind of business document. As I record these observations, there may be readers who recognize overlap between my morning environment here at Excelsior Café's ThinkPark location and their current situation. "Carriable" (mobile) media, such as books, have the characteristic of essentially enabling "other places and times" to exist in the actual here-and-now. This book calls this state engendered by mobile media the "doubling of place and time" and engages in a discussion on this topic.

In this chapter, I want to address a conceptual extension of this doubling of time and place, namely, the "doubling of social relationships." This social-relationship doubling is a contemporary phenomenon not seen previously in mobile media and is characteristic of the use of mobile communications media such as cellphones or smart phones are. "Behind" the smartphone's display screen are people, who are involved in the phone's communications via a variety of social networking services (SNS), messaging tools, etc. In today's communications environment, such social relationships go beyond what is visible on a phone display: They create intricate circumstances which, in turn, impact mutual, face-to-face interactions. Consider, for example, the businessman referenced above, creating a business document. He has placed his smartphone next to him, and even as he creates the document, his seriousness apparent in his face, he is surely communicating with his boss, receiving instructions and criticism on his work, causing him to revise his document accordingly. At least this is what one imagines, and given his current state, no doubt his own colleagues would hesitate to talk with him now. This may be an imagined construct, but the social reality is that the businessman's boss does in fact exist.

Meanwhile, what kind of person is this boss who appears (via imagination) through the smartphone medium? Is she a boss who would interrupt a face-to-face communication carried on with the same kind of seriousness described above? Would she be the kind who supports and encourages such interpersonal communications, carefully following up with her subordinate as necessary? The reality of their relationship (here, with the superior "actually" existing) is surely a matter of personal interpretation. That is, people linked via media can participate in different kinds of "doubled relationships" depending on how the social context of the interacting participants is understood.

Thus, the relative social status of the people involved is the most fundamental information needed to consider the differences in the "doubled relationships" the art manifested through the (smart) phone medium. This paper seeks to investigate the role that social status plays in these relationships.

## 2 Conceptual Framework

Below is a summary of prior research useful in discussions of the "doubling of social relationships" in terms of time and place. This will serve as the conceptual framework for this paper. Then, this conceptual framework will be used to draw out a more specific research question.

### *2.1 The Formation of Intermediate Spaces via Mobile Media*

John Urry's discussion of "mobility" is indispensable for considering the doubling of social relationships in time and place. According to Urry, mobile media has enabled people to perform activities "on the move," making for "intermediate spaces" (Urry 2015:15) from which various urban systems are accessible, which are "intermediate" in the sense that they are neither at home nor at work nor at other fixed sites. These intermediate spaces are considered to be the fields where "doubling" occurs. This is because doubling, and the interactions which serve as its premise, are considered difficult to conduct at "dominant" times and sites. Contexts which already distinctly exist, and which have been historically and socially defined —places where "culture" occurs, at home, at work, at school, and so on—do not readily serve as sites for explicit negotiations of novel meanings and values. In social contexts, doubling does not exist at sites of dominant meaning and value, but easily occurs in spaces where, via mobile media carried by each person, a variety of social values are evoked—that is, in intermediate spaces.

This intricate intertwining of communications performed as "interfaced" interactions on and through media has been labeled the "techno-social situation." Prior research by Ito and Okabe (2006), which sought to clarify the systemic "order" of such situations, focused on mobile communications conducted on city bus lines. Amagasa (2016) studied mothers of preschool children as these mothers performed strategic communication, keenly aware of the social networks existing on their screens as they used smartphones in interfaced interactions. This research studied people's behaviors in their online communities, conducted as they were in public spaces and constantly on the move.

Thus, prior research on interfaced interactions and their connections to social relationships studied intermediate spaces involving mobility. Interpersonal contexts within intermediate spaces fostered by mobility are intertwined with virtual relationships via media, and as broadband has become the norm for communications lines thanks to technological advances and mobile devices have featured ever larger screens, these interlocking relationships become ever more apparent.

## 2.2 Formation of Intermediate Zones and Their Localities

In the above discussion of the circumstances in which the doubling of human relationships occurs in terms of time and space, and I have made it clear that such doubling can most easily occur in intermediate spaces, formed "on the go." Below, I will focus on "localities (regions) and cities," elements which impact the formation of intermediate zones, and I will also describe why I came to emphasize these aspects.

First, inasmuch as intermediate zones are "fields" created when moving, then one can easily imagine how their characteristics can be influenced by the types and methods of movement. Whether walking, riding on public transportation, or using a private means of transportation (such as a personal car), the public nature of surroundings will change depending on speed and space, making for large differences in the nature of intermediate zones.

The degree of the local area's "urbanism" has the greatest impact on mobility methods. The reason we can use public transportation in our daily lives is due to the high-speed urban infrastructure already in place in any one specific district. Outside of such areas, private means may be our only choice. Prior research has also made it clear that the form and quality of social relationships and social networks differ according to degree or extent of urban development (herein called "urban extent"), one of the themes of this paper.

Shinji Nozawa, for example, a pioneer in social network analysis, found that people who live in districts with a high level of "urbanism" have more geographically scattered and varied networks compared with people who live in less urban areas (Nozawa 1995). His analysis results demonstrated that Japan also fits into the broad framework depicted in the findings of social network studies in Europe and North America, including the subculture theory (Fischer 1982) and community openness theory (Wellman 1979). Incorporating these research trends, Harada and Sugisawa (2014) studied personal network characteristics within urban "gradations"; their results supported those of Harada, finding that networks tend to be geographically distributed in areas of high urban extent. Miyata (2006) used a questionnaire survey to investigate relationships between media usage and the geographical distribution of human relationships.

## 2.3 Research Question

The above summary of prior research made it clear that in numerous cases, doubling of time, place, and relationships occur in intermediate zones. We also found how the "urban extent" of localities where intermediate zones occur have a large influence on the nature of the intermediate zone, as well as the nature of the human relationships and social networks linked within that intermediate zone. Based on these findings, this chapter takes as its hypothesis that urban extent is a factor that engenders differences in the social position/status and interpretation of people linked by media in situations where there is a "doubling" of human relationships. It aims to, via survey, examine to what extent differences in the social significance of human relationships and social networks linked by media are due to locality. Using the data collected, it also aims to consider factors that cause such differences.

This chapter also considers the extent that social relationships and networks play a role in the life stage of surveyed individuals, specifically that of women who are currently raising children. In Japan, the idea that each gender has separate roles and responsibilities is still deeply rooted, and most of the work necessary for raising children is still the burden of mothers. There are limits to public support and services available to these mothers, meaning that no matter how much effort they make, they are still forced to rely on their own personal social relationships and networks (Sekii et al. 1991; Kubo 2001). Regional differences in the ways that Japanese women effectively utilize their human relationships and social networks have been identified (Matsuda 2008). Nevertheless, no investigation has yet been made as to the nature of the relationships as they exist and unfold via media. The described conditions demonstrate that women currently raising children are an appropriate subject target for an investigation of local (regional) differences in human relationships intermediated via media.

## 3 Survey Overview

To answer the above research question, a questionnaire-based survey was conducted using the Internet. Specifically, the data used for analysis in this paper were drawn from an online questionnaire survey performed using "Fastask," a questionnaire platform provided by JustSystems Corporation, in the period from February 22, 2017 through March 4, 2017. The created survey form was distributed by a JustSystems research panel to people meeting the following conditions: "resident in Japan's Kanto Region," "individuals with parental rights of a child or children living with them," and "women between the ages of 18 and 39 years." As a result, responses were received from 723 sampled individuals. Of these, 680 samples deemed to be valid responses were used for analysis. The mean age of valid respondents was 33.9 years (SD 3.75), of which 6.9% were unmarried. It is thought that these "unmarried" people were either single mothers or people in common-law marriages.

### *3.1 Characteristics of the Tokyo Metropolitan Area, the Surveyed Site*

This paper seeks to investigate functional and social differences resulting from differences in the urban extent of social networks connected via mobile media.

To do so, a summary is first made of the characteristics of the metropolitan (capital) district (the Kanto region), with Tokyo as its center.

According to the United Nations (2018), Tokyo is the world's largest metropolitan area. The Tokyo metropolitan area and adjacent prefectures (Chiba, Saitama, and Kanagawa prefectures) form a district called "Greater Tokyo" with approximately 37.0 million residents. For perspective on the massive size of Tokyo, consider that the second most populated metropolitan area is Delhi, India, with approximately 29.0 million residents. Meanwhile, the area of Greater Tokyo is 13,562 $km^2$, not a considerably broad area, although somewhat larger than Paris and London, which each have around half the population of Tokyo. Tokyo is second in size among the world's four largest "mature" cities: New York (population: approximately 20.0 million people/land area 21,482 $km^2$); London (population: approximately 14.0 million people/land area 12,109 $km^2$); Paris (population: approximately 12.0 million people/land area 21,012 $km^2$) (Tokyo Metropolitan Government 2018: 54–55).

This relatively large metropolitan area with its high population density gives the Tokyo city region two special characteristics. The first is its wide-ranging public transportation infrastructure, centered on rail transport, a carefully designed urban system to effectively address the transportation needs of Tokyo's large population. The second is the development of the city in a concentric manner, which itself enables the wide-ranging public transportation system.

Tokyo's core area is comprised of 23 urban wards (districts; recently called "cities") in which underground rail is also developed, such that there is an average of one railway station per square kilometer (Japan Ministry of Land, Infrastructure, Transport and Tourism (MLIT) 2016: 6). Thus, most people can meet all their daily transportation needs using rail lines. The "bedroom communities" in the greater metropolitan area are also linked via the railway system, including private rail companies. With "supplementary" public bus lines and other alternatives also in place, most locations can be reached using public transportation alone.

The next section will describe in more detail the concentric nature of the Tokyo area, with Chiyoda ward (city) serving as the center. This is the location of the main Tokyo Station, as well as government and administration buildings and offices clustered in Nagata-cho ("cho" is a subdistrict of a ward/city). Outside of Tokyo proper, the metropolitan district generally takes on more of a mosaic configuration, and Tokyo has fixed clusters of one or more densely urban districts, from which railway lines radiate over the surface to connect outside areas.

This type of connected geographic outspreading from Tokyo is an important point to consider in a discussion of social network functions mediated via the use of mobile social media for each residential area with its characteristic urban extent. Lack of a certain degree of homogeneity in residential environments would immediately invalidate any statistical comparison of residential zones by district. If a zone with high-urban concentration is located adjacent to a zone with low-urban extent, and when travel to and from each respective zone is extremely smooth and easy, then classification and analysis of the comparative "urban extent" in each zone would be meaningless. In this sense, the Tokyo metropolitan area is thus an appropriate zone for examining this paper's research question by means of statistical survey.

It should be noted that while the Tokyo metropolitan district is ordinarily taken to be comprised of the four autonomous administrative areas mentioned above, namely, the Tokyo metropolitan area, Chiba Prefecture, Saitama Prefecture, and Kanagawa Prefecture, this paper includes analysis of areas not fully developed in terms of urban services. However, given that all these areas lie within the Kanto Plain area (Kanto Region), the region surveyed in this study, the following prefectures adjacent to the previously named four areas are also included in this survey: Ibaraki Prefecture, Tochigi Prefecture, and Gunman Prefecture.

## 3.2 Area Divisions Used in the Analysis

As described above, areas where there is ready access to the urban system (called here "urban extent") are used as a key index in this chapter. Next, an index is needed for classifying and evaluating the "degree" of urban extent of each zone. To do so, this paper employs the most general and simple index, that of population density in the residential district of each respective survey respondent.

Here, the definition of "urban" regarding population density is that used by the Japan National Census that of "densely inhabited district" (DID). In the National Census, when adjacent "basic unit zones" with population densities greater than 4000 people/km$^2$ have an overall population greater than 5000, the area is known as a "DID" (Statistics Bureau, Japan Ministry of Internal Affairs and Communications 1996) (Table 1).

Due to the survey design, this study was not able to obtain residential addresses according to basic "zone units" (i.e., an area comprising a city, town, or village) of the National Census. It was thus determined that strict application of the DID standard would indicate any location within an administrative district (city, town, village) with a population density of 4000 or more people/km$^2$ as "urban" (here, zones designated as "Area 2: Middle Density"). Zones designated as administrative districts with lower population densities (less than 4000 people/km$^2$) were designated as having a relatively low degree of urban extent (zones designated as "Area 1: Low Density"). Among administrative districts with 4000 or more people/km$^2$, a region comprised chiefly of the 23 wards of Tokyo Metropolitan Area were deemed as having a high degree of urban infrastructure (Area 3: High Density). The

**Table 1** Definitions of areas 1–3 and sample sizes

| | Population density in administrative area | Sample size |
|---|---|---|
| Area 1 (low density) | Less than 4000 people/km$^2$ | 223 |
| Area 2 (mid density) | 4000 people/km$^2$ to less than 10,000 people/km$^2$ | 263 |
| Area 3 (high density) | 10,000 or more people/km$^2$ | 194 |

**Fig. 1** Area surveyed, and local zones with the area

high-density standard was 10,000 or more people/km$^2$, and virtually all the 23 Tokyo wards fell within this standard.

Figure 1 illustrates the categorization of the areas surveyed on a map. White shading designates Area 1 (Low Density), light gray Area 2 (Middle Density), and dark gray Area 3 (High Density).

As stated above, Area 3 (High Density) covers virtually all the 23 wards of Tokyo. The only exception is Chiyoda ward (city), the "center of Japan," with its concentration of government buildings and office towers and its few permanent residents. In addition to the 23 wards of Tokyo, Area 3 extends to adjacent areas where railway networks are extensively developed, chiefly to the east of Tokyo, as well as Yokohama, Urawa, etc. Tokyo, where the author lives, is recognized for its underground (Metro) stations located near each other, making for ready mobility; it is also always easy to hail a taxicab in Tokyo. There are few real benefits to car ownership, and having your own automobile is viewed as a kind of "luxury." Tokyo has numerous commercial districts, with a choice of places to do one's daily grocery shopping. It can be said to be optimal for consumption. In this survey, Area 3 had 194 samples.

Area 2 (Middle Density) is centered on the western part of Chiba Prefecture, the southern part of Saitama Prefecture, and the western part of Kanagawa Prefecture, as well as the center part of Tokyo. Geographically, it "encircles and encloses" Area 3 in this region, public transportation, including buses, can be used to move around practically the entire area. Here, however, many families own their own cars, for shopping, leisure, etc. Consumption mainly takes place in large-scale commercial zones near main stations; while most of the goods and services available in Area 3 are also found in Area 2, without a car, one has fewer choices than in the more urban wards of Tokyo. This is a region of high homogeneity, in which one can fully accomplish one's daily mobility needs by walking or using a bicycle. In this survey, Area 2 had 263 samples.

Area 1 (Low Density) includes all survey areas located outside of Areas 2 and 3. Using public transportation alone in this area would involve some inconveniences, and most homes have an automobile. Main commercial facilities are not found near the closest train station, but are mostly roadside, with a car as the chief means of transport for consumption. The car and its wider area of coverage mean that Area 1 residents have more consumption choices; prices are generally lower than in Area 3, but the products available are characterized by less diversity and cutting-edge fashionability. In this survey, Area 1 had 223 samples.

This paper thus examines the gradation in degree of urban extent as found in these three areas and investigates the status of media usage by surveyed mothers and the related issue of social relationships and social network functions.

## 4 Survey Results

In the employed questionnaire, based on the research question, respondents were asked about their personal attributes, including place of residence, their media usage status, and the functions of their social relationships and social networks. This section discusses the survey results.

### 4.1 Basic Attributes for Each Analysis Area

#### Family status

Table 2 shows results for respondents' age and items that indicate the basic status of their families: household income, number of children, age of youngest child, and marital status. To examine differences in unmarried rates, the chi-square test was used, while for all other data, analysis of variance (ANOVA) was performed.

No significant differences were found for age of survey respondents (mothers), number of children living with each respondent, or unmarried rate by area. Differences were seen in household income and age of youngest child. Differences in annual income were as follows: more than ¥350,000 between Area 1 and Area 2, and a larger difference, just under ¥1.5 million, between Area 2 and Area 3. This result shows that as "urban extent" (here, population density) increases, household income levels also increased, particularly in income levels for household units in Area 3 with the highest level of urban extent. The age of youngest child was also shown to have significance, although at the 10% level, with children in Area 3 being younger by about 0.5 years. This is thought to be due to the fact that as

**Table 2** Basic status of survey respondents and their families by area

| | N | | Age | Annual household income(\) | No. of children living with respondent | Age of youngest child | Unmarried rate |
|---|---|---|---|---|---|---|---|
| Area 1 (low density) Less than 4000 people/km$^2$ | 223 | Mean | 33.8 | 5,595,855 | 1.73 | 3.72 | 6.28% |
| | | SD | 3.9 | 2,422,203 | 0.71 | 2.85 | |
| Area 2 (mid density) 4000 people/km$^2$ to less than 10,000 people/km$^2$ | 263 | Mean | 33.9 | 5,951,754 | 1.76 | 3.79 | 6.84% |
| | | SD | 3.6 | 2,682,107 | 0.79 | 2.75 | |
| Area 3 (high density) 10,000 or more people/km$^2$ | 194 | Mean | 34.1 | 7,436,782 | 1.75 | 3.21 | 7.73% |
| | | SD | 3.8 | 3,801,281 | 0.92 | 2.68 | |
| | | Test | | ** | | † | |

(Mean values are shown, though not for the unmarried rate)
Test: ** 1% significance level, * 5% significance level, † 10% significance level

children in a family get older, the family tends to look for less expensive residential environments, especially in suburbs or outlying areas.

***Employment status***

Figure 2 shows differences in employment status among the three districts. Of interest is the fact that while Area 2 had a somewhat higher percentage of "homemakers," there were no major differences between the three areas. As for full-time workers, percentages in Areas 1 and 2 were lower, especially in Area 2, with an approximate 10-point spread from the 55% of Area 3. It could be said that Area 3 is the zone where the work-family balance is roughly equal. Meanwhile, given that it had the highest percentage of homemakers and the lowest percentage of full-time employees, Area 2 could be said to be the zone with the most "family centered" lifestyle.

This data provides a rational explanation for the significant difference in annual household income noted above. Dual incomes exist when both married partners work, and this is thought to have raised mean income values in Area 3. Furthermore, it is assumed that salary levels are also the highest in Area 3. Nevertheless, because Japan is a country with relatively small salary variations, salary levels alone cannot explain the large difference of nearly ¥2.0 million between Area 1 and Area 3. The above-described difference in employment status, then, is thought to be largely implicated in this annual income disparity.

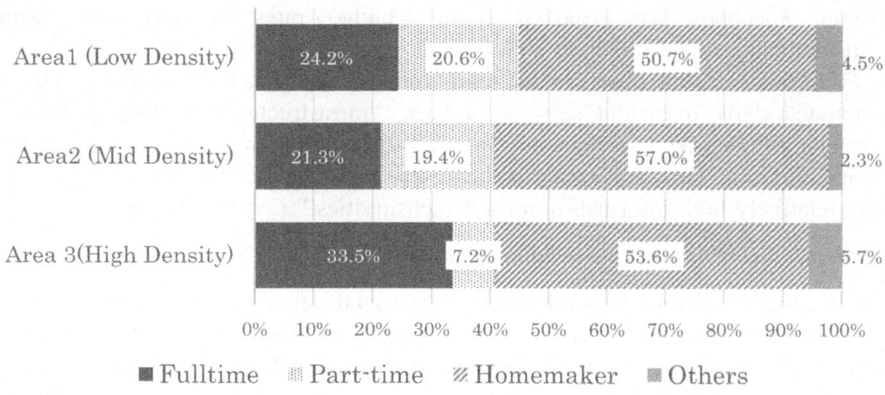


**Fig. 2** Employment status of survey respondents by area

### *Media usage status*

Figure 3 shows the usage status of each media type by survey respondents. There was especially high usage of social networking services (SNS), mobile media that can be used "on the go." This aspect of "using while doing something else" makes it difficult to pinpoint "pure" usage frequencies and usage times. Thus, in this survey, four choices were provided regarding usage. Results showed that messaging applications were used most frequently, with over 90% of surveyed people using them, and with just under 70% using messaging applications at high frequencies. This was, followed by electronic mail (e-mail), used by approximately 85% of respondents, with around 35% using this at high frequencies (defined as "use a lot" and "cannot live without it"). Conversely, mothers raising children did not have very high usage rates for SNS-type services in this survey. Twitter and Instagram usage were approximately 30%, with high-frequency usage at less than 15%

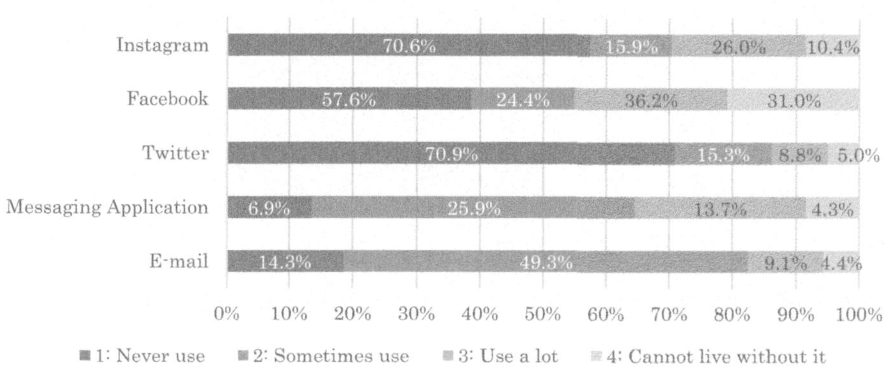


**Fig. 3** Media usage status by type

overall. Facebook was used at slightly higher rates, at over 40%, with high-frequency usage less than 20% overall.

From this data, one observes that mail-type services (email and messaging) have penetrated daily lives and serve as a basic "infrastructure" in daily practices. Meanwhile, SNS-type services are not well-diffused among this generation busy raising children, with the assumption being that these are more often used by people with relatively high information-related "sensitivities."

***Status of social networks and human relationships***

Finally, Fig. 4 shows structural elements of social networks and human relationships, with respondents' "degree of reliance" on them (here indicating how dependent people are on these networks and relationships by attributes as surveyed). First, there is 70% overall reliance (responses of "rely on" and "very much rely on") on one's parents. Over 25% said they "very much rely on" their parents, indicating that parents are an essential relationship for women when they are raising children. Meanwhile, respondents' reliance on neighborhood friends was approximately 35%, with government workers and specialists at closer to 40-plus %. Compared with women's parents, these people had little impact on child-rearing, but for some people, important relationships are formed with members of these two "groups"; it is thought that mothers raising children could be selective in choosing their relationships with people in these groups.

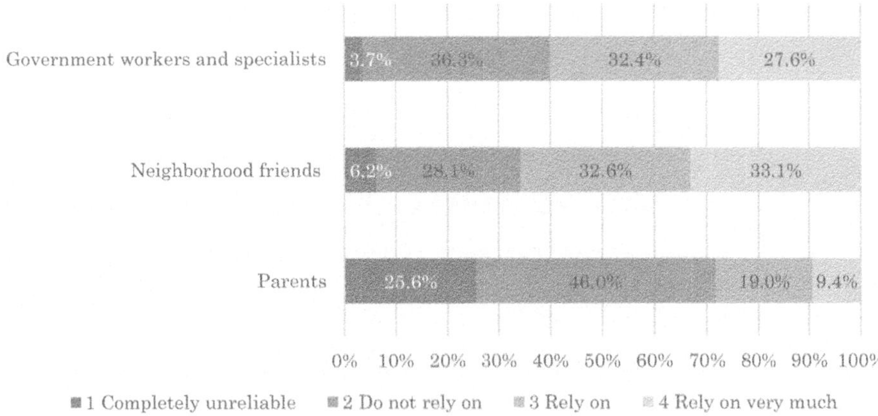


**Fig. 4** Structural elements of social networks and reliance rates

## 5 Discussion

Using the data discussed in Sect. 3 above, this chapter next investigates differences in extent, by area, of the relationships between media usage and social network functions.

To do so, it is first noted that analysis was made by broadly dividing "media" into the separate categories of email, mail-type messaging applications, and various SNS, namely, Twitter, Facebook, and Instagram. "Heavy users" ("use a lot" and "cannot live without it") of "mail-type" services (either email or messaging applications) were 72.1% of respondents (490 samples), while people responding that they "use a lot" or "cannot live without" an "SNS-type" media (Twitter, Facebook, or Instagram) were 26.8% (182 samples). Looking at these "heavy users" by area, results were as follows for "mail-type" media: Area 1 = 69.1%, Area 2 = 73.4%, and Area 3 = 73.7%. Thus, while Area 1 (with its lower urban extent) was somewhat lower, overall, there were no significant differences. As for "heavy users" of "SNS-type" media, results were: Area 1 = 22.9%, Area 2 = 26.6%, and Area 3 = 31.4%. Thus, the greater the "urban extent" of an area, the higher the usage rate of SNS-type media.

The next analysis was of the extent of reliance of these "heavy users" of mail-type and SNS-type media on social networks with different social characteristics, namely, parents, neighborhood friends, and government workers and specialists.

### *5.1 Relationships via Media with "Parents" by Area*

Figure 5 shows the rate of reliance, expressed as percentages, on parents by area. Area 1, with the lowest "urban extent" had the highest rate of reliance on parents among "heavy users" of both mail-type and SNS-type media. In fact, the rate of reliance on parents among heavy users of mail-type and SNS-type media in Area 1 was actually higher than the reliance-on-parents rate for survey respondents overall. This data shows, at least, that in areas of low-urban extent, the use of mail-type and SNS-type media does not have negative effects on the establishment and maintenance of relationships with parents.

### *5.2 Relationships via Media with "Neighborhood Friends," by Area*

Figure 6 shows rates of reliance on neighborhood friends by area. As for "heavy users" of "mail-type" media, the reliance percentage increased as "urban extent" increased. This, however, was the same trend shown overall, and there was not much

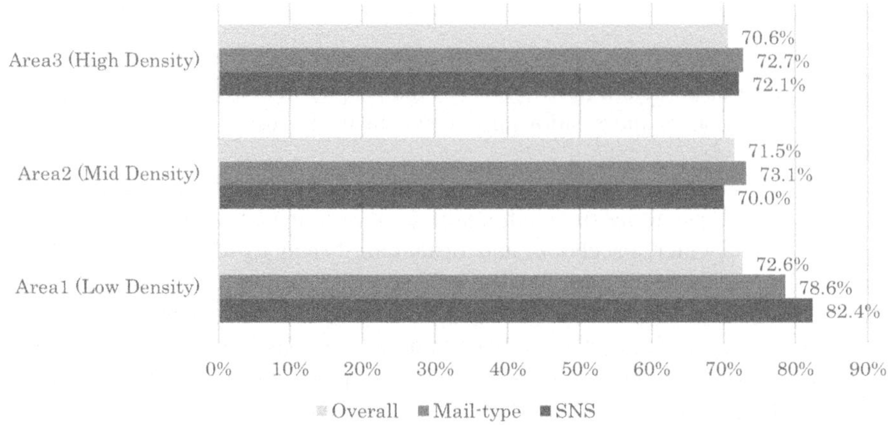


**Fig. 5** Percentage of reliance on parents for each "level of urban extent" and media type

difference in levels by media usage. In other words, as urban extent increased, so did the importance of neighborhood relationships for users of mail-type media. As for "heavy users" of "SNS-type" media, in Area 3 the reliance rate on friends was higher compared to the other areas. The rate for Area 3 was 47.5%, or 10 points higher than that of the overall reliance rate (37.6%). These results suggest that within Area 3, with its higher level of "urban extent," the use of media—especially SNS—is effective in establishing and maintaining relationships with neighborhood friends. Also, unlike with heavy mail-type media users, little difference was seen between Area 2 (middle-level urban extent) and Area 1 (low-level urban extent) in terms of reliance rate on neighborhood friends. This point indicates with high probability that unlike mail and messaging, SNS usage does not function effectively in establishing reliable relationships with neighborhood friends in areas with lesser urban extent.

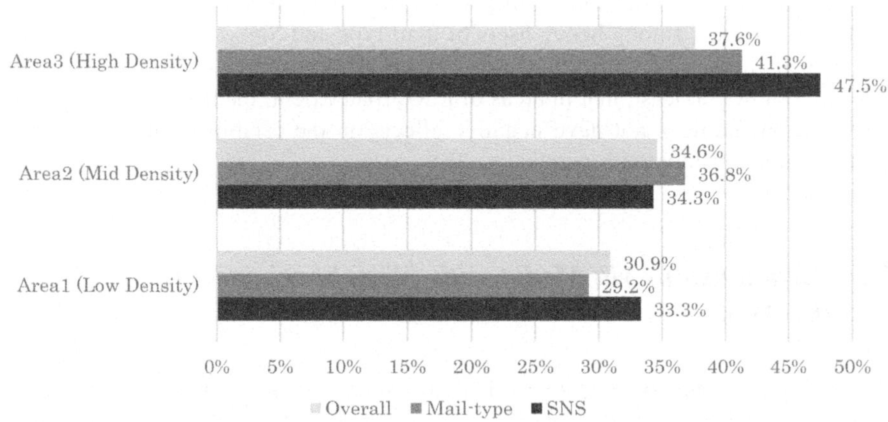


**Fig. 6** Rate of reliance on neighborhood friends for each "level of urban extent" and media type

### *5.3 Relationships via Media with "Government Workers and Specialists" by Area*

Figure 7 shows rates of reliance on government workers and specialists by area. Area 2, with its "middle urban extent" compared with Area 3 (high-urban extent) and Area 1 (low-urban extent), was somewhat lower in this general tendency. As for heavy users of mail-type and SNS-type media, there were practically no differences in rates of reliance. Meanwhile, Area 1 had the highest overall reliance rate. In Area 1, reliance rates on specialists by heavy media users were higher than the overall rate (44.4%), and the rate was particularly high among heavy SNS users (64.7%). The same tendency was observed for Area 3. In fact, the reliance rate of SNS heavy users was statistically significant by area. Considering this point, results indicated that government workers and specialists have a larger impact on mothers raising children in Area 1 (low-urban extent) and Area 3 (high-urban extent) than in Area 2 (middle urban extent); also demonstrated was that the use of SNS-type media in particular has a positive impact on the formation and maintenance of connections with government workers and specialists.

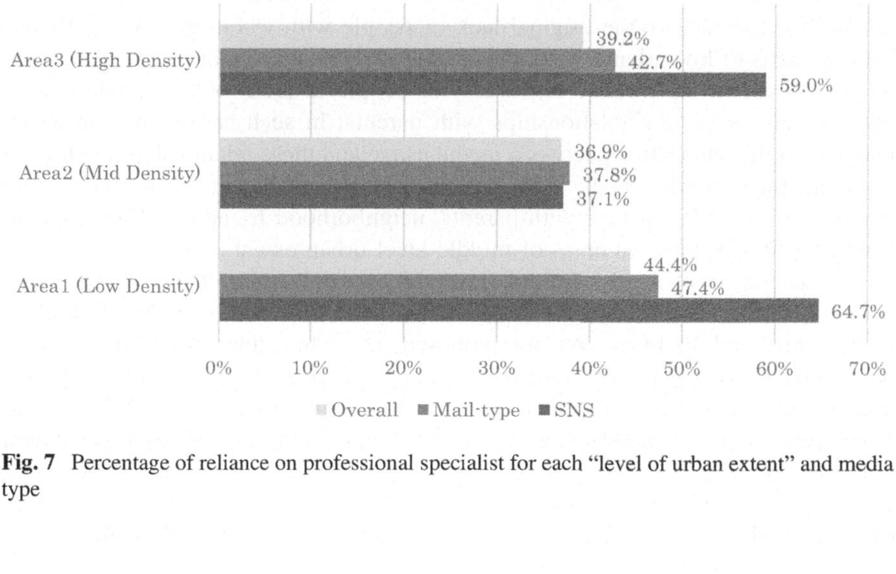


**Fig. 7** Percentage of reliance on professional specialist for each "level of urban extent" and media type

## 5.4 Summary: Who Does One See "Behind" the Smartphone Screens of Mothers?

The above analyses of the results of this study clarify that human relationships mediated by mail, messaging, and SNS-type media have, at least for mothers currently raising children, differing tendencies by level of urban extent.

People living in areas of high urban extent (in this survey, Area 3, comprised of the 23 Tokyo wards and central portions of Saitama and Yokohama) can, if they are "heavy users" of media, especially SNS, more easily establish relationships with "neighborhood friends" and with "government workers and specialists" than can people with comparatively lower usage of SNS. Also, in areas with low-urban extent, such that without car ownership there are certain limitations to daily life, a tendency was seen that heavy media users could more easily forge and maintain relationships with "parents" and with "government workers and specialists" than can less-heavy users. Here, it is thought the results point to cases where, rather than making direct contacts through SNS, relationships are sustained as a result of collecting information via SNS. Whatever the case may be, in areas of high and of low urban extent, then, it is these categories of people who can be "seen" on the "other side" of the smartphone.

Meanwhile, in areas of "middle-level" urban extent, where life can be lived within a walking radius, heavy media users did not show any special tendencies toward positive effects on human relationships compared with people who had relatively lower rates of media usage. Compared with the other areas of this survey, in Area 2 media usage is not readily linked with human relationships, and one finds it difficult to see specific people "behind" the screen of the smartphone.

In areas of low-urban extent, it is relatively difficult to form friendly relationships effectively with neighbors, either with or without media usage. This can be rationally explained by the original lack of people with whom to develop friendships in areas of low urban extent. Nozawa (1995) indicated that relationships with relatives form an "alternative resource" for people in areas of low urban extent, characterized by strong relationships with parents; in such cases, one can easily understand the connections between media usage and these relationship bonds. The question, then, is why media does not function effectively in the formation and maintenance of relationships with parents, neighborhood friends, and government workers and specialists in areas of middle-level urban extent.

Characteristics of Area 2 (middle-level urban extent, as defined by population density) in this study are among its limitations, in terms homogeneity of employment status and mobility. As for employment status, this area had the most homemakers and the fewest full-time workers. As for mobility, the use of public transportation is not as convenient as in areas of high-urban extent (Area 3), and other areas are not as accessible as they are to people in the area of low-urban extent (Area 1), where car ownership is generally a necessity. This is not to say, however, that daily life in Area 2 is "inconvenient." This area does include areas of concentrated "urban-like" facilities, with all basic shelter, food, and clothing necessities sufficiently supplied within walking or bicycle-riding distances. Mobility limitations in Area 2, however, do have some merits for mothers busy raising children. Such merits are thought to be related to the fact that mothers in Area 2 are able to construct relationships without reliance on media.

Meanwhile, material choices available within walking distance are limited in Area 2, both "formally" (in terms of urban systems) and "informally" (in terms of social relationships). In this sense, Area 2 has a certain homogeneity due to its lack of diversity. Because of the dearth of the mobility provided by urban systems, there are fewer opportunities to be "on the move," and even in intermediate spaces created by mobility, there is a uniformity of local culture, meaning that the "negotiation of meaning" due to human interactions within these spaces does not easily occur. Homogeneity also implies the existence of dominant methods of interpreting meaning, meaning that people, who may individually oppose such interpretations, are readily frustrated in any efforts to change or "overturn" dominant concepts, even with the use of diverse contacts and contexts. Compare such an area, then, to highly urban areas encompassing diversity, or to non-urban spaces where, although individuality may be advanced, there may be insensitivity to diversity. Certainly, a living space that is urbanized but with high homogeneity has, by its very nature, a tendency to reject doubling of social meaning, in terms of both space and time. The fact that SNS, with its visible and open relationships, was found in the current survey data to serve fewer functions in the area of middle urban extent than in the other areas certainly supports the conclusions presented above. Amagasa (2016) also indicated in prior research that "mothers who secretly use their smartphones to visualize people beyond the screen" are indeed found in areas like this; to avoid conflicts that can easily occur with the doubling of social meaning, such mothers are thus thought to use personal, individualized communication strategies.

## 6 Conclusion

The development of technology has engendered the "doubling of social relationships" in our society, both in terms of time and place. Against this backdrop, this study hypothesized that there would be differences in the social status and interpretation of people linked with media depending on the factor of their "locality/ level of urban extent." Thus, this study investigated the extent of regional differences regarding the social meaning of human relationships and social networks as linked via media.

Study results showed that useful human relationships and media usage were not linked in the same way in each area (region) studied. It was found that in an area of middle-level urban extent with a high degree of homogeneity, it is easier for a unique culture to take root; in such an area, doubling—with its inherent denial of unique, individual culture—does not easily occur, even in face-to-face communications.

The doubling of social relationships does not happen universally, in every society and in every situation, simply due to the existence of media technology. This doubling is a product of our communications which are embedded in the politics of our mutual interactions.

## References


Amagasa K (2016) Relationships in child-rearing spaces and media usage. In: Post-mobile society (in Japanese) (ed) Tomita H. Sekaishisosha, Tokyo, pp 108–124

Fischer CS (1982) To dwell among friends: personal networks in town and city. The University of Chicago Press, Chicago

Harada K, Sugisawa H (2014) Urban extent and personal networks: multilevel analysis of relationship between relatives, neighbors, and friends. Japanese Sociol Rev (in Japanese) 65(1):80–96

Kubo K (2001) Child-raising support via personal networks of working mothers. J Home Econom Japan (in Japanese) 52(2):135–145

Matsuda S (2008) What can support child-raising? The strength of middle-level networks (in Japanese). Keiso Shobo, Tokyo

Miyata K (2006) Mobilizing Japanese. In: Matsuda M et al (eds) An environment with cell phones (in Japanese), pp 99–120. Kitaohji Shobo, Tokyo

Nozawa S (1995) Married couple relationships in personal networks: comparative study of urban areas of family and community issues. In: Matsumoto Y (eds) Proliferating networks (in Japanese). Keiso Shobo, Tokyo, pp 175–233

Sekii S et al (1991) Views of division of roles by gender of working women, and child-raising support networks. Japan Soc Family Sociol (in Japanese) 3:72–84

Statistics Bureau, Japan Ministry of Internal Affairs and Communications (1996) What are 'population density areas? (in Japanese). http://www.stat.go.jp/data/chiri/1-1.htm. Accessed on 1 Dec 2017

United Nations (2018) World urbanization prospects: the 2018 revision/key facts. https://population.un.org/wup/Publications/Files/WUP2018-KeyFacts.pdf. Accessed on 21 Oct 2018

Urry J (2007) Mobilities. Polity Press, Cambridge

Wellman B (1979) The community question: intimate networks of east yorkers. American J Sociol 84(5):1201–1231


**Kunikazu Amagasa** is an Associate Professor of the Faculty of Humanities and Social Sciences at Showa Women's University in Tokyo, Japan. He Specializes in media studies, with a focus on social network theory, and has engaged in ethnographic research on mobile media usage in local communities, such as mom friends' local network. His Publications include 'Polyreality: Sociological imagination evoked by smartphones' in The Post-Mobile Society: From the smart/mobile to second offline (Routledge, 2016).

# Social Media Usage and Translocality Among Japanese Young Adults

**Ichiyo Habuchi**

**Abstract** The chapter examined correlations between geographical proximity and intimacy among young adults living in provincial cities. How do social media enhance their intimacy? It is particularly examining the question of whether social media use age can help young adults transcend the constraints of physical distance and play a part in forming and maintaining interpersonal relationships. The study's results showed that LINE and Facebook were used by people living in their hometowns used LINE and Facebook to maintain local interpersonal relationships, and Twitter use was negatively correlated with their satisfaction with the current situation or optimism about the future. The study found that young adults' interpersonal relationships and life satisfaction were affected by the characteristics of every social media platform used by them.

## 1 Introduction

Since its advent, the mobile phone has been used to maintain intimate networks, such as those between close friends and families (Okada et al. 2000; Nakamura 2001; Tsuji 2008; Sakaguchi 2016). The advance of mobile phone technologies has been bewildering, with the explosive spread of mobile phones in the late 1990s, the diffusion of internet-connectable technologies, and the rapid rise of smartphones in the second decade of the twenty-first century. Communication via mobile phone has also changed in terms of application usage in accordance with the times. With the transition from the late 1990s to now, people now communicate with each other not only through telephone or email but also through other kinds of simple and inexpensive social media. The result of this transition is the present situation with its development of relevant technologies.

As an example of these developments, the 2017 Survey on Usage Time and Information Behavior with Regard to Telecommunications Media, carried out by

I. Habuchi (✉)
Faculty of Humanities and Social Sciences Section, Hirosaki University, Aomori, Japan
e-mail: ichiyo@hirosaki-u.ac.jp



H. Tomita (ed.), *The Second Offline*, Advances in Information and Communication Research 3, https://doi.org/10.1007/978-981-16-2425-4_15

the Ministry of Internal Affairs and Communications Institute for Information and Communications Policy, found that the usage rate of LINE is higher (75.8%) than Facebook (31.9%) and Twitter (31.1%) (Ministry of Internal Affairs and Communications Institute for Information and Communications Policy 2018). It is important to mention the situation of the younger generation which this study focused on (people in their 20 s and 30 s): over 90% were LINE users, and 52.3% of those in their 20 s and 46.6% of those in their 30 s were Facebook users. There was a large difference in Twitter usage between people in their 20 s and 30 s: 70.4% of the younger group used Twitter, while only 31.7% of the older group did.

A large amount of empirical research on social media usage has been conducted both in Japan and internationally, including a few qualitative studies that focus on the degree to which social media plays a role in maintaining intimacy across physical distance (Sample 2014). For example, the interaction with friends in a distant location through social media makes it possible for mothers to reduce their mental stress resulting from childrearing (Amagasa 2016). On the contrary, it is reported that even people in the same room sometimes communicate with each other through email in order to maintain interpersonal relationships (Ito 2016). It is easy to imagine social media other than email being used in similar ways. Some physical distance between people imposes constraints on their life circumstances and forms a barrier to communication regardless of the size of the distance, but the use of mobile phone-based social media can break down such barriers. Qualitative research concerning whether social media can transcend a physical distance to promote communication and thus help maintain intimacy has been accumulating, but quantitative research into this area has not been conducted enough to capture how intimacy can be affected by communication between people in some distance through mobile phone-based social media. In this connection, this study conducts a quantitative analysis, focusing on the relation between social media usage and the maintenance of close interpersonal relationships with a physical distance.

First, let us discuss some problems caused by the existence of physical distance: differences in lifestyle between urban and regional areas, and unfavorable geographical conditions. As for the former, the following issues have been discussed in modern Japan: depopulation, a rapidly aging society, and abandoned villages (Yamashita 2012, 2014). They are related to the scarcity of employment opportunities and estrangement from consumer life. As for the latter, it should be noted that there are a wide range of region-specific issues, such as the lack of institutions of higher education, the unavailability of medical and judiciary services, and problems related to nuclear power plants and Self-Defense Force facilities. It is natural to consider that residents put an emphasis on employment opportunities, education, and medical services. However, recent migration research has shown increases in young people's desire to return to their hometowns, despite the difficulties mentioned above (Abe 2013; Tsuji 2016; Kutsuwada 2017). Kutsuwada's (2017) study on regional satisfaction levels suggests that their desire to return to their hometowns is not affected by the unfavorable conditions of the countryside, in contrast to the past situation. According to this study, whether a regional satisfaction level is high or not depends on the differences in the consumer environment and the convenience of access to public transport, while there was no difference between regions in terms of life satisfaction. In fact, the life satisfaction depends on the existence of a spouse and activities related to work, as suggested in recent literatures of Japanese youth.

If life satisfaction is not determined by the unfavorable nature of one's area of residence but rather by consumption and intimacy, then in present-day Japanese society, it should be possible to consider that the same conditions hold on life satisfaction wherever one lives. This suggests the possibility that the development of media technologies and logistics systems enables people to resolve some of the problems of locality caused by the physical boundaries of their regions. This chapter refers to such a locality as "translocality." That is, it is an individual's occupation and level of intimacy that determines life satisfaction levels. As noted above, it goes without saying that there are challenges regarding employment opportunities and population in the regional areas. If such an environment in general is a locality, then translocality may be considered to be a useful concept for indicating the commonalities among non-central areas.

The "translocalized" situation is related to the doubling of time/place that this book is concerned with (see Tomita chapter). If life satisfaction can increase through resolving the relevant problems of locality, enabling employment, and maintaining intimacy, then mobile media can play an even more important role than would previously have been ever expected. In fact, it must already be playing such a role!

Then, let us consider social media usage and lifestyles, as well as the intimacy and well-being, of young people living in a specific region.

## 2 Aomori Prefecture: Mutsu City and Oirase-Cho

Mutsu city is a provincial city situated on the Shimokita Peninsula in Aomori Prefecture, a northernmost prefecture of the island of Honshu. It is a municipality with a population of approximately 60,000, with 20% of them in their 20 s or 30 s (the age groups that are the target of this study).

In this area, fisheries and agriculture are thriving, with approximately 10% of the workforce engaged in primary industries, approximately 20% in secondary industries, and approximately 70% in tertiary industries. Some amounts of workers in their 20 s and 30 s migrate to Mutsu city from other Japanese municipalities because it is home to a Maritime Self-Defense Force base and its neighboring municipalities host facilities such as nuclear power plants (Figs. 1, 2 and 3).

Oirase-cho, a municipality which is adjacent to Hachinohe city, has a population of approximately 25,000, containing 4000 young people in their 20 s or 30 s. Approximately, 10% of its workforce are involved in primary industries, approximately 30% in secondary industries, and approximately 60% in tertiary industries. It is located within the employment catchment area of Hachinohe city, and its employees can be considered to be employed in the secondary and tertiary

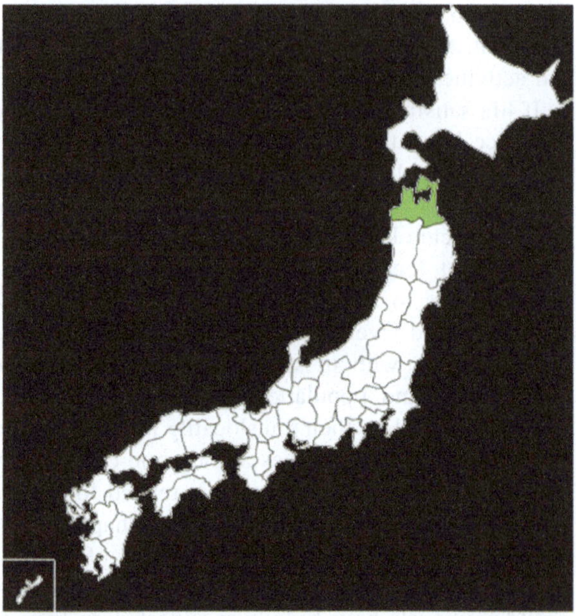

**Fig. 1** Aomori Prefecture

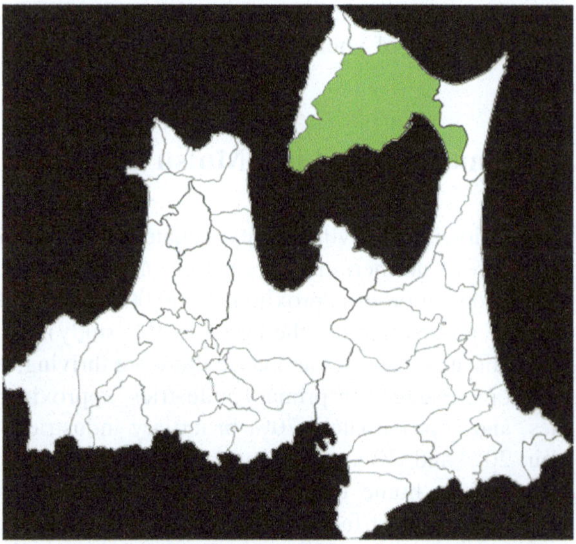

**Fig. 2** Mutsu city

industries of Hachinohe city. The proportion of employees who work in secondary industries is relatively high in Aomori Prefecture.

As Mutsu city includes areas with unfavorable conditions and Oirase-cho is adjacent to a regional urban center, selecting these two areas as the targets of the

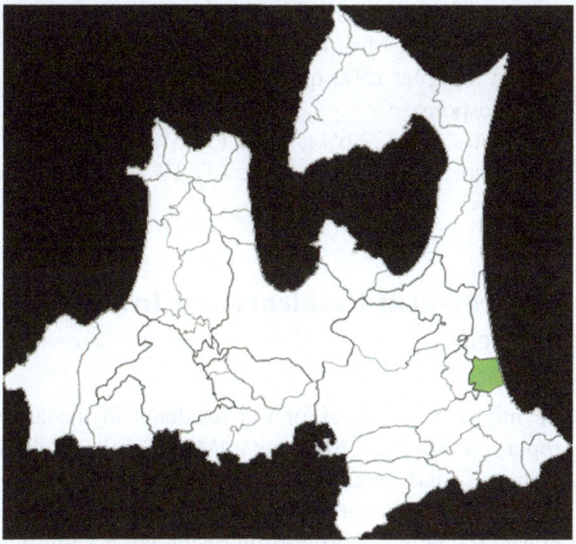

**Fig. 3** Oirase-cho

survey should enable us to examine the lifestyles in the peripheral areas on the northernmost point of the main island of Honshu.

## 3 Thesis, Data, and Variables

This study treats social media usage as a target variable and attempts to answer the following questions: (i) to what extent do migrants and permanent residents differ in their use of social media; (ii) whether their use of social media enables them to maintain relationships with people from their hometown with whom they grew up, far away from where they currently live; and (iii) whether or not their use of social media is corelated with their life satisfaction. Accordingly, the main questionnaire items are as follows: behavior and values among Japanese local youth, such as social media usage, impressions of the area, and residence history; values concerning living in the area and one's state of employment; values regarding employment and self-evaluation; values regarding one's life; values regarding lifestyle and interpersonal relationships; and their behavior on society and politics. This chapter investigates what determines the well-being of residents in regional areas, focusing on whether it is related to their social media usage or whether the well-being depends on where they live (in terms of urban/regional areas). If the well-being is not determined by the region in which one lives, then what does determine it? This study seeks to specify the process of the translocalization of a regional area through the media use. An overview of the survey is as follows:

Survey Period: April–May 2018
Target Locations: Mutsu city and Oirase-cho (Aomori Prefecture)
Target Age: 20–39

Survey Method: Questionnaire survey (postal) employing random sampling (systematic sampling) from the electoral register.
Planned Sample: 1500 questionnaires for each area (Total: 3000)
Valid Responses:
Mutsu city: 340 (22.6%); Male (55.3%), Female (44.7%)
Oirase-cho: 340 (22.6%); Male (47.1%), Female (52.9%)

## 4 Permanent Residents and Inward Migrants in Regional Areas

The migration histories of the residents in the areas are shown in Table 1. The proportion of inward migrants to Mutsu city, which includes areas with unfavorable conditions, and Oirase-cho, which is located near a regional urban center, is 30–39%. The reasons for inward migration to Mutsu city are different from those to Oirase-cho, with the proportion of the latter slightly higher than that of the former. As for the former, migration is motivated by the need to transfer to the area with the branch of the Self-Defense Force or for Japan Nuclear Fuel Limited. On the other hand, as for the latter, they are attracted by the convenience of the area, which is located on the outskirts of Hachinose city and has "Aeon Mall Shimoda," the largest shopping mall in Aomori Prefecture.

**Table 1** Migration patterns

| % | | | Mutsu city | | Oirase-cho | |
|---|---|---|---|---|---|---|
| | | | (N = 323) | | (N = 320) | |
| Locals | Pemanent Residents | Never lived in another area | 24.8 | 24.8 | 25.3 | 25.3 |
| | U-Turn | Moved back after graduating (or dropping out of) a school in another area | 25.1 | 45.2 | 20.6 | 36.9 |
| | | Moved back after working in another area | 20.1 | | 16.3 | |
| Inward Migrants | I-Turn | Moved to current area due to marriage | 4.6 | 30.0 | 11.6 | 37.8 |
| | | Moved to current area due to employment | 19.8 | | 9.4 | |
| | | Moved to current area due to education | 1.5 | | 0.9 | |
| | | Moved to current area due to relocation | 0.9 | | 11.6 | |
| | | Moved to current area due to family circumstances | 3.1 | | 4.4 | |

Approximately, one quarter of the residents in both areas have never left the area they were born in—they are called permanent residents. Table 1 shows that the proportion of U-turners (those who have returned to the areas after leaving) is slightly higher to Mutsu city (45.2%) than to Oirase-cho (36.9%). There is no conspicuous difference between permanent residents and U-turners in Mutsu city and Oirase-cho (see the part of U-Turn in Table 1). What is important in Table 1 is that the proportion of inward migrants is the highest who moved for work to Mutsu city which is close to areas with unfavorable conditions, and the proportion of inward migrants is the highest who moved to Oirase-cho in order to get married and construct their houses. This would lead us to conclude that the inward migrants to Mutsu city are different from those to Oirase-cho in whether they can make their own choices to migrate or not.

## 5 Where Is a Local Area for Inward Migrants?

What exactly is a local area? Simply put, it is one's hometown. Locals live in their hometown and think of the place where they live as a local area, but do inward migrants think so? Their hometown is geographically far from where they live. Do they think the local is their hometown or the area where they live? Table 2 shows where the local area is for inward migrants. Most inward migrants think the local area is their hometown, but 23.5% of them think the local area is Oirase-cho. This percentage is higher than in Mutsu city. This difference in results suggests the possibility that local consciousness varies according to the reason for movement.

I am additionally concerned with why the satisfaction of living in a given area is different. The highest ratio of inward migrants to Oirase-cho moved to the area due to marriage and relocation, while in Mutsu city, the highest ratio of movement is due to employment (Table 1). Table 3 shows the area satisfaction for inward migrants. Inward migrants in Oirase-cho are more satisfied with the area they live in compared to Mutsu city.

**Table 2** Where is a local area for inward migrants?

| % | Mutsu city | Oirase-cho |
|---|---|---|
| I think local area is my hometown | 83.9 | 71.5 |
| I think local area is where I live now | 12.1 | 23.5 |
| Others | 4.0 | 5.0 |
| N | 99 | 119 |

**Table 3** Area satisfaction for inward migrants

| % | Mutsu city | Oirase-cho |
|---|---|---|
| I am satisfied with the area I live | 31.7 | 73.0 |
| I am not satisfied with the area I live | 68.3 | 27.0 |
| N | 101 | 122 |

## 6 Social Media Usage

It was found in this study that usage rates for social media were 92.3% in Mutsu city and 90.0% in Oirase-cho. Table 4 presents the usage rate of each of the social media in Mutsu city and in Oirase-cho. According to the results given in Table 4, in both areas, around 90% of respondents used LINE, making it the most popular service, while Facebook and Twitter were used by around 40% of respondents. These results indicate that there is not much difference in social media usage between the two areas. To briefly outline the characteristics of these social media services, LINE can be thought of as an instance of personal media with extended functions of email or a telephone. Conversely, Twitter can be regarded as mass media, enabling the transmission of one's thoughts that happen to come to mind to a large and unspecified number of recipients. Facebook can be used as both personal and mass media, depending on a choice of usage.

It would be natural to assume that the differences in the architectures of these media come from those of the form of well-matched networks (i.e., intimate interpersonal relationships) and the purposes of communication. Ogasawara (2016) proposed the relevant analysis of the relationship between knowledge of social issues and contact with shared news in these three social media services. In the case of media such as LINE—which reinforces strong social ties and close communication—decreases in knowledge about social issues were found to be related to frequencies of use. This result indicates that usage of LINE, but not Facebook and Twitter, may cause a disparity in the knowledge of social issues between individuals. As mentioned by Ogasawara (2016), the social medium LINE reinforces strong social ties, such as familial relationships, romantic relationships, and friendships, which can be formed by territorial and blood-based bonds, as well as

**Table 4** Social media usage (%)

| SNS利用% | | |
|---|---|---|
| | Mutsu city | Oirase-cho |
| LINE | 90.2 | 84.1 |
| Facebook | 38.7 | 35.6 |
| twitter | 39.3 | 34.7 |
| mixi | 5.1 | 4.0 |
| N | 336 | 329 |

bonds formed through education. Both Mutsu city and Oirase-cho have low population densities and relatively small workforces in Japan. There are few higher education institutions, meaning that it is necessary to leave these areas for education or employment purposes.

As discussed above, Mutsu city has a high proportion of people aged in their 20 s and 30 s who moved to the area for work while Oirase-cho has a high proportion of those who intend to make their family in the area. This leads us to observe the increase and decrease in a certain local population: some people come to these areas (increase) but other people leave them (decrease). The same phenomenon in these areas makes it possible to compare two groups in terms of social media usage, lifestyle, and views: one consists of people who are close to their hometown and the other consists of people who are distant from their hometown. The goal of this chapter is to make it clear whether the inward migrants and local residents use social media to maintain interpersonal relationships with local people, and how such usage is related to life satisfaction and well-being.

Let us now examine, in particular, whether social media also supports communication to maintain "local friendships" that have been formed from one's hometown bonds. Table 5 presents the frequency of interaction with local friends on social media. Approximately, 30% of the respondents interacted with local friends on social media every day. The frequencies of interaction on social media in Mutsu city and in Oirase-cho are not significantly different (Chi-square test). Furthermore, no significant differences are found among the four types of social media.

**Table 5** Frequency of interaction with local friends on social media

| % | | Interact everyday | Interact once or more a month | Interact once or more every six months | Interact once or more every year | No contact or discussion at all | N |
|---|---|---|---|---|---|---|---|
| Mutsu city | LINE | 27.9 | 41.5 | 13.6 | 8.5 | 8.5 | 294 |
| | Facebook | 26.2 | 50.0 | 10.8 | 5.4 | 7.7 | 130 |
| | Twitter | 28.2 | 43.5 | 9.9 | 8.4 | 9.9 | 131 |
| | mixi | 23.5 | 64.7 | 5.9 | 0.0 | 5.9 | 17 |
| Oirase-cho | LINE | 29.6 | 42.3 | 10.2 | 6.9 | 10.9 | 274 |
| | Facebook | 32.8 | 44.5 | 11.8 | 4.2 | 6.7 | 119 |
| | Twitter | 35.3 | 41.4 | 6.9 | 3.4 | 12.9 | 116 |
| | mixi | 15.4 | 61.5 | 7.7 | 0.0 | 15.4 | 13 |

## 7 Who Interacts with Local Friends on Social Media?

This study investigated the demographic distribution as to whether social media was being used to interact with local friends. The result of this investigation did not find any correlations with age, gender, annual income, marital status, cohabitation with family, or experience of moving. On the other hand, it is found that living in one's hometown is related to using social media to interact with local friends. People living in their hometowns were found to be using social media to interact with their local friends more than inward migrants (Table 6). This result supports the findings of existing mobile media research, showing that mobile phones are used among geographically and psychologically close people. This suggests that social media cannot be considered to expand social network in psychological and geographical terms, like mobile media. In other words, while social media can function to enforce communication in existing interpersonal relationships, they cannot expand the network. Now note that no significant differences were found between Mutsu city, in which young inward migrants experience frequent transfers, and Oirase-cho, in which young inward migrants expect to live in the area for a relatively longer period. Therefore, it is summarized that the important aspect of communication on social media is whether users live in their hometowns or not. It can be posited that being in one's hometown, rather than transferring many times, is correlated with the maintenance of one's local networks.

Furthermore, the existence of local friends with whom one can relax and hang out is of relevance with the observed usage of social media, as clarified in Table 5.

According to Tables 6 and 7, the high frequency of interaction on social media is related not only to the absence of physical distance between respondents and their local friends but also to the presence of their local friends. A correlation between the frequency of interaction on social media and the presence of close local friendships was found in Mutsu city, where young migrants move inward as employees who move frequently, but a weaker correlation between them was found in the case of Oirase-cho, where young migrants inward move for marriage and private lives and are expected to live in the area for a longer time.

**Table 6** Residence in one's hometown and interaction with local friends on social media (%)

| % | | Interact everyday | Interact once or more a month | Interact once or more every six months | Interact once or more every year | No contact or discussion at all | N |
|---|---|---|---|---|---|---|---|
| Mutsu city* | Migrants | 20.8 | 35.4 | 21.9 | 12.5 | 9.4 | 96 |
| | Locals | 30.3 | 44.8 | 9.5 | 6.0 | 9.5 | 201 |
| Oirase-cho* | Migrants | 26.9 | 37.5 | 9.6 | 12.5 | 13.5 | 104 |
| | Locals | 30.8 | 43.0 | 10.5 | 3.5 | 12.2 | 172 |

Chi-square test: * = $p < 0.01$

**Table 7** Existence of many local friends with whom one can relax and hang out and interaction with local friends on social media (%)

| % | | Interact everyday | Interact once or more a month | Interact once or more every six months | Interact once or more every year | No contact or discussion at all | N |
|---|---|---|---|---|---|---|---|
| Mutsu city* | Existence | 36.2 | 43.0 | 12.1 | 3.4 | 5.4 | 149 |
| | not so many | 18.7 | 40.7 | 14.7 | 12.7 | 13.3 | 150 |
| Oirase-cho† | Existence | 35.5 | 42.8 | 8.0 | 5.1 | 8.7 | 138 |
| | not so many | 23.2 | 39.1 | 12.3 | 8.7 | 16.7 | 138 |

Chi-square test: * = p < 0.01, † = 0.05

The above results show that, first of all, people living in their hometown have a higher frequency of social media usage to interact with local friends than inward migrants. It is not the case that social media tools are used to maintain some friendship between people in physical distances. Additionally, the quality of intimacy with local friends is related to the frequency of interaction with such friends on social media.

## 8 Relationships with Local Friends and Social Media Usage

No striking relationship was found between the social media types (LINE, Facebook and Twitter) and the frequency of communication with local friends. We would like to examine the difference between their types in detail, focusing on how social media types are corelated with the formation of interpersonal relationships and satisfaction with interpersonal relationships and life (Table 8). First, no correlation was found between the use of any of the social media services and the satisfaction with parent–child relationships, and the interest in interaction with people in one's residence. On the other hand, a correlation was found between the use of LINE, Facebook, and Twitter and interpersonal relationships and life satisfaction. Let us discuss in the following with what variables LINE, Facebook, and Twitter are corelated.

First, we describe the LINE usage. Approximately, 90% of the respondents used LINE, meaning that non-users can be considered to be categorized as a minority in young Japanese. The LINE users are more likely to think that they are "blessed with a wealth of opportunities to meet people broadening their sphere of activity and their perspective" (Chi-squared test: $p < 0.001$). The correlation of the LINE usage with close friendship satisfaction was found (Chi-squared test: $p < 0.005$), but the

**Table 8** Social media usage and behaviors

| | | LINE | | Facebook | | Twitter | |
|---|---|---|---|---|---|---|---|
| | | Mutsu | Oirase | Mutsu | Oirase | Mutsu | Oirase |
| Satisfaction | In general, I am satisfied with my current situation | n.s. | | n.s. | ** | **neg. | n.s. |
| | In general, I am satisfied with my current life | n.s. | | *** | | n.s. | |
| | In general, I am satisfied with my relationships with friends | ** | | ** | | n.s. | |
| Relationships | I am blessed with a wealth of opportunities to meet people outside of one's own sphere and that one's perspective is broadening | ** | | *** | | † | |
| | I am blessed with a wealth of opportunities to interact with people close to me and I am deepening our relationships | ** | | *** | | n.s. | |
| Perspect one's futture | I am optimistic about my future | * | | *** | | † neg. | n.s. |
| Happiness | I am happy | † | | n.s. | ** | n.s. | |

Chi-square test: *** = $p < 0.001$, ** = $p < 0.005$, * = $p < 0.01$, † = $p < 0.05$

difference was not significant between the LINE usage and the satisfactions/ happiness of the user. The results thus show that LINE users are more satisfied with their friendships than non-users.

Next, let us turn to the Facebook usage and the interpersonal relationships/life satisfaction relevant to it. There are fewer users of Facebook than LINE, and in international terms, the proportion of users of Facebook in Japan is lower than that in other countries. The general image of characteristics of Facebook users in Japan is that users are outgoing and have a preference for foreign culture because of the lower rates of domestic users. As such, the Japanese users may be thought of as having an interest in foreign countries and having friendships with non-Japanese individuals. This general impression is incompatible with the results of this study. We found that in Oirase-cho, the Facebook usage is corelated to the feeling that one is blessed with a wealth of opportunities to meet people outside of one's own sphere and that one's perspective is broadening (Chi-squared test: $p < 0\ .001$), whereas in Mutsu city, it is not, and that in both areas, it is corelated with the feeling that "I am blessed with a wealth of opportunities to interact with people close to me and I am deepening our relationships"(Chi-squared test: $p < 0.001$). The summary can be drawn that Facebook users may tend not only to search for opportunities to interact with people outside of their area of residence and to try to expand their networks overseas but also to place emphasis on interacting with those who they are in close interpersonal relationships with. Facebook helps Japanese younger people make friends and care for their relationships among geographically neighboring people.

Additionally, a correlation with life satisfaction was partly found (Chi-squared test: $p < 0.01$). Facebook users have high life satisfaction. A striking result was that compared to non-users, Facebook users tend to have an optimistic view of their future (Chi-squared test: $p < 0.001$). This is a different result to what was found for Twitter users, as discussed below.

Twitter usage exhibits a different tendency to LINE and Facebook usage. Most correlations with interpersonal relationships were found in Mutsu city but not so in Oirase-cho. First of all, only significant differences were found with regard to the relationship with life satisfaction in Mutsu with a proviso that a significant negative correlation (Chi-squared test: $p < 0.005$) was found with the item "In general, I am satisfied with my current situation." In a point probably related to this negative tendency, a relationship with well-being and optimism about one's future was also found. The correlation was weak but compared to non-users, Twitter users in Mutsu were found to have a tendency to respond in the negative to the statement "I am optimistic about my future" (Chi-squared test: $p < 0.05$).

In regards to correlations observed only in Mutsu city, Twitter use had a negative relation with whether they were satisfied with their current situation or whether they were optimistic about their future. The Twitter user is dissatisfied with their present situation of life and seems to tend to have uneasiness about the future. While most young migrants who flowed into Mutsu city did so for reasons of work, the young migrants who flowed into Oirase-cho did so to better their life. The young migrants in Oirase-cho have social networks and supportive neighborhoods more so than in Mutsu city. Therefore, it is thought that Twitter users in lack of social relationships gave negative evaluation of their life and future.

Furthermore, Twitter use was weakly correlated (Chi-squared test: $p < 0.05$) with the statement "I have a wealth of opportunities to meet people outside of my own sphere, and my perspective is broadening." It is a negative interpretation, but Twitter users may search outside friendships because of the dissatisfaction for their existing human relations and uneasiness about the future.

## 9 Type of Social Media and Well-Being

The above results show that social media displays similar characteristics and trends in usage behaviors as early stage mobile phone use. In short, social media is used in interpersonal relationships where distances are close in psychological and/or physical terms. Furthermore, it was shown that interpersonal relationships and views regarding one's life differed between social media types.

LINE, Facebook and Twitter users have the self-awareness that they were blessed with opportunities to meet people from outside of their own sphere and felt as if their perspectives are broadening. LINE and Facebook users also had relatively high levels of life satisfaction compared with Twitter users. Facebook users, in particular, reported that they were optimistic about the future. Conversely, it appeared that Twitter users partly were not satisfied with their current situation and were not optimistic about the future.

The results of this study show that if it is the case that individuals have different views depending on the type of social media that they use, then talking about social media as one coherent whole will result in scattered responses depending on what the respondent is imagining. This indicates that social media functions differently according to type and that communication with differing aims is being carried out on different types of social media.

A particularly interesting result was that LINE and Facebook usage showed that while LINE is regarded as having communication functionality that specializes in communication between close networks and Facebook has an image of functioning to promote communication with spheres that are not close in Japan, it is not always the case that actual use reflects such an impression. In general, social media is used for geographically close interpersonal relationships and while use objectives differ according to functionality, it may be that it is actually quite difficult to use social media in a way that transcends locality. In this study, Twitter's comparatively high (if not total) anonymity and ability to disseminate opinions and feelings broadly may be the reasons for it being used to transcend locality. Furthermore, the weak correlation with well-being and non-positive views about the future prospects not being positive indicated that dissatisfaction with local circumstances may drive users to the online space of Twitter. This is similar to the tele-cocoon model, which was observed in the early 1990s with regard to email usage (Habuchi 2005). The concept of the tele-cocoon concerns the development of interpersonal relationships in online space as a result of dissatisfaction with existing interpersonal relationships, but the similarity in this case relates to Twitter being used for online communication due to maladaptation not to local interpersonal relationships but to the local environment. This may also be an element of translocality and also be related to doubling space.

## 10 Conclusion

The present study focused on young people living in provincial cities in an investigation of geographical proximity and social media usage—particularly the question of whether social media usage can help transcend the constraints of physical distance and play a part in forming and maintaining interpersonal relationships. The results showed that LINE and Facebook were used by people living in their hometowns to maintain local interpersonal relationships. Connections between these social media services and satisfaction with life and interpersonal relationships were also observed. In short, LINE and Facebook possess the characteristic of reinforcing positive existing local interpersonal relationships.

On the other hand, while Twitter was not found to help in maintaining existing interpersonal relationships or to have a connection with satisfaction, it was found to have a negative correlation with satisfaction with their life situation and one's optimistic feeling for the future. Further, Twitter users were found to show as a weak tendency that they were blessed with a wealth of opportunities to meet people from different spheres and that their perspectives were broadening. If it is the case that Twitter is fulfilling the role of a tele-cocoon, as discussed above, then this cyber space should be functioning as a comfortable one. However, there was no strong evidence that this is the case.

Previous studies of the idea of tele-cocoon have produced some mix results (Kobayashi et al. 2015). One of them is smartphones can be used to meet a necessary condition for accessing social capital contrary to the tele-cocooning hypothesis, however the principle of homophily as a driving force of tele-cocoon is still relevant with the widespread use of smartphones. This result suggests that Twitter users would like to search for new networks of the filter bubbles (Pariser 2011), but these user's challenges are almost lost. They are not satisfied with their current situation and have tried to express their opinions and behaviors on Twitter. But we cannot obtain evidence to say with certainty that Twitter users have a wealth of opportunities to meet people from different spheres.

As a general rule, no internet paradox (Kraut et al. 1998) caused by the use of social media was found to exist in this research, but the influence of social media type and area of residence was found to have slightly different effects on feelings of well-being and the maintenance of interpersonal relationships. Past surveys on social media usage behavior have found that communication on social media is carried out through existing interpersonal relationships (Kawai 2014) and that, in relation to selective contact behavior on Twitter, Twitter enables a greater degree of selective information consumption in line with one's desires compared to other media (Ogawa et al. 2013). The findings of this study provide further evidence of the trends observed in the existing literature.

In Mutsu city, the fact that Twitter use was inversely correlated with living area satisfaction and one's feelings of well-being indicates the existence of young people who wish to engage in communication that transcends geographical constraints. The people that they want to engage in such communication with, however, are not local friends or those in close interpersonal relationships with them.

Additionally, there is a certain proportion of young people in Mutsu city for whom relocation is common. Such people move to different areas for work every few years. They have a low level of satisfaction with the living area, which is close to areas with unfavorable conditions (Habuchi 2018). Further, it is those with low levels of satisfaction who tend to use Twitter. However, even though they use Twitter, they do not believe that they are blessed with a wealth of opportunities to meet people from differing spheres or that their perspectives are broadening.

To re-emphasize, while young people who are dissatisfied with their current situation, and in particular with the area they live in, may use Twitter, it is not the case that they are using it to transcend such circumstances and communicate with close friends or acquaintances in geographically distant locations. However, an analysis of the functioning of the Twitter use of young people that are dissatisfied with the area in which they live is beyond the scope of this study. As the existing literature indicates, however, the fact that Twitter is a form of media where it is possible to selectively acquire the information one wishes to consume means that we can assume that young people in Mutsu city are transcending location to consume the information that they desire. It may be that, through the consumption of desired information and the performance of a tele-cocoon-like public space, that users are reducing the feelings of dissatisfaction caused by migration.

**Acknowledgements** This study was supported by the Matsuda Foundation and JSPS (Grant no.18H00917). I received generous support for English writing from Dr. Ryoichi Kondo and Dr. James Alastair Butler. This is also a product of research which was financially supported by the Kansai University Fund for Supporting Outlay Research Center "Sociology reserach onmobile media society" 2019–2020.

## References

Abe M (2013) Youth hiding in the regions: the new society which emerged between city and countryside. Asahi Shinsho (in Japanese)

Amagasa K (2016) Connection and media usage in the childrearing space: the smartphone as a ventilator for social imagination. In: Tomita H (ed) Post-mobile society: towards the second offline age. Sekaishisosha (in Japanese)

Habuchi I (2005) Accelerating reflexivity. In: Ito M, Okabe D, Matsuda M (eds) Personal, Mobile Phones in Japanese Life. MIT Press, Portable, Pedestrian

Habuchi I ed (2018) Report of a study funded by the mazda foundation—opinion poll on aomori residents in their 20 s and 30 s. Translocality study group. http://mzaidan.mazda.co.jp/publication/index_s9.html (in Japanese)

Ito K (2016) The future of mobile content: towards a richly contextualized "me". In: Tomita H (ed) Post-mobile society: towards the second offline age. Sekaishisosha (in Japanese)

Kawai D (2014) Social media paradox: does social media reduce friends relationship and psychological well-being? Socio-informatics 3(1), the Society of Socio-Informatics (in Japanese)

Kobayashi T, Boase J, Suzuki T, Suzuki T (2015) Emerging from the cocoon? Revisiting the tele-cocooning hypothesis in the smartphone era. J Comput-Med Commun 20(3):330–345

Kraut R1, Patterson M, Lundmark V, Kiesler S, Mukopadhyay T, Scherlis W (1998) Internet paradox. A social technology that reduces social involvement and psychological well-being? Am Psychol 1017–1031

Kutsuwada R (2017) Youth and well-being in the regions. Keisoshobo (in Japanese)

Ministry of Internal Affairs and Communications Institute for Information and Communications Policy (2018) 2017 Survey on usage time and information behavior with regard to telecommunications media. URL: http://www.soumu.go.jp/main_content/000564530.pdf (in Japanese)

Nakamura I (2001) Interpersonal relationships in email on the mobile phone. In: The University of Tokyo institute of socio-information and communication studies (ed) Japanese Information Behavior 2000, University of Tokyo Press (in Japanese)
Ogasawara M (2016) Might news-sharing and retweeting on social media be bringing about social fragmentation? In: Tomita H (ed) Post-mobile society: towards the second offline age. Sekaishisosha (in Japanese)
Ogawa Y, Yamamoto H, Miyata K, Ikeda K (2013) Association between selective exposure and attitude on Twitter. In: The proceedings of the 27th annual conference of the Japanese society for artificial intelligence, the Japanese Society for Artificial Intelligence (in Japanese)
Okada T, Matsuda M, Habuchi I (2000) Characteristics of mobile phone-based media and interpersonal relationships: from a survey of university students. In: 1999 Annual report of the japan society of information and communication research, the Japan Society of Information and Communication Research (in Japanese)
Pariser E (2011) The filter bubble: what the internet is hiding from you. Penguin Press, New York
Sakaguchi Y (2016) Correlations and changes in youth media and lifestyle: a comparison between 2002 and 2012. In: Fujimura M, Asano T, Habuchi I (eds) The well-being of modern youth: living in the anxious society, Kouseisha Kouseikaku (in Japanese)
Sample M (2014) Location is not compelling (until it is Haunted). In: Farman J (ed) The mobile story: narrative practices locative technologies. Routledge
Tsuji D (2008) New media and changes in youth communication. In: Hashimoto Y, Funatsu M (eds) Communication of children and adolescents. Hokuju Shuppan (in Japanese)
Tsuji I (2016) Hometown orientation and youth culture: a comparative survey of regional areas and large cities. In: Kawasaki K, Asano T (eds) Dissolution of "The Youth" Keisoshobo (in Japanese)
Yamashita Y (2012) The truth about marginal settlements: will depopulated villages disappear? Chikuma Shinsho (in Japanese)
Yamashita Y (2014) The trap of regional extinction: the "masuda report" and the truth about the shrinking society. Chikuma Shinsho (in Japanese)

**Ichiyo Habuchi** is a professor at Hirosaki University in Aomori, Japan. Her study focuses on youth, particularly the impact of mobile media technologies on their intimacy since 1998. She has tested the Telecocoons hypothesis proposed in her article (in Personal, Portable, Pedestrian: Mobile Phones In Japanese Life, MIT Press, 2005). Her survey research "the media usage and intimacy with physical distances" is under investigating.

The manufacturer's authorised representative in the EU is Springer Nature Customer Service Centre GmbH, Europaplatz 3, 69115 Heidelberg, Germany. If you have any concerns regarding our products, please contact ProductSafety@springernature.com

Printed and bound by CPI Group (UK) Ltd, Croydon, CR0 4YY
30/09/2026
02225293-0007